Easy Gardens

Other Publications:

Easy Gardens

by
DONALD WYMAN and CURTIS PRENDERGAST
and
the Editors of TIME-LIFE BOOKS

TIME-LIFE BOOKS, ALEXANDRIA, VIRGINIA

Time-Life Books Inc.
is a wholly owned subsidiary of
TIME INCORPORATED

FOUNDER: Henry R. Luce 1898-1967

Editor-in-Chief: Hedley Donovan
Chairman of the Board: Andrew Heiskell
President: James R. Shepley
Vice Chairmen: Roy E. Larsen, Arthur Temple
Corporate Editors: Ralph Graves,
Henry Anatole Grunwald

TIME-LIFE BOOKS INC.
MANAGING EDITOR: Jerry Korn
Executive Editor: David Maness
Assistant Managing Editors: Dale M. Brown,
Martin Mann, John Paul Porter
Art Director: Tom Suzuki
Chief of Research: David L. Harrison
Director of Photography: Robert G. Mason
Planning Director: Thomas Flaherty (acting)
Senior Text Editor: Diana Hirsh
Assistant Art Director: Arnold C. Holeywell
Assistant Chief of Research: Carolyn L. Sackett
Assistant Director of Photography:
Dolores A. Littles

CHAIRMAN: Joan D. Manley
President: John D. McSweeney
Executive Vice Presidents: Carl G. Jaeger,
John Steven Maxwell, David J. Walsh
Vice Presidents: Peter G. Barnes (Comptroller),
Nicholas Benton (Public Relations),
John L. Canova (Sales), Herbert Sorkin
(Production), Paul R. Stewart (Promotion)
Personnel Director: Beatrice T. Dobie
Consumer Affairs Director: Carol Flaumenhaft

THE TIME-LIFE ENCYCLOPEDIA OF GARDENING
EDITORIAL STAFF FOR EASY GARDENS
EDITOR: Robert M. Jones
Assistant Editors: Sarah Bennett Brash, Betsy Frankel
Text Editors: Margaret Fogarty, Bonnie Bohling Kreitler
Picture Editor: Jane Jordan
Designer: Albert Sherman
Staff Writers: Bobbie Conlan-Moore, Susan Perry,
Mark M. Steele
Researchers: Diane Bohrer, Marilyn Murphy,
Susan F. Schneider
Art Assistant: Santi José Acosta
Editorial Assistant: Maria Zacharias

EDITORIAL PRODUCTION
Production Editor: Douglas B. Graham
Operations Manager: Gennaro C. Esposito
Assistant Production Editor: Feliciano Madrid
Quality Control: Robert L. Young (director),
James J. Cox (assistant), Michael G. Wight
(associate)
Art Coordinator: Anne B. Landry
Copy Staff: Susan B. Galloway (chief), Elizabeth Graham,
Lynn Green, Florence Keith, Celia Beattie
Picture Department: Barbara S. Simon
Traffic: Jeanne Potter

CORRESPONDENTS: Elisabeth Kraemer (Bonn); Margot
Hapgood, Dorothy Bacon (London); Susan Jonas, Lucy T.
Voulgaris (New York); Maria Vincenza Aloisi, Josephine du
Brusle (Paris); Ann Natanson (Rome). Valuable assistance
was also provided by: Diana Asselin (Los Angeles); Carolyn
T. Chubet, Miriam Hsia (New York). The editors are
indebted to Margaret M. Carter, Michael McTwigan, Rona
Mendelsohn, Jane Opper, Maggie Oster, Karen Solit,
Lyn Stallworth and Anne Weber, writers, for their help
with this book.

THE AUTHORS: Donald Wyman was for 33 years the horticulturist of Harvard University's Arnold Arboretum. The recipient of many horticultural awards in both the United States and Great Britain, he is a past president of the American Horticultural Society. Dr. Wyman has shared his extensive knowledge with gardeners in numerous books, including Wyman's Gardening Encyclopedia. Curtis Prendergast is a former TIME-LIFE correspondent who, during his years abroad, visited and reported on gardens in Japan, England, France and South Africa. Research for this book took him as well to gardens in many parts of the United States. In addition to tending his own 4½-acre garden in Maryland, he has contributed to other volumes in The TIME-LIFE Encyclopedia of Gardening.

CONSULTANTS: James Underwood Crockett, author of 13 of the volumes in the Encyclopedia, co-author of two additional volumes and consultant on other books in the series, has been a lover of the earth and its good things since his boyhood on a Massachusetts fruit farm. He was graduated from the Stockbridge School of Agriculture at the University of Massachusetts and has worked ever since in horticulture. A perennial contributor to leading gardening magazines, he also writes a monthly bulletin, "Flowery Talks," that is widely distributed through retail florists. His television program, Crockett's Victory Garden, shown all over the United States, has won countless converts to the Crockett approach to growing things. Dr. Robert L. Baker is an Associate Professor of Horticulture at the University of Maryland, College Park. Dr. Conrad B. Link is a Professor of Horticulture at the University of Maryland, College Park.

THE COVER: Weathered boards set off a simple and care-free bed of perennial orange coneflowers, golden calamagrostis grass and an Adam's-needle yucca. The bed is mulched with a 3- to 4-inch layer of pine-bark mulch to hold down weeds and retain moisture.

Library of Congress Cataloging in Publication Data
Wyman, Donald (1903)
    Easy gardens.
    (Time-Life encyclopedia of gardening)
    Bibliography: p.
    Includes index.
    1. Landscape gardening. I. Prendergast, Curtis, joint author. II.
Time-Life Books. III. Title.
SB473.W95   635.9   78-23434
ISBN 0-8094-2639-0
ISBN 0-8094-2638-2 lib. bdg.

CONTENTS

Gardening that is easy on the gardener 1

"What a man needs in gardening," the 19th Century American author Charles Dudley Warner once ruefully observed, "is a cast-iron back, with a hinge in it." Rudyard Kipling, Warner's contemporary across the ocean, seconded the motion with a bit of wry verse, describing men at work in England's stately gardens, "grubbing weeds from gravel paths with broken dinner knives." Concluded Kipling, in the meter that stirred millions:

Oh, Adam was a gardener, and God who made him sees
That half a proper gardener's work is done upon his knees;
So when your work is finished, you can wash your hands and
     pray
For the Glory of the Garden that it may not pass away!

A good many similar sentiments, including some unprintable ones, have been uttered by less illustrious gardeners. Almost everyone enjoys a beautiful garden, but not everyone enjoys the work—the digging, planting, watering, fertilizing, weeding, mowing, mulching, raking, pruning, clipping, pinching, spraying, not to mention cleaning up debris, putting the tools away, and washing off the mud.

Many who garden as an avocation—80 million Americans, according to U.S. Department of Agriculture estimates—accept such chores more or less willingly as the price they pay for gardening's rewards. A lot of gardeners, however, would just as soon spend part of that time playing golf, or fishing, or relaxing in the shade reading a book. It is to both kinds—those who enjoy gardening but are working harder than they need to and those who would really rather not do nearly so much work—that this book is sympathetically addressed.

Gardening, of course, can be as time consuming as you make it. Many people find it a source of deep satisfaction, as well as a form of light exercise. To others, chopping brambles and pulling weeds is a grim, unending war. To still others who once had more energy,

A lush array of easy-upkeep plants decorates this walled garden—a Japanese snowbell tree, ground covers of lily-turf and bergenia, wild geraniums, coneflowers and cascading masses of eulalia grass.

things appear in a different perspective with the passing of years. Retirement or the departure of the last child from home may present new options, including a chance to travel without worrying about lawns and flower beds, which cannot get along on their own.

But there is no such thing as a totally work-free garden. Ask a horticulturist or a nurseryman and he will probably answer: show me one. Even if you let your property go completely wild—in theory, at least, the ultimate in naturalized gardening—you will soon find that you have traded your lawn mower for a machete and a tank of herbicide to keep the advancing jungle at bay. A low-maintenance garden is not a bit of nature raw and rampant but a bit of nature matched to your soil and climate, and kept under strict control.

PERFECT VERSUS PRACTICAL

At the other extreme, a low-maintenance garden is not likely to rival the great gardens of the world for formal elegance and dazzling floral displays. Inevitably, it involves weighing the effect desired against the effort required, trade-offs between the perfect and the practical, a willingness to compromise.

Finally, the concept of minimum maintenance recognizes that people today are not necessarily more slothful than in the good old days. But they are a good deal more mobile, they have a wider range of interests and they are largely obligated to do their own gardening. Gone is the time when a young man would come by after school to mow the lawn or clip the hedge for a dollar or two. More likely he will charge 10 dollars, if not more, if he is interested at all.

"There is no easy solution to low maintenance," concedes Richard Lighty, University of Delaware associate professor of plant

A RAMP FOR STEPS

To ease the strain of moving a heavy load up garden steps, cover them with a portable ramp. Nail two 2-by-8-inch boards to 2-by-2-by-16-inch cleats positioned so the top cleat will catch the edge of the top step. Add extra cleats, if needed, for more strength. Use the ramp when you roll a wheelbarrow up (left) or slide a heavy object such as a large potted plant (right). For sliding, place heavy canvas under the object to reduce friction and provide a better grip.

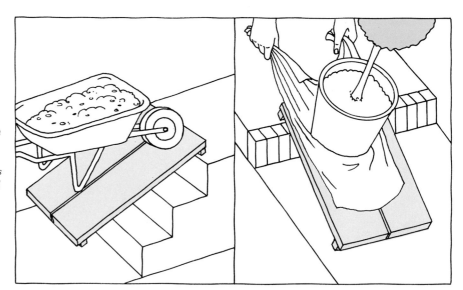

science, who is himself a low-maintenance gardener. "It is all a matter of balance; the goal is to achieve the highest level of interest with the least maintenance throughout the growing season."

Moreover, what constitutes low maintenance varies with the locality. In New England, some perennial borders virtually maintain themselves, emerging each year from their winter blankets of deep snow, but the same perennials lead a chancier existence in Mid-Atlantic states where winter is a damaging succession of freezes and thaws. Low maintenance in many parts of California requires drought-resistant plants. In the Southwest, gardeners must consider the problems of soil that is very low in organic content. Where icy streets are salted in winter, gardeners must set their shrubbery well back to avoid the destructive salty splash. A terrace of loose bricks, which can be laid on 6 inches of sand in a mild-winter state, may heave erratically unless it has four times that much base sand and gravel in a frigid area.

But regardless of soil or climate, garden design concepts have changed with the times. Liberty Hyde Bailey, a great American horticulturist, once wrote, "One plant in a tin can may be a more helpful and inspiring garden to some mind than a whole acre of lawn and flowers may be to another. The satisfaction of a garden does not depend on the area, nor, happily, on the cost or rarity of the plants. It depends on the temper of the person."

What Bailey was saying has even greater validity in today's atmosphere of competing interests, high costs and diminishing privacy. The most successful garden is no longer the one planted to dress up a house or impress the neighbors. Rather, it is one designed to provide the greatest possible pleasure for the gardener, one that involves only the kind of plants and the kind of gardening work he enjoys. Planning, then, must start with self-examination, plus consultation with any family members who will be involved in enjoying the garden and in keeping it up. With ideas compared and a goal defined, a gardener can consider the three elements—plants, design, and laborsaving techniques—that will bring the goal within reach.

"If a person wants to show his skill," Bailey observed, "he may choose the balky plant; but if he wants fun and comfort in gardening he had better choose the willing one." Not too willing, Bailey might have added, lest the gardener find it overrunning his yard.

The smallest plant, grass, is probably the easiest ground cover to grow in a level, sunny garden, but it also has a big headache potential. Grass is remarkably willing to grow, considering the repeated beatings it takes from mowing, drought and the patter of little feet. But even more willing are the plants that move in with it.

PLEASING YOURSELF

9

The American homeowner runs his power mower again and again through waving fields of dandelions, the national flower, and does battle with crab grass, the national weed. What has become a relentless schedule of lawn care for millions of gardeners has also become a vast industry for the makers of mowers, trimmers, fertilizers, weed killers, lawn sprinklers, aerators, dethatchers, leaf brooms and assorted other weaponry, all designed to keep a 2-inch-tall plant weed free and emerald green.

LESS TIME ON THE TURF

There are things a gardener can do to ease his lawn work. One is to use only the best seed mix designed especially for his region. With care, it will produce a dense, low-growing, drought- and disease-resistant turf that will repel weeds. Another is to cut that grass no shorter than 2 inches—and somewhat higher in midsummer. A third is to take advantage of such modern aids as fine-chopping mulching mowers, herbicides and slow-release fertilizers.

Even such a lawn may require more work than you are willing to give it, especially if it was designed with little forethought. To cut the labor further, consider these added steps: first, reduce the lawn to a single area instead of two or three separate ones; second, locate that area adjacent to the main outdoor living space; third, make it a simple shape without awkward projections; fourth, keep it free of all internal plant beds and other obstacles that impede mowing; and finally, rim its edges and any obstacles you cannot remove with mowing strips (page 52) to reduce tedious hand trimming.

If you follow this plan, you can forget about planting grass where it would only add work. Do not try to maintain grass in an

MAKING A DRAWSTRING SACK

An old piece of canvas or a large rectangle of heavy-duty plastic can be converted into a handy device for moving loads of leaves and other garden debris. Sew the canvas or staple the plastic to make a hem around three sides. Through the hem run a length of rope to serve as a drawstring (left). Rake or pile the debris onto the cloth (center) and, when you have a full load, tighten the drawstring (right) to hold the debris as you drag it to a disposal area.

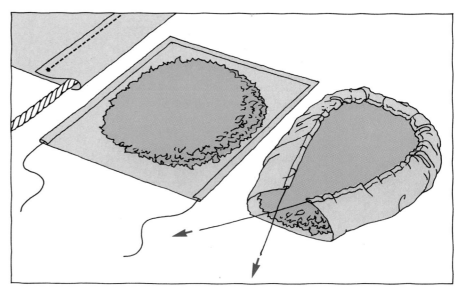

area of constant foot traffic, under the eaves of the house, under trees that cast dense shade or have shallow roots that monopolize moisture and nutrients, or near streets where salt used to melt ice will be sprayed onto it. In such places, use a paving material or a ground-covering mulch of gravel, stones or wood chips.

Nor is it wise to plant grass on a slope. Even a moderate incline makes mowing hard work and can pose a hazard for the person behind the mower. On a slope, as well as under trees and in other problem areas, use a low-growing ground-cover plant such as pachysandra, periwinkle or English ivy; their deeper roots will hold the soil against erosion better than grass.

Many gardeners interested in lower upkeep reduce the sizes of their lawns and concentrate instead on the largest plants in the garden, the trees and shrubs. Major woody plants not only improve the livability of a lot and increase its real-estate value but are willing plants that deliver much enjoyment with very modest care over the years. Here, with a little prudence, you can select species and varieties that are naturally resistant to pests and diseases (*encyclopedia, Chapter 5*), thus eliminating the perpetual battle of the spray gun. You can also choose shrubs and trees well suited to your climate, so you will not need to provide special winter or summer protection. If the plants you choose will thrive in your soil as it now exists, you will not need to modify its chemistry or composition. Good shade trees especially are a sound investment if they are selected with care, trained when young, and placed where neither litter nor invasive roots will become a problem.

While trees, shrubs and ground covers are the basic elements of a low-maintenance garden, other plants fill particular needs. A gardener interested in minimizing his chores will have to weigh the considerable pleasures of eating fresh produce against the work of planting, watering, fertilizing and pestproofing fruits and vegetables. A good compromise is to have a single small, easily managed bed in a sunny place near the kitchen for a few easy-to-grow vegetables such as lettuce and cucumbers plus a handful of indestructible herbs like mint, chives, thyme and sage. Let the commercial growers provide you with perfect, worm-free pears, apples and peaches.

Flowers also can be approached from a low-maintenance standpoint and still provide all of the color and fragrance most gardeners want. For seasonal color, you can rely on flowering shrubs like azaleas, spireas, abelias and crape myrtles, or on hardy, no-work perennials like peonies and day lilies that will blossom every year with little or no effort on your part. In northern climates, avoid plants like dahlias whose roots must be dug up, dried, stored and

THE PERMANENT PLANTINGS

Accents that add little labor

Rare indeed is the low-maintenance gardener who is not tempted occasionally to augment his basic collection of easy-care trees, shrubs and perennials with a brilliant bulb, a splashy annual or an exotic wildflower. The following lists of such enticing plants are made up of the easiest of their kind to grow. But be sure not to let them become the siren song that will lead you to the more work-intensive members of their families. If the enticing flavor of an herb or the color of an annual erodes your resolve to avoid nonessential gardening chores and lures you to the tool shed with ever-greater frequency, you have met your easy-gardening Waterloo.

Two bright annuals, dwarf and African marigolds, flaunt their colors against the greenery of a 20-year-old easy-care garden.

8 easy herbs

You can skip fertilizing any of these sun-loving easy-care perennial herbs. Peppermint and bee balm prefer moist garden spots, but all the others thrive in places where the soil is dry.

ARTEMISIA
Artemisia species

BEE BALM
Monarda didyma

GERMANDER
Teucrium chamaedrys

LAVENDER COTTON
Santolina chamaecyparissus

PEPPERMINT
Mentha piperita

ROSEMARY
Rosmarinus officinalis

THYME
Thymus species

TRUE LAVENDER
*Lavandula angustifolia angustifolia,
L. angustifolia 'Nana'*

11 easy annuals

Easy annuals seed themselves and reappear voluntarily the following year, with no extra work or expense on your part. The plants that are marked with an asterisk in the list below flower better when they are planted in a heavy clay soil or light sandy soil than in one that is rich with humus. Buy started plants from a local nursery and plant them in full sun, mulching them to minimize weeding and watering.

AGERATUM
Ageratum houstonianum

BABIES'-BREATH
Gypsophila elegans

BELLS-OF-IRELAND
Moluccella laevis

* CALIFORNIA POPPY
Eschscholzia californica

CANDYTUFT
Iberis amara

* COREOPSIS
Coreopsis tinctoria

COSMOS
Cosmos bipinnatus, C. sulphureus

MARIGOLD
*Tagetes erecta, T. patula, T. hybrids,
T. tenuifolia pumila*

MIGNONETTE
Reseda odorata

PETUNIA
Petunia hybrids

* PORTULACA, MOSS ROSE
Portulaca grandiflora

12 easy bulbs

Once they have been planted, these easy spring-, summer- or fall-blooming bulbs will return for years without ever being dug up for storage or for division. They form neat clumps that slowly increase in size; those marked with asterisks also seed themselves.

* ARMENIAN GRAPE HYACINTH
Muscari armeniacum

AUTUMN CROCUS
Colchicum autumnale

CROCUS
Crocus species

DAFFODIL, JONQUIL, NARCISSUS
Narcissus species

FAWN LILY, DOG-TOOTH VIOLET
Erythronium species

GLORY-OF-THE-SNOW
Chionodoxa species

LILY
Lilium species

ORNAMENTAL ONION
Allium species

* SIBERIAN SQUILL
Scilla siberica

* SNOWDROP
Galanthus elwesii, G. nivalis

SPANISH SQUILL, SPANISH BLUEBELL
Endymion hispanica

STAR-OF-BETHLEHEM
Ornithogalum umbellatum

8 easy ferns

Although most ferns are quite particular about temperature, humidity and other growing conditions, these eight require only a shady location with moist, acid soil. All of them are hardy, pest-free perennial plants that establish themselves quickly, spread readily and never need to be divided.

CHRISTMAS FERN
Polystichum acrostichoides

CINNAMON FERN
Osmunda cinnamomea

INTERRUPTED FERN
Osmunda claytoniana

JAPANESE PAINTED FERN
Athyrium goeringianum 'Pictum'

LADY FERN
Athyrium filix-femina

NEW YORK FERN
Thelypteris noveboracensis

OSTRICH FERN
Matteuccia struthiopteris pensylvanica

ROYAL FERN
Osmunda regalis

5 easy grasses

Unlike lawn grasses, these decorative perennial grasses are pest free and form clumps that return year after year with little care. They turn brown with frost but may remain standing well into winter. Some types of ornamental grasses are quite tall—ravenna grass, for instance, can reach 12 feet.

BLUE FESCUE
Festuca ovina glauca

EULALIA GRASS
Miscanthus sinensis

OAT GRASS
Arrhenatherum elatius bulbosum

PAMPAS GRASS
Cortaderia selloana

RAVENNA GRASS
Erianthus ravennae

5 easy succulents

Drought-, pest- and disease-resistant succulents are so easy to care for that they do not even need watering once they are established. Snow does not injure these species, which are hardy from Zone 4 south *(map, page 148)*. Give them a sunny spot in well-drained soil.

ADAM'S NEEDLE
Yucca filamentosa

COBWEB HOUSELEEK
Sempervivum arachnoideum

HEN AND CHICKENS, COMMON
HOUSELEEK
Sempervivum tectorum

OCTOBER PLANT
Sedum sieboldii

SHOWY STONECROP
Sedum spectabile

5 easy wildflowers

By definition, a wildflower is one that grows without man's aid. But many are difficult to domesticate unless the garden environment exactly matches their native one. Those listed below are all hardy perennials that are native to both woodland and prairie environments over a wide range of climate zones. Give them full sun and a neutral to slightly acid soil that is moist but well-drained.

BLUEBELL, HAREBELL
Campanula rotundifolia

BLUE-EYED GRASS
Sisyrinchium angustifolium

BUTTERFLY WEED
Asclepias tuberosa

CANADA LILY
Lilium canadense

NEW ENGLAND ASTER
Aster novae-angliae

replanted. Instead use hardy daffodils, crocuses and grape hyacinths that need only be planted once and left to bloom again and again.

For concentrated splashes of color where you can enjoy them the most, do not overlook annuals. They need replacement every year, but they have long seasons of bloom with little care. Rather than starting annuals from seeds, buy them in flats or pots at the garden center; nothing could be easier. One Boston gardener does this every spring, setting out several dozen petunias, marigolds and ageratums near her terrace, then covering the soil around them with leaf mold. For contrast, she masses a dozen potted geraniums on a low wall nearby. In one afternoon she has her whole flower garden in place, with little to do for the rest of the warm season except to water, pinch off faded flowers and pull an occasional weed that struggles up through the mulch. When the plants cease blooming, she pulls them and throws them away. The next year she can repeat her arrangement, try a different one or forget about it entirely.

Everywhere the trend is toward simpler landscaping. Gardening with nature—using native plants to re-create at home the look of the countryside—has become popular in some regions. To simulate a bit of pristine landscape, whether woodland or grassland, wetland or desert, can be exhilarating. Almost everywhere you have a rich choice. The variety of the land astounded early settlers. The Spaniards were overwhelmed by the California hillsides that seemed on fire with the glow of wild poppies. The tall grass of the Midwest prairies, the flowering shrubs and trees of the Appalachian chain, the evergreens of the Pacific Northwest are all horticultural treasures.

AT HOME, NATURALLY

In a return of these natives there is much opportunity for easier gardening, since the plants are of proven suitability for local climate and soil conditions. Caution is in order, however. Endangered species must not be moved. Among those still abundant, not every wild plant will adjust to a garden. Some can take over your garden completely, some have a naturally short life, many will not survive domestication. So research is in order; from lists available from botanical gardens and arboretums or from your county agricultural agent, you can select native plants likely to do well in a garden.

If you live in the South, for example, Callaway Gardens in Pine Mountain, Georgia, offers information on the growing of the native azaleas and rhododendrons in their spectacular collection. For Midwest gardeners, the Boerner Botanical Gardens near Milwaukee publishes a guide to the growing of prairie grasses and flowers. For Northeastern gardeners, the Connecticut Arboretum at Connecticut College in New London has a booklet of native plants including easily grown ferns, grasses, ground covers, vines, wildflowers, shrubs and trees. A booklet on native plants of California is available from the Rancho Santa Anna Botanic Garden in Claremont.

Choosing the right plants for a low-upkeep garden, whether native to your region or not, is a valuable first step. But before permanent planting is done, determine their ultimate sizes and growth habits. Locate them according to the functions you want them to perform. This requires a landscaping plan. A few gardeners are lucky, finding the elements of an attractive, easy-maintenance garden on the property they have just purchased. But others, not so blessed, must create their low-maintenance gardens by design.

Functional areas—a floored patio for outdoor sitting and dining, a play area for children, a service yard—will have to be located on a paper plan. Traffic patterns will need to be studied—how one gets from kitchen to patio to serve an outdoor meal, from parking area to front door without brushing against wet bushes or walking on wet grass, from sandbox to bathroom without tracking sand on the living-room rug. All such details need to be considered in plotting an organized, long-range landscaping plan. A well-designed garden has an advantage that goes beyond just saving work. Against a strong, pleasing overall design, the eye will tend to overlook imperfections, making day-to-day maintenance less critical. Even if you do see a few weeds sprouting in your flower beds, or a shrub in need of pruning, chances are that no one will notice but you.

Finally, with a good layout and well-chosen plants, you can ease the weekly work load by using low-upkeep gardening techniques and tools. Among these are long-range soil preparations for planting; the use of mulches to keep weeds down and reduce watering; scientific methods of controlling pests and diseases; and modern ways of feeding, watering and accomplishing other garden chores with the fewest steps in the least amount of time.

Gardening can be made easier and more enjoyable by all of these techniques, but perhaps the most effective of all is simply one of restraint. Avoid trying to landscape everything in sight, or trying to maintain a garden larger than you need, or getting into projects you cannot easily sustain, or striving for a formal perfection when informality is so charming—and so much easier.

"Praise a large estate, but farm a small one," was the advice of the eminent Roman poet Vergil, himself a farmer, to the would-be easy gardeners of his day 2,000 years ago. More recently, a lesser gardening light named Reginald Arkell put it this way:

> A garden should be rather small
> Or you will have no fun at all.

A HOMEMADE HOSE GUIDE

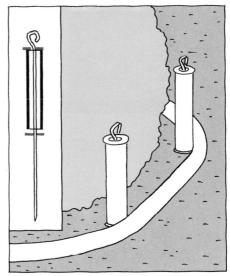

Easily assembled guides keep a garden hose from dragging across flower beds or damaging shrubs. For each guide, start with a tent stake 18 inches long. Slip on a large washer, a 5-inch section cut from an old hose, and a second large washer (inset). Push guides into the ground. When the hose is pulled past, the guides will rotate on the stakes.

Natural designs to let nature do the work

A compromise between the chaos of the wilderness and the clipped perfection of the conventional garden, a garden that is based on the concept of naturalized landscaping offers both orderliness and easy care. By imitating nature's way with plants, and capitalizing on irregular shapes and soft flowing lines, it does away with the tedious chore of maintaining symmetrical shrubs and borders. By following nature's lead in the choice of plants, and relying heavily on native or naturalized trees, shrubs, grasses, ground covers and perennials, it cuts down on the watering and fertilizing required by more finicky plants. The naturalized garden gets its color from shrubs and perennials that flower dependably year after year with only nature's nursing, not from annuals that need to be planted each spring. And in place of the lawn, with its weekly summertime schedule of care, the naturalized garden substitutes evergreen ground covers. Where appropriate, the lawn may even be reborn as an uncut meadow.

Though the look is casual, the design of a naturalized garden is often carefully calculated. Indeed, the gardens pictured here, all created by experts, make use of the design elements associated with formal gardens—such considerations as unity, balance, accents, repetition and variety of color and texture. But in a natural garden planned for easy maintenance, some of these elements play a bigger role than others. For example, repetition is emphasized. To cut down on the separate chores required to maintain many different plants, fewer kinds of plants are grown. The textures and shapes of leaves, bark and ground covers also become more important in a low-maintenance garden without bright annuals for visual contrast.

"Keep it simple," advises one landscape architect, "and learn to be flexible." That is good advice. Do not be afraid to break away from the tradition of wide green lawns, meticulously clipped hedges and foundation shrubs, and beds bursting with annuals.

"It took some getting used to," said one owner of a natural, easy-to-care-for garden, "but now that I've adjusted, I wouldn't trade it for any other."

A thick evergreen ground cover of English ivy blankets a shady garden slope. The small trees at left are vine maples that produce spring flowers and brilliant autumn foliage.

Grace notes for all seasons

Although they require no seasonal care, the gardens of landscape architects Wolfgang Oehme and James Van Sweden offer year-round beauty. "We try to strike a balance," explains Van Sweden, "using plants that offer something in all four seasons." Perennial ornamental grasses, such as fountain grass and blue wild rye, combined with evergreens such as leatherleaf viburnum, are his particular favorites.

Coneflowers, fountain grass and a broad-leaved yucca soften the sharp edges of a walkway. In winter, the dark centers of the coneflowers remain on their stems and become a rich brown, the fountain grass turns a copper color, and the yucca remains blue-green. The tall golden grass is calamagrostis.

Perennials, including (right to left) coneflowers, rose mallow, blue wild rye and calamagrostis grass, arch toward their reflections in a garden pool. A sheet of stainless steel, 2 feet wide and buried vertically, prevents the bamboo behind the coneflowers from spreading.

A grassy dune garden

Once part of a New Jersey bay, the natural garden below was barren dredged soil when landscape architect Arthur Bye began to develop it. He shaped the land into dunes, then seeded them with dune grass. For dark, dramatic accents, he planted bayberry shrubs and Japanese black pines in undulating masses over the dunes. "We are trying to reinforce the natural character of the area," he says.

Bayberry shrubs, which thrive in sandy soil, form a half circle in a meadow of shimmering dune grass. At right are jagged Japanese black pines; near the house are Andorra junipers and dwarf Japanese yews.

The contrasting textures of bumpy Mascarene grass and low shore juniper create an unusual pattern in this coastal garden.

Textured landscapes

The strong, dry winds that sweep along the coast of Southern California would dismay many gardeners, but not landscape architect Fred Lang. The wind helps to sculpt his highly textured gardens, shaping, for example, the finger-like branches of Hollywood junipers *(opposite)*. "To mitigate the problems in your garden," he advises, "take advantage of the opportunities that nature has already provided."

Mondo and Mascarene grasses (foreground) are salt-tolerant evergreen ground covers that spread slowly, requiring little upkeep.

Rosettes of agave, filmy asparagus ferns and day lilies give varied color and texture to a Western garden. An undulating concrete

mowing strip keeps the flower bed's ground cover in check while eliminating the need to hand-clip the edge of the lawn.

Plants that keep their place

For the luxuriant gardens of the Pacific Northwest, landscape architect A. Rex Zumwalt selects plants that will develop their natural shapes without outgrowing their allotted spaces. In a small garden bordering a lake *(below)*, he planted compact shrubs and trees, including dwarf evergreen azaleas and a Japanese threadleaf maple; both remain small without laborious pruning.

Pearlwort, a thick, mosslike ground cover sprinkled with white flowers, softens the edge of a lakeside garden. Contrast is provided by dwarf azaleas (right), a Japanese maple (center) and several taller vine maples.

Choosing plants that care for themselves 2

Ironclads. Cast iron plants. Old ironsides. Thus some nurserymen label those garden indestructibles that seem to endure the worst weather, the most outrageous neglect, the most pernicious pests, and still flourish year after year. Half the secret of saving time and work in the garden lies in selecting plants with such virtues, plants that require neither coddling nor disciplining.

Yet surprising numbers of gardeners ignore this possibility. They buy plants on impulse, on the basis of bits of information from nursery tags or catalogues. The information may be accurate as far as it goes, but it falls far short of giving a complete picture of the plants' staying power or of describing what some of their more peculiar, if not downright objectionable, habits might be.

Take, for example, the ailanthus—the tree of heaven celebrated in *A Tree Grows in Brooklyn,* Betty Smith's classic novel of tenement life in early-20th Century New York. In its brief era of glory, this fast-growing and exotic Asian import, with its parasols of large, graceful leaves, was all the rage among proper Victorian homeowners, thousands of whom bought it to ornament their gardens. Gradually, however, some of the tree's less heavenly characteristics were revealed.

Though the ailanthus obligingly grew anywhere, even in smoky air and meager soil, it soon was growing all over the place, its Gorgon-like roots breaking pipes and drains in a voracious need for water, its winged seeds floating far and wide to send up groves of unwanted progeny. The male trees had a foul odor when in bloom, and the fast-growing branches of both sexes were so brittle they constantly littered the best-kept Victorian lawns. The tree even produced a toxic chemical in its leaves; washed to the ground by rain, it inhibited the growth of other plants. As the evidence against it mounted, admiration for the ailanthus waned. Today it is generally scorned as a "trash" tree. Though it continues to sprout stubbornly

A sea of peonies engulfs an ornamental beehive in the gardens at Winterthur, Delaware. Peonies are remarkably free of pests and diseases; some of those at Winterthur were planted in the 1880s.

in vacant lots, it is a species of choice only for beleaguered city dwellers who simply can get nothing else to grow.

For less spectacular but equally valid reasons, anyone interested in a trouble-free garden should approach other plant species with caution. To plant roses, probably the most popular flowers in American gardens, is to sign up for an exacting program of spraying several times each year. The same is true of fruit or nut trees. Mulberries grow rapidly and provide welcome shade, but they can be a nuisance; fruiting varieties drop their plump berries on sidewalks and terraces, leaving messy, stubborn stains. Still other plants create more work than some gardeners will think they are worth. Lilacs must be pruned to keep them flowering, and they must be protected from scale and borer attacks. Like the ailanthus, willows and poplars grow rapidly, but they are so brittle they require a constant cleanup of their litter. Chrysanthemums must be divided periodically to keep them blooming well. Regal delphiniums must be staked to keep their stems from breaking in the wind. Some plants can even be a menace—a wisteria vine cascading over a sturdy pergola can be a garden delight, but its muscular shoots can loosen the shingles on the side of a house.

A LIST TO CHOOSE FROM

No plant is completely well-mannered, of course, and thus no garden is work free. But you can greatly decrease the amount of work you must do by choosing plants that have few bad habits and by matching their natural needs to your local conditions. To help you make such choices, the characteristics of over 200 trees, shrubs, perennials and ground covers, selected for their low maintenance, are described in the encyclopedia chapter that begins on page 91. These plants constitute a basis for permanent landscaping. All have been chosen for their adaptability to a wide range of climate and soil conditions, for their general resistance to common pests and diseases and for their relatively modest demands on your time. In addition to qualities that make upkeep easy, most have other outstanding virtues, such as shade and screening qualities, attractive flowers or brilliant autumn color.

In many of the encyclopedia entries, you will note that some familiar species have been omitted. As in human families, the characteristics of individuals can vary widely, and not all are equally well behaved. Among the deciduous trees, for example, the Amur maple is recommended but the silver maple is not. Although the latter grows with gratifying speed for those who want quick results, it can quickly become too large for the average suburban lot, and its weak branches are prone to split under high winds and ice. Similarly, the Swiss stone pine is recommended, but not the Swiss mountain or Mugo pine, a frequent victim of scale insects. You will find the thornless honey locust listed, but not those locusts whose thorns are hazardous or whose seed pods drop, requiring frequent raking.

Among the shrubs, only a handful of roses is included, the tough old-fashioned species roses. Omitted are all the beloved hybrid teas, which require a regular program of pruning, fertilizing, spraying and winter protection. Flowers such as day lilies and hostas, which seem to thrive on neglect, get top billing on the list of perennials, but irises do not make it; they are too vulnerable to invasion by the iris root borer.

(The plants that will form a less permanent part of your landscape—such as annuals, herbs, ferns, ornamental grasses, vines and bulbs—can also be evaluated on the basis of the care they demand; lists of relatively care-free choices appear on page 13.)

When you select plants for minimum maintenance, you should not only look through the encyclopedia chapter but also look around you, exploring the local scene. Drive around town and out into the country. Note what plants are prevalent in gardens, which kinds seem especially handsome and healthy, where and how each has been used. Look also in patches of meadow or forest, noting which plants grow there naturally, in what combinations with other plants and under what conditions of moisture, sun or shade. You are likely to discover some local star performers that are not listed in this book's encyclopedia, perhaps so common that to you they seem almost like weeds. Their very profusion is a good guarantee that they will grow well in your own garden. But keep in mind that some

HOMETOWN FAVORITES

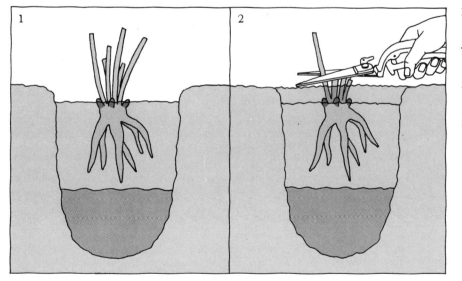

PERSUADING PEONIES

Peonies flower faithfully for many years, but only if they are planted at the right depth. Plant in early fall, when the red buds of next year's growth are visible on top of the crown. Set the roots in a hole 1½ to 2 feet deep, half filled with peat moss and soil mixed with a double handful of bone-meal fertilizer. Position the roots so the buds are 2 inches or a bit less below the soil's surface; when buds are too deep, peonies fail to flower. Fill the hole with soil to the level of the buds and water thoroughly. When the water drains away, press out any air pockets, then add soil up to the ground level. Trim off stems close to the surface of the soil.

native shrubs and vines grow so rampantly in good garden soil that they may quickly get out of hand.

Visit an arboretum or botanical garden if there is one in your area. You will find plants of particular interest around the grounds, and horticulturists on duty may be willing to tell you a great deal about your native plants and their habits, good and bad, as well as about special varieties particularly suited to your area. However familiar, take a fresh look at plantings in public places like town parks, school campuses, golf courses and cemeteries. Especially rewarding are highway borders and median strips. Increasingly, roadsides are being turned into showcases for local trees, shrubs, grasses and ground covers, all chosen by professionals for their appearance and for the lowest possible upkeep. Note particularly plants that flourish under conditions similar to those in your garden: which ones grow well in sun and which in shade, which prosper in windy, exposed positions and which prefer low, swampy ground.

DETECTIVE WORK   In your horticultural explorations, take a camera along with you. If you cannot identify a tree or shrub that interests you, take a few pictures of it. Pick a sprig, too, if picking is permitted. A sprig with several leaves on it is essential for identification; if you can include some flowers or fruit or seed pods, so much the better. Press the leaves and flowers so that they dry flat; otherwise identification may be difficult.

You may be able to match your photographs and samples with the paintings in this book. In any case, when you are ready to start buying you will have something to show a knowledgeable nurseryman. Unless you are starting a garden from scratch or planning an extensive remodeling, the advice of such a nurseryman is all you are likely to need when you select plants.

Start with initial visits to local nurseries and garden centers. Examine plant tags and prices and note the merchandise in stock. If you want to talk with someone about particular plants or specific problems in your garden, plan a second visit, preferably on a weekday afternoon. On a spring weekend, everyone on the nursery staff is likely to be busy just taking orders and loading plants in the backs of cars and station wagons.

NINE VITAL QUESTIONS   You can get an idea of what will grow well in your area just by examining the rows of plants lined up at the nursery and by checking the plant tags. What the tags will not tell you, however, are the answers to nine vital questions bearing on any plant's need for upkeep in your garden:

1. What will be the plant's function in your garden? "Amateur gardeners think about plants as isolated specimens, not about the purposes they will serve," says one gardening authority, deploring the tendency of beginners to buy plants that catch their fancy and only later wonder where to plant them. There are, of course, some superb trees and shrubs whose beauty of form, texture or color permit them to stand alone as focal points in a landscape. But most plants are not works of art to be collected like statuary or China teapots. As they grow and change, they will add the most delight to a garden if they have been wisely chosen to serve utilitarian as well as esthetic functions.

If your garden needs shade, for example, you will do yourself no favor by rushing to the nursery and blindly buying a pair of bargain trees. Precisely what kind of shade do you need? If you want to shield your terrace from the afternoon sun, try to select a tree that will not only cast a generous circle of shade but will look well with high branches so you can walk under them comfortably. This rules out such species as pin oak or weeping birch, which have low and trailing branches.

Consider too the quality of shade you want. A tree like a Norway maple, with large, flat, overlapping leaves, will cast dense shade, giving maximum protection from blazing midsummer sun. On the other hand, a tree like a honey locust, with finely cut compound leaves, is a better choice if you want light, filtered shade that will not black out the interior of your house. If you live in the South, where shade is welcome much of the year, an evergreen tree may be the best choice. In the North, however, deciduous species are usually preferred because they provide shade in summer when you need it but drop their leaves in autumn to admit welcome light and warming sun. Refining your choice one step further, you might select a deciduous tree like the ginkgo that tends to lose all of its leaves at one time, so only one raking is needed in the fall. Or you might prefer a mountain ash, with leaves so fine they tend to disappear under shrubs and ground covers, thus needing little raking at all.

In similar fashion, the natural growth habits of other trees, shrubs and even ground covers can serve whatever particular purposes you have in mind. You can choose plants to block a view of the neighbors or the street or to reduce the force of prevailing winds. You can create a barrier to keep out wandering dogs or children. And there are plants whose roots will hold a bank against erosion and others that can be used to divide a garden into separate areas for different uses *(Chapter 3)*.

2. Will the plant find the climate of your garden suitable? Though a few tough species will grow almost anywhere, most plants will flourish only in an environment similar to that of their native regions. Plants recommended in the encyclopedia chapter are keyed to the U.S. Department of Agriculture climate map *(page 148)*, which divides the United States and Canada into 10 zones according to the severity of winter cold. A plant's resistance to cold—its winter hardiness—is indicated in each encyclopedia entry by the numbers of the zones where it can be expected to grow and thrive. A plant that is suited to the warmth of Zones 9 and 10 (Florida, southern Texas and California) might also be able to survive in a protected spot in neighboring Zone 8. But some plants—shrubs like mock oranges and weigelas, for example—might suffer winter dieback in the northern reaches of their recommended zones if they are grown in exposed locations; the dead branches that result could necessitate extra pruning work.

CLIMATIC HIGHS AND LOWS

These local variations within zones known as microclimates can be created by differences in altitude, the nearness of bodies of water or exposure to strong winds. An extreme example is the Grand Canyon, where there are four distinct microclimates between the canyon floor and its rim. If you live at the bottom of a hill it can make a difference in the way your garden grows. Nights will be cooler there than farther up the hill, frosts will end later in the spring and come earlier in the fall, your plants' growing season will be shortened, and there will be some plants your neighbor up the hill can grow but you cannot. By contrast, if you live near the ocean or some other large body of water, the water temperature will tend to moderate changes in air temperature, and your garden will be favored, because plants withstand gradually changing temperatures better than sudden sharp rises and falls.

(continued on page 38)

Self-sufficient serenity

Hostas, also known as plantain lilies, will brighten a garden's shady corners for many years with their dramatic leaves, which are usually deeply grooved, often very large and sometimes marked with white or yellow. "A hosta clump really looks its best if it is left undisturbed for 10, 20 or even 30 years," says one expert. "I have seen many hostas flourishing in gardens long abandoned."

In recent years hybridizers have created more than 200 varieties of this handsome import from the Orient, confusing the nomenclature mightily but giving gardeners an enormous choice. The newer hostas shown here carry on a tranquil tradition with fresh dashes of spice. On some, yellow or white markings decorate giant frosty blue-green clumps; on others, flowers dance above leaves that have a seersucker texture. Massed in a bed, used as a ground cover in deep shade or planted in a row as an informal hedge, the hosta's overlapping leaves so nearly eliminate any need for weeding that it has won the sobriquet, "the old people's plant."

Prized for the beauty of their foliage from spring until frost cuts them down, hostas add a bonus of delicate summer flowers.

Diversity on display

HOSTA TOKUDAMA AUREO NEBULOSA
Yellow-flushed leaves thrive in deep shade or sun.

H. NIGRESCENS ELATIOR
These clumps may grow 6 feet wide, with flower spikes 9 feet tall.

H. FORTUNEI NORTH HILLS
This hosta flaunts an imposing clump of lance-shaped leaves.

H. GOLDEN PRAYERS
Puckered, gold-capped leaves suggest upright hands.

II. KROSSA REGAL
This large, silvery hosta spreads vigorously.

H. FLORAL MASS
The buds will soon become a profusion of purple blossoms.

H. BLUE WHIRLS
Swirling tiers of leaves look like petticoats.

H. FLAMBOYANT
Many-hued leaves are almost luminous at dusk.

H. LANCIFOLIA HAKU-CHU-HAN
The leaves are eye-catchers.

H. LANCIFOLIA KABITAN
This small hosta keeps its yellow glow all season.

H. FORTUNEI GLORIOSA
Sharply outlined leaves seem carved in jade.

PLANTING UNDER OVERHANGS
To avoid the need for hand-watering where eaves of the house prevent rain from reaching the ground, plant shrubs so their centers are well outside the edge of the eaves. The roots exposed to rain will provide water to the sheltered portion of the plant. Also allow ample space for growth so branches of the shrub will not rub against the house when the plant is mature.

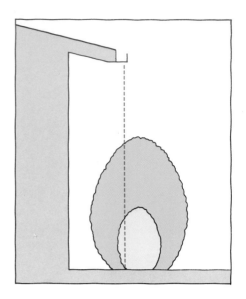

Winter hardiness can also be affected by local heat, humidity and rainfall. The moisture-loving Douglas fir that thrives in the rainy Pacific Northwest would have no chance to survive in the dry climate of Nevada, only a few hundred miles away. Many bulbs benefit from lying dormant under a continuous blanket of winter snow; but in regions where the cold is broken by intermittent winter thaws, the soil heaves, and bulbs may be moved and damaged. Unusual amounts of summer rainfall can force soft new growth on plants that are normally winter hardy, making them most vulnerable to cold damage.

Thus, when you are checking the climate-zone map, let what you see growing well in your immediate neighborhood be a cross-check on your zone reading. If you need additional information, consult the local office of the Cooperative Extension Service, which is usually listed under the county government in the telephone book.

3. Will your soil suit the plants? Soils also vary geographically. But most of the plants commonly grown in American gardens grow well in the moderately acid to neutral soils that prevail throughout the East, the prairie states and the woodlands of the West Coast. A smaller range of plants will tolerate the alkaline soils of the Southwest. City soils vary greatly, but generally they are poorer than average. In some suburban developments, the rich topsoil has been scraped away—"scalped"—for sale elsewhere, leaving a thin layer of sod as a temporary mask over poor subsoil. If building rubble such as scraps of plasterboard is buried on the site, the soil may be more alkaline than normal for the region.

If you have doubts about your soil, or if your plants fail for no apparent reason, a soil test is in order. Local offices of the Cooperative Extension Service will test soil, though you may need to wait several weeks for a report. Alternatively, you can take a reading yourself with one of the test kits sold at garden centers. If you find that the soil is too alkaline for a particular plant, you can modify it by adding ground sulfur or iron sulfate; if the soil is too acid, you can sweeten it by applying ground limestone. Such amendments are only temporary solutions, however. It is better to match your choice of plants to the soil's natural chemistry and save your energy for a more important task: improving the soil's tilth, its physical qualities as a growing medium for your plants.

Preparing soil for planting is certainly one of gardening's most arduous tasks, but it cannot be skipped. There is no shortcut unless you are extremely lucky and a previous owner of your property has done it for you. For any plant to thrive, especially a permanent addition to the landscape such as a tree, shrub, perennial or ground cover, you must dig deeply, loosening the soil and blending in a generous measure of such organic matter as peat moss or leaf mold to lighten the soil and improve its drainage. Though this involves hard work initially, it will eliminate endless problems later with weak, struggling, unhealthy plants. Techniques for improving your soil, even if it is very poor and compacted and underlaid with impervious rock or clay, are described in Chapter 4. As an alternative, you can simply ignore the existing soil and grow your plants in raised beds filled with rich topsoil.

4. Does the plant have special requirements for moisture, for wind protection, or for sun or shade? Garden centers are filled each weekend with gardeners happily loading their cars with unhappy surprises. A plant's preference for sun or shade, its need for a moist or dry location and its vulnerability to wind or snow damage are all characteristics that should be considered before you buy. Fragile, fast-growing trees, shrubs and perennials are bound to require extra work in areas where winds are strong and persistent. Some plants cannot stand wet roots without rotting, while others are almost continuously thirsty. And while most plants grow best in full sun, there are exceptions. Small trees like dogwoods and shrubs like rhododendrons that are natives of the forest floor not only tolerate partial shade but may prefer it. Several ground covers—sweet woodruff, galax, pachysandra, periwinkle and English ivy among them—do with so little sun they are regularly used instead of grass for carpeting under shade trees.

5. Is the plant resistant to pests and diseases? This may be the most important single work-saving question to ask at the time of purchase. If the plant you buy is not subject to malaise or pest attack, it will not require all the mixing, application and cleanup that go with a regular program of spraying. The environment and you will share the benefits.

The species listed in the encyclopedia chapter are generally free of the most common afflictions. In addition, it is a good idea to check with local horticulturists, nurserymen or a county agent concerning the susceptibility of any particular plant to current local blights or infestations. Fruit-bearing plants, whether trees, vines or shrubs, should be viewed with special caution; these almost guarantee that you will be out with a spray canister or hose attachment on a systematic, time-consuming schedule.

6. How large will the plant be when it matures? Countless picture windows have been engulfed by dandy little plants that looked tame and manageable in their containers at the nursery. Who would guess that such a soft, tiny hemlock could become a 40-foot monster in less than 25 years. Plants that swiftly outgrow their assigned spaces require constant, merciless, time-consuming and often unattractive pruning to keep them in bounds. Most of these lusty offenders are foundation plantings that have been set close to contemporary, ground-hugging ranch houses whose foundations actually need very little camouflage. For such houses, compact, dwarf or trailing species with predictably low mature heights are appropriate and work-saving choices.

If you select such plants, have the courage to space them well apart and far enough out from the house so they have room to grow. The shrubs should be spaced to accommodate their mature sizes. If they seem small and lonely, fill in around them with flowering annuals for the first few years.

7. Does the plant have special pruning needs? Like the little evergreen that swallowed the house, any plant that needs frequent pruning to limit its size is bothersome. All fruit trees, especially those that are espaliered, fall into this category. Grapes also need much pruning. So does any tree or shrub that has been propagated by grafting; it must be pruned to keep suckers from the understock from taking over. Any ground cover that needs shearing is likely to be more work than grass, since the trimming involved is handwork. A flowering shrub that benefits from the removal of faded flowers, one by one, will take many hours of your time if you groom it properly. And if you want a formal privet hedge like the one grandmother had, be prepared to clip it every few weeks. Actually, the pruning needs of many such plants are primarily related to their purpose and placement. As a single ornamental with plenty of space, a California privet is a care-free plant; it is only when it is used in a formal hedge that it makes extra work for you.

8. *How aggressive is the plant?* As one landscape architect observed, you have to know which plants are the Huns. A number of otherwise appealing species can be backyard barbarians if given half a chance. These are the aggressive rooters, spreaders and climbers that plunge beyond their allotted spaces, crowd out less combative plants, overgrow paths and patios, or even close in on the house itself. Willows and poplars are notorious for their water-seeking roots, which sometimes range up to 100 feet to clog underground pipes and drains. In some parts of the Northeast, overrun woods are ample testimony to the tree-climbing vigor of Hall's honeysuckle, a delightfully fragrant species introduced from Japan a century ago. Some ground covers like the handsome flowering crown vetch will invade nearby flower beds and lawns, though it can be very useful in a broader, more open area—on a sunny bank, for example, where its tough, far-ranging underground stems penetrate deeply to form an erosion-resistant cover.

9. *Does the plant have other undesirable traits?* Periodic clean-up is a chore that cannot be avoided entirely, even in the best designed of low-upkeep gardens. But it can be made easier if you avoid plants that are notorious litterbugs. In addition to weak trees that constantly shed twigs and small branches on the lawn, there are others that perpetuate the family line by promiscuously dropping objectionable fruits or exceptionally fertile seeds. One, the female ginkgo, drops round, juicy fruits that smell, in the words of one plant

PACHYSANDRA PROPAGATION

1. *To plant a single-rooted cutting of pachysandra, wrap an 8- or 10-inch length of the white underground stem into a spiral. Set it in a small hole in loosened soil mixed with leaf mold or peat moss. For even distribution, plant cuttings 6 to 12 inches apart. Rooted cuttings can be taken from a thick existing bed for starting a new bed elsewhere.*

2. *For faster cover, plant several cuttings at once in a larger hole. Loop the stems of several plants into a loose overhand knot, taking care not to break either stems or the hairlike roots.*

Judging nursery trees and shrubs

The trees and shrubs you plant in a low-maintenance garden should be the best you can afford. Since it takes the same amount of labor to plant a poor specimen as a superior one, you gamble with your future gardening work load when you buy a dubious bargain. Use these guidelines to choose well-proportioned, vigorous plants that will ensure less pruning, fertilizing and spraying. Quality plants will more than repay their premium prices by saving you time and effort later.

Appraising the shape

PROPORTION OF ROOTS TO TOP

A medium-sized shade tree with a root ball roughly two-thirds the width of the tree's crown (near right) has the healthiest proportion of roots to top growth. A tree with a small crown in comparison to its root ball (center) may be weak and stunted. But avoid the temptation to buy the largest plant in order to have an instant tree. A small root ball cannot support an excessively large crown (far right). The tree would need severe pruning to keep new growth from dying due to lack of nutrients and water.

SHRUB SYMMETRY

Look for a deciduous shrub with many stems that start to branch close to the ground and grow symmetrically around a central point (left). A shrub that is misshapen (right) may have grown under crowded conditions or may have suffered from injury or disease; it will need severe pruning.

EVERGREEN SILHOUETTES

An evergreen should present a small-scale version of the mature shape you desire. Its branches should be evenly and closely spaced along its entire trunk (left). New growth may not fill in gaps left by missing branches (center). A tree that has lost its topmost shoot (right) may develop an undesirable shape.

Studying the top

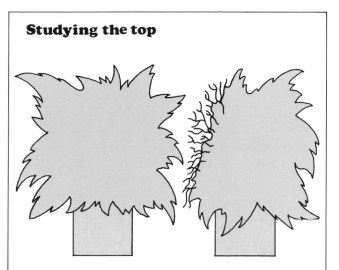

SIGNS OF EVERGREEN VIGOR
Choose bushy conifers with short spaces between branches and with undamaged new growth at branch tips (left). Avoid those with broken branches on shoots, yellowed tips or dead patches of brown needles (right). Foliage should be healthy and colored a shade of green appropriate to the species.

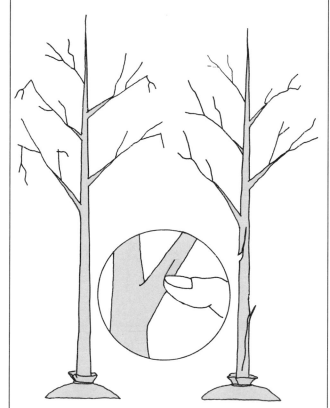

SOUND DECIDUOUS TREES
Broken twigs will not set back a deciduous tree (left). But avoid trees with broken branches or gouged, split or sunburned trunks (right), or with wilted or discolored leaves. If the tree is not in leaf, gently scratch the bark of a finger-thick branch (inset) to see if the tissue below is a healthy green.

Evaluating roots

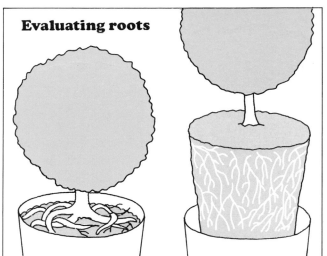

CONTAINER-GROWN PLANTS
Pass up container-grown plants with many roots poking through the soil's surface (left). If possible, lift the plant to look for a network of white or light tan roots evenly distributed through the root ball and firmly holding the soil (right). Reject plants that have black or brown roots, loose soil, or girdling roots.

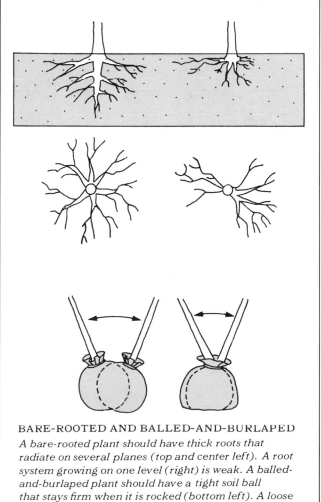

BARE-ROOTED AND BALLED-AND-BURLAPED
A bare-rooted plant should have thick roots that radiate on several planes (top and center left). A root system growing on one level (right) is weak. A balled-and-burlaped plant should have a tight soil ball that stays firm when it is rocked (bottom left). A loose ball (right) indicates too few roots.

expert raised on a Midwestern farm, much like the inside of an uncleaned chicken coop. Some plants like white baneberry and Japanese yew have poisonous berries that may pose a danger to curious children. Female honey locusts, except those of the seedless, thornless kind, drop seed pods up to a foot long, as do coffee trees. And weedy trees like the wild cherry and the sassafras spread their seeds so widely and root so readily that you will spend much time yanking up the seedlings.

Finally, a word about acquiring new plants. In any garden, the most costly maintenance item of all is the plant that dies, the one that must then be dug up or cut down and replaced. Very few bargain plants are really bargains, and gathering plants in the wild, even where it is permissible, can be a risky business. The safest course is to purchase plants from a reputable nursery or garden center in your area or from one of the large mail-order companies that also have reputations to protect.

Your own nurseryman will normally sell only plants that are reliably winter hardy in your area. He may grow his own stock, which is all to the good, or he may import it from a place where growing conditions favor the propagation of certain plants. Along the shores of Lake Erie, for example, there is a belt of sandy loam that produces shrubs with superior root systems. Oregon and Washington have superior tree farms; a maple seedling grown there and cut back in its second or third year can be expected to shoot up a whip 6 or 8 feet tall in a single season.

THE INSTANT GARDEN

Few questions are put more often to nurserymen than "How fast will it grow?" Instant privacy behind a tall hedge, instant shade beneath a soaring tree, instant coolness within a vine-covered bower—all these can be had, but at a price. In gardening, there are two sides to this coin. One way to an instant garden is to choose fast-growing plants, the kind that are advertised as living fences or miracle trees. Speedy results can be had with such plants, but often at the sacrifice of long-term satisfaction. As a general rule, the faster a plant grows, the more likely it is to have weak, brittle wood, a higher-than-average susceptibility to insect damage and fungus disease, and a short, sometimes messy life.

Another formula for quick results is to balance time against money and buy the largest trees and shrubs you can afford. Transplanting is more difficult, however, because more of the root system must be pruned away in getting a plant out of the ground. It is likely that you will have to face the extra cost of professional help with the entire project. Dollar for dollar, a small tree or shrub gives you more for your money than a large one.

Yet another solution to the dilemma is to buy a few fast-growing species as temporary fillers to make a bare lot livable and add more desirable species when possible, eventually removing the fillers when the long-term garden mainstays have grown to an appreciable size.

The ultimate compromise is to choose species that combine a reasonably fast growth rate with adequate sturdiness, neatness and longevity, plus a pattern of growth that will level off at a predetermined point without getting out of hand. Among the shade trees that are described in the encyclopedia chapter that suit this good-compromise description are the green ash, little-leaved linden, Norway maple, katsura, red oak and Amur cork; among the shrubs are cornelian cherry, beauty bush, Tatarian and fragrant honeysuckle, weigela, viburnum and mock orange.

When money is of no concern, of course, many such problems become moot. One Florida millionaire ordered, and got, a 12-foot-high hedge of oleander, telescoping eight years of growth into a two-day moving job. A Georgia landscape contractor will transplant magnolia trees 35 to 40 feet tall; the cost of planting two about equals the price of an automobile. And a client of a Connecticut landscape architect found a way to buy an instant woodland garden. A crew of gardeners was dispatched to cut 4-by-8-foot segments from the forest floor. These were eased onto sheets of plywood—flowers, ferns, fallen leaves and all—and were carried to the home-site. There they were reassembled like a giant puzzle atop previously prepared patches of ground. It was not a cheap operation.

COMPROMISE CANDIDATES

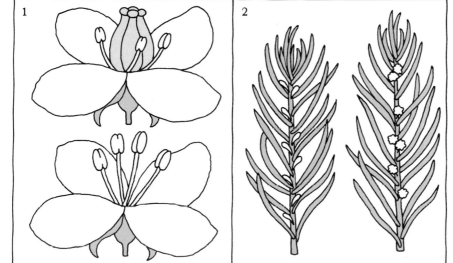

SEX DISCRIMINATION

1. *The fruit-bearing flower of the female holly (top left) has a large central pistil surrounded by nonfunctioning small stamens. The male holly's flower (bottom), needed to fertilize the female, has four large stamens. If you plant at least one of each sex in the spring, you can be confident of getting berries in the fall.*

2. *On the yew, buds of the fruit-bearing female (left) are narrow, pointed and not so plentiful as on the male. The male flower buds (right) are numerous and rounded.*

Planning ahead to save falling behind 3

Some homeowners are lucky. They find the elements of an easy-upkeep garden already in place when they acquire their property. Perhaps they have bought a wooded suburban lot that naturally lends itself to the creation of a garden of ferns and other native plants, one that will need only occasional management rather than constant maintenance. Perhaps they are city dwellers like the couple in Philadelphia who bought an 18th Century townhouse and acquired, thanks to a previous owner, a walled garden with brick-enclosed, waist-high flower beds, the perfect arrangement for no-stoop gardening.

Not many homeowners, however, are so fortunate. More commonly they must deal from the beginning with a garden that is difficult to maintain. The soil may be poor, the lot awkwardly shaped. There may be too few or too many plants, including several of the wrong kind. Yet even in such circumstances gardening can be made less time consuming. The trick is to substitute brainwork for back work—and the brainwork starts with planning. It is surprising how badly planned many gardens are.

Perhaps the main reason why so many gardens are so disorganized is that their owners have never decided what kind of garden they really wanted. They have collected plants haphazardly, or they have inherited someone else's landscaping notions, complete with mistakes, and have unwittingly become slaves of the status quo. It takes ingenuity, not to mention fortitude, to tear out an unsatisfactory garden and start over to create one that is tailored specifically to your needs. But there is no question that such a major decision can pay off handsomely, not only in lower upkeep but in greater enjoyment of the garden itself.

The first step in this process of redesign is analytical. Landscape architects, who are all too familiar with the difficulty of getting clients to identify their real interests and desires, have likened this

Drought-resistant African daisies hug a steep coastal hillside in Southern California. At the top of the stairs geraniums are flanked by wind-tolerant myoporum shrubs. At lower left is a lemonade-berry shrub.

analysis to the agonies of the psychiatrist's couch. Compared to it, they say, preparing drawings and specifying plants seem simple. Atlanta landscape architect Edward Daugherty begins a garden renovation by taking his clients on a garden tour. "I wander over the whole site with the clients, observing how they live, what their children do, what functions they want their garden to serve. I explore alternatives with them verbally for as much as three hours. Only then, in the final hour, do I begin to draw up a sketch. 'Now,' I say, 'let's focus on that area of most concern to you.'"

Whether or not you seek professional advice, the same principle applies to your own search for an easier garden. Concentrate on garden areas and functions that are important to you, and focus your redesign on them. Maintaining these areas will not seem like hard work because they give you pleasure. The rest of the garden can be relegated to a secondary role, even to a measure of benign neglect. Do not worry about what others may think. "Gardeners fuss too much over details that most people never notice," observes one Connecticut nurseryman.

FIRST THE BIG CHANGES

In planning for low upkeep, then, do not concern yourself at first with the day-to-day shortcuts, saving 15 minutes here and 10 minutes there, until you have taken a concentrated look at the big picture. Try first to find those major changes that will make your garden more livable and at the same time eliminate major chunks of work. If you would rather relax on your terrace than mow a large expanse of lawn, it stands to reason that you should reduce the amount of lawn and enlarge the terrace. Most terraces are too small to be comfortable anyway. By expanding your terrace and adding plantings around it, you will not only gain more useful outdoor living space but you may be able to settle for a much smaller area of lawn. In fact, you may be able to eliminate grass completely in favor of a no-care ground cover.

If, on the other hand, your lawn is manageable but you are tired of dragging out the hose every few days and maneuvering it around to water the grass and a dozen different shrub borders and flower beds, consider installing a built-in sprinkler system with strategically placed heads and an automatic timer. Or, if you are losing a long-standing war with rabbits and raccoons in your vegetable patch, consider enclosing the garden with wire-mesh fence—and add a base that extends a foot into the ground to discourage the raiders once and for all.

Having determined what areas to concentrate on, think next about garden design. Here, you will need to balance effort (and cost) against effects. A certain amount of simplification is likely to be in order, but not necessarily at the expense of beauty. Some of the loveliest gardens are simple, almost sparse, in conception.

First priority should be given to trees and shrubs. These long-lived plants are the framework, the bones of the anatomy of your garden. They give the garden its essential and lasting character over the years and through all seasons. Even in the winter their bare branches and stems create graceful patterns when they are silhouetted against snow and sky. And once they are established, most of these plants require virtually no maintenance.

Gardens consisting solely of woody plants—ground covers as well as trees and shrubs—are in fact popular for their combined advantages of simple, handsome design with minimum upkeep.

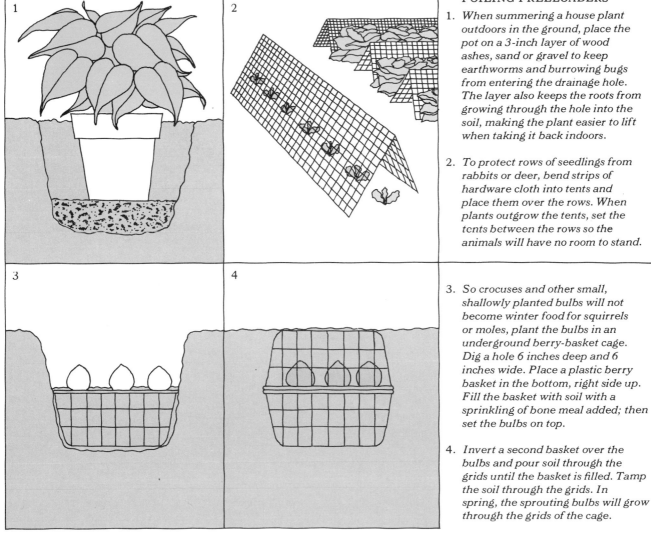

FOILING FREELOADERS

1. *When summering a house plant outdoors in the ground, place the pot on a 3-inch layer of wood ashes, sand or gravel to keep earthworms and burrowing bugs from entering the drainage hole. The layer also keeps the roots from growing through the hole into the soil, making the plant easier to lift when taking it back indoors.*

2. *To protect rows of seedlings from rabbits or deer, bend strips of hardware cloth into tents and place them over the rows. When plants outgrow the tents, set the tents between the rows so the animals will have no room to stand.*

3. *So crocuses and other small, shallowly planted bulbs will not become winter food for squirrels or moles, plant the bulbs in an underground berry-basket cage. Dig a hole 6 inches deep and 6 inches wide. Place a plastic berry basket in the bottom, right side up. Fill the basket with soil with a sprinkling of bone meal added; then set the bulbs on top.*

4. *Invert a second basket over the bulbs and pour soil through the grids until the basket is filled. Tamp the soil through the grids. In spring, the sprouting bulbs will grow through the grids of the cage.*

Landscape architects call them green gardens. The essential design exploits the textures, patterns and shadings of a variety of leaves, branches and bark. But a green garden need not be totally green; it can also provide the added delights of flowers, berries and brilliant autumn foliage. Thousands of miles of federal and state highways have been landscaped with such green-garden plants, and the effect can be strikingly beautiful. As one gardening authority observed, "It is possible for someone not interested in gardening for its own sake—who wants to do the work once and then forget it—to stop right there, with woody plants."

A LIMITED NUMBER

Whatever plants you choose, do not use too many of them. One of the most common problems encountered by gardeners is the plant that has outgrown the space allocated to it—and this is a problem that is avoidable. The average mature height and spread of any tree or shrub is known, so you can place it where it will not interfere with others. When trees or shrubs have to fight for space, they usually end up misshapen.

Even when there is no question of crowding, you probably need fewer plants than you think. On a typical suburban plot, four or five trees are usually sufficient for shade and screening. The rule of thumb used by some landscape architects, that a tree will dominate an area whose radius is equal to the tree's height, is convenient for judging the number of trees you need. (The exception is a grove, where the goal is to have a thicket of trunks and the contours of the individual trees blend together.)

A LIMITED VARIETY

Do not mix too many different kinds of plants, either. Over the years your garden, like so many others, could develop into a miniature nursery, a miscellaneous collection of plants bought on impulse, brought home as souvenirs of a vacation trip, or given to you by friends. A garden that includes too many plant varieties can have a maintenance schedule booked solid from spring to fall. There will always be something needing attention—fertilizing, spraying, staking, disbudding, dividing—and usually at different times. Moreover, too much variety in a garden can be distracting, "jumpy," as one garden designer puts it. Most landscape architects work with a fairly small plant list. "With a dozen plants you can create some very nice compositions," says Connecticut landscape architect Arthur Bye. The dune garden on page 20, whose maintenance, according to its designer, "hardly goes beyond clipping a branch or two," contains just five plant varieties.

A garden speckled with individual plants virtually guarantees hours of busywork. But if you limit the number of planted areas as well as the number of plant varieties, you will also limit the need for maintenance. Moreover, except for a few specimen shrubs like beauty bush and linden viburnum, most plants look better grouped in clusters of three or more than they do when standing alone. By grouping, you can get more design impact with fewer plants; seen en masse, a group registers more forcefully than single plants scattered around the lawn like marbles. In fact, one of the simplest ways to improve a garden's design is to tie the plant materials into groups, either by transplanting them or by linking them visually with ground covers or mulches.

In designing such massed plantings, group trees and shrubs wherever possible in company with their own kind. If you group together plants that have identical requirements for fertilizing, watering and spraying, you automatically shorten maintenance time. Plants that need the most tending should have a place conveniently near the house. Those that need to be watered frequently, for example, should be close enough to an outside faucet to be reached with a single 50-foot length of hose.

Other guidelines for locating the structural elements on your garden plan are equally sensible. Trees and shrubs that are grouped at the periphery of your property will extend its apparent size, block out unattractive views, and at the same time act as focal points for your own view from the terrace or house windows. But wherever you place a tree, remember that its fallout can create a nuisance. Minimize the litter problem by keeping fruiting trees away from areas that are paved. If you have a pond or a swimming pool, keep trees that shed their leaves in autumn some distance away. Plan to

GROUPED FOR CONVENIENCE

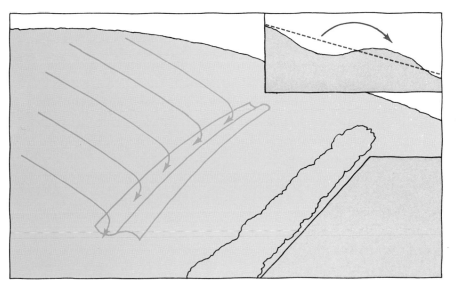

SWALE-AND-BERM DRAINAGE

To curb soil erosion and prevent rain-water runoff from drowning plants at the bottom of a slope, dig a shallow interceptor ditch—called a swale—to redirect the flow of water diagonally down the slope. An easy project, the swale need be only 2 to 5 inches deep, depending on the steepness of the slope, and about the width of a shovel. Pile dirt removed from the ditch on the downhill side to form a low dam—the berm (inset). Test the swale's internal slope by rolling a basketball down it, then line it with gravel and topsoil and plant grass or ground cover. The swale and berm will be nearly invisible.

51

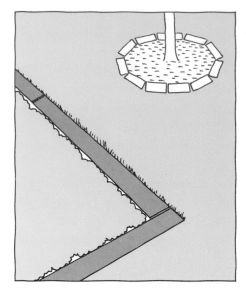

use thick ground-cover plantings under trees to swallow dead leaves, seed pods and fruit.

Next to trees and shrubs, the most important element of most garden designs is the lawn *(page 9)*. No gardener needs to be reminded of the work involved in caring for turf grass. For that reason alone, it should be part of a low-upkeep garden only if its function there, like that of any other plant, justifies the effort spent in maintaining it. But a lawn can be a poor design choice for other reasons. Sometimes it is simply not suited to the natural features of the site. For example, do not try to maintain a lawn on ground that slopes more steeply than one vertical foot in every three. Such a slope is hazardous to mow and prone to erosion. Instead, you should choose a deep-rooted ground cover that will hold the soil and break the force of the rain.

SLOPES AND SWAMPS

On a steeper slope, forget ground covers and consider installing a retaining wall. Built on a slope without mortar, such a wall will provide chinks for rock plants on its face as well as along its top. If the site has natural rock outcroppings, count yourself fortunate. By digging around the rocks, hosing them clean, and tucking some low-growing plants into the crevices, you can turn an eyesore into a dramatic focal point that will require almost no maintenance.

Similarly, the solution for a low, swampy place need not be loads of landfill. With some minor excavation and perhaps an underground supply pipe to provide water during dry spells, you can transform the low spot into an attractive bog garden or woodland pool, rich with ferns and aquatic plants.

Finally, do not overlook the advantages of paving, decking and other constructed elements as a substitute for a lawn. Judiciously used, especially in small urban and suburban gardens, they not only reduce maintenance but decrease the number of plants needed and make fewer plants go further by giving them greater impact. Gravel, crushed rock, river stones and wood chips are some of the simplest of these alternatives to grass. In Washington, D.C., one gardener carpeted his walled garden with pine needles laid thickly over builders' tar paper (which he used as a weed barrier). The tar paper disintegrated long ago, but the weeds never reappeared. "Got tired waiting, I guess," the owner remarked. On uneven ground, a deck is often the easiest and the cheapest alternative to costly grading, and in some shady locations a deck can raise container-grown plants up into the sunlight.

Heavy-duty surfaces such as bricks, flagstones or poured concrete cost considerably more initially than the other grass substitutes, but they hold up better, especially in areas of heavy traffic, such as walkways and terraces. One particular hard surface that is a true work saver is the mowing strip. It consists of a border of brick, stone, wood or concrete, 6 to 12 inches wide, set flush with the ground along the edges of flower beds and gravel paths or driveways. Not only does it neatly separate the areas but it allows you to run one wheel of the mower along the top of the strip, thus eliminating hand trimming and edging.

If you elect to use one of the lawn substitutes in your garden plan, there are certain practical matters to keep in mind. A paved surface close to the house will reflect summer heat indoors, while turf will absorb heat and stay cool. Also, some paving materials, notably pine boards, glazed tiles and smooth flagstones or concrete can be dangerously slippery when wet. Bricks are handsome, but they may absorb food stains that cannot be scrubbed out. Gravel scattered from a pathway onto a lawn can become a hazardous projectile when it meets the high-speed blades of a rotary lawn mower.

There are other garden structures that can save you work. Instead of blocking out an undesirable view with a tall hedge or a row of trees, you may find that a wooden fence or a masonry wall will do the job more effectively and will require much less maintenance. It will also take up less room in cramped quarters. In similar fashion, a canvas awning or a slatted roof structure over a terrace can provide shade faster than a slow-growing shade tree—and without the litter from the tree.

Among construction projects, raised planting beds deserve special mention. Framed with brick, wood, stone or concrete and

HARD-SURFACE HAZARDS

filled with rich, humus-laden soil, they offer an ideal setting for a great variety of plants. The soil in raised beds tends to warm up earlier in the spring, so cultivation can begin sooner, an advantage if you are planting a kitchen garden with vegetables that will take several months to reach maturity. But the big advantage of a raised planting bed is that it is so easy to care for without stooping or getting down on your knees.

A simple raised bed can be made of 2-inch-thick boards of rot-resistant redwood or preservative-treated lumber, set on edge on level ground and fastened at the corners with galvanized angle irons. A sturdier, longer-lasting version can be built of one or more tiers of railroad ties or landscape timbers, drilled with vertical holes and anchored with lengths of galvanized pipe pounded through the holes into the ground beneath.

TENDING PLANTS IN POTS

Do not, however, confuse raised-bed gardening with container gardening as a laborsaving device. On city terraces and rooftops a container garden may be the only option, but containers create work. Their soil dries quickly and needs frequent watering. One New York suburbanite raised a few impatiens in containers on his patio. Delighted with the results, he decided to go into full-scale container gardening—and ended totally exhausted. "I was hauling water like a coolie all summer long," he complained.

With these landscaping principles in mind, you can begin to draw up a plan for your own low-maintenance garden. This plan is another important preliminary, almost as important as understanding the basics of garden design. If you lay out your garden on paper,

GIVING THE GARDEN A LIFT

Where soil is packed hard, is low in nutrients or is always soggy, fast-draining raised beds are an easier solution than wholesale soil conditioning or an elaborate drainage system. With a series of different beds, you can group plants that have the same soil, water and fertilizer requirements. A basic mix of 2 parts topsoil, 1 part sand and 1 part humus, suitable for most plants, is easily altered to meet special needs. Doubling the proportion of sand, for instance, makes a bed that is ideal for succulents. Adding ground sulfur to acidify the mixture readies another bed for such broad-leaved evergreens as azaleas and mountain laurels.

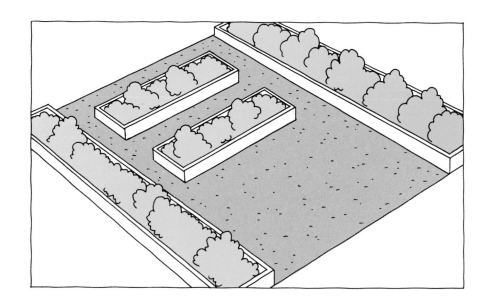

the actual installation will go more smoothly. You can even break up the job into manageable fragments, doing first one area and then another, as time and money permit. Pencil and paper also help you clarify your thinking. The planting mistakes you may make with a pencil are easy to erase and will cost you nothing at the garden center. And working with a pencil is obviously a lot less strenuous than working with a spade.

So start your new garden by going to a stationery or art supply store and buying graph paper. If your lot is no larger than 136 by 176 feet, 17-by-22-inch paper ruled eight squares to the inch will do; let each square represent one foot, and everything will fit comfortably. If your property is larger than that, let each square equal two feet or more, or use graph paper ruled 10 squares to the inch.

Start by drawing a map of your property as it looks now, with the house, entrance walk, garage and driveway, utility areas and property boundaries all properly positioned. Include all existing trees, shrubs, flower beds and any other garden features, such as fences and pools. Be sure to indicate the house doors and view windows, and show the location of outdoor faucets and electrical outlets. When you draw trees, show their trunks as black dots and the approximate spread of their branches as circles of dotted lines. Also put on the plan any underground obstructions that you may have to deal with, such as water and sewer pipes, utility lines, oil-storage tanks, septic tanks and drainage fields. Stories abound of expensive concrete patios, poured unknowingly over septic systems, that later had to be torn up with jackhammers when access to plumbing became necessary. Finally, your site plan should indicate features that might limit your choice of plants, such as the way shade falls on your garden in the morning and in the afternoon, and the existence of any high or low ground that could restrict your freedom to plant where you would like.

In making this map, the architect's or builder's plan for your house and lot can be useful. Also helpful is a copy of your deed survey, filed at the local tax assessor's office. You can simply transfer any relevant information from them onto your sketch. Otherwise, take garden measurements with a 50- or 100-foot carpenter's tape, enlisting a helper to hold one end or pegging the end to the ground with a screwdriver stuck through the loop. Alternatively, you can simply pace off the garden area. Pin-point accuracy is not as important as completeness.

In mapping your garden, you are likely to see a number of problems that you overlooked in casual strolls or that you knew were there but preferred not to think about—angles around flower beds

PENCIL-AND-PAPER PLANS

MEASURE FOR MEASURE

55

that are too tight for a lawn mower to negotiate easily, a bush that has outgrown its allotted space, a shrub growing under the drip line of the roof that is slowly being broken to pieces by rain water cascading off the shingles. The mapping process will take time. It will be time well spent, however, since it will save you labor, not to mention cash, later on.

DOODLING DREAMS

Your site map will form the basis for your garden planning. As you begin to develop ideas about what improvements you would like to make, place tracing paper over the map and doodle. Draw in the pattern of foot traffic across the lawn where the soil is packed hard and a paved walkway might save constant lawn repairs. Sketch in a new or enlarged patio; position it close to the kitchen door if you like to eat alfresco. Plot the location of a new tree for afternoon shade, or of a fence or a tall hedge to screen out an unwanted view. In this paper exercise you can let your imagination soar; you are not contracting to buy anything. If some of your ideas do not work, simply discard the tracings one after another until you arrive at a plan that is right.

As your plan develops, try to visualize how it will look in three dimensions. Such mental pictures are not everyone's forte. It is a good idea to take snapshots of your house and garden from several directions, looking toward the house and from the house toward the garden. Then place tracing paper over the photographs and draw in the trees and shrubs you are thinking about planting, or the placement of a wall or terrace. Even on a snapshot, such a tracing-paper drawing is often clear enough to tell you whether or not you are on the right track.

As a further aid to visualization, you can drive stakes in the ground to indicate the height of a shrub, or use a beach umbrella to suggest the dimensions of a small tree, or stake out a proposed terrace with a string, or outline a proposed flower bed by snaking a length of rope or garden hose into various positions until the curve looks exactly right. To gauge how high or how far from a sitting area a hedge should be in order to block out an undesirable view, put poles in the ground, run string between them and drape folded newspapers over the string. To test the placement of trees or shrubs near a garage or driveway, insert a row of sticks there too; then back the car out to see if you bump them.

FREEDOM FROM WATERING

Finally, if you want to add the ultimate in work-saving devices to your garden plan, lay out an automatic underground watering system. Such systems, long used on golf courses and in public parks, are popular with gardeners too, especially in hot, dry regions. They are not inexpensive, but there is probably no single piece of equipment that offers as much liberation from the drudgery of gardening. Lightweight, durable plastic pipe, dependable sprinkler heads and compact controls have reduced the costs of installation and operation. You may find the job of installation exacting enough to warrant turning it over to a professional, though many dealers are more than willing to help you do it yourself. In fact, most dealers will design the system for you free of charge in return for the purchase of their parts. You must, however, furnish them with an accurate plan of your property, along with detailed information on your plumbing system, soil, exposure and the nature of the various planting areas that will need to be watered.

A plan for the sprinkler system should be laid out on tracing paper placed over your final site plan. On lawn areas you will want retractable sprinkler heads that lie flush with the ground when you mow, but pop up to deliver spray. They cast a circular pattern and are placed so the circles overlap, but the diameter of each circle varies with the size of the head and your water pressure.

Around the edges of lawns and in corners or irregularly shaped areas, sprinkler heads are available that cast half-circle, quarter-circle and three-quarter-circle patterns. For long, narrow strips, there are heads that cast rectangular patterns. Flower beds, ground covers and foundation plantings are watered with special bubbler heads designed to penetrate mulch and soak the ground beneath the plants with gentle streams.

All these heads are arranged on a branching layout of main pipes and side spurs that are connected to the house water supply, often through an existing outside faucet. The different lines may be programed to different watering schedules by shutoff valves hooked to an electric control box.

Generally, the entire system is hooked up and tested aboveground; then it is buried in slit trenches 6 or 8 inches deep. The trenches are dug with a power trencher that leaves only narrow scars over which the sod is easily replaced. Good plastic pipes expand without rupturing when the water inside them freezes, but winter drainage is necessary to protect the fittings.

Once installed, a sprinkler system needs only fine tuning to adjust the amount and frequency of watering. You can set the various heads to turn on for periods ranging from two minutes to an hour, from one to as many as eight times a day, on as many days a week as you want. Then you sit back and relax. When you come home from the office, or even from a vacation trip, the garden will be there to greet you, watered and green and ready for you to enjoy, without your having lifted a finger.

PROGRAMED FOR ACTION

Structures that please the eye and ease the job

Raised flower beds, patterned and textured paving, wood decks and other types of garden structures can reduce wearisome chores even as they perform visual miracles such as opening up a small urban lot or unifying a spacious but sprawling backyard. Such structures will help to reduce and concentrate the planted areas of your garden, a major goal in low-maintenance planning. But man-made additions must be thoughtfully chosen and installed with care. Paving, for example, is often a practical alternative to grass, but if it is located in a place that is usually sunny and left completely without shade, it can reflect unwelcome heat indoors.

As the owners of the walled retreat opposite decided, however, paving can rival living ground covers for attractive patterns and textures, and it certainly stands up better under heavy use for outdoor entertaining. They covered the center of the yard with several inches of loose gravel and surrounded it with a paved brick border. Then, by confining the plantings to beds along the sides of the garden, they transformed the entire area into a living stage for a bright Chagall mosaic on one wall.

On terrain that is uneven or steeply sloped, a wood deck is a practical alternative to a paved terrace, serving many of the same purposes. Without expensive grading and filling, wooden platforms give sure and level footing. Whether your garden is restrained or prodigal, a silvery weathered deck helps tie all the elements together—and it will never need mowing.

Finally, you may want to consider the virtues of raised flower beds and airy trellises. They can often bring attractive plants into closer focus and also give additional control over the kind of soil or shade that specific plants may require. You can banish backaches by raising a flower bed 30 inches and capping the walls so that you can pull weeds without stooping or admire your azaleas while comfortably seated. If you hang house plants from a well-designed arbor, you can dream in the shade all through the summer without having to rake a single leaf in the fall.

A chartreuse hosta echoes the mosaic leaves above it and—with woodruff, ferns, mahonia and a fringed bleeding heart— forms a no-fuss border for an urban garden.

On the level with decks

A bridge joining two decks crosses crushed stone simulating a dry stream. Near the bridge are black pines and golden junipers.

Slatted platforms and concrete paths cross a creek to banks of red-berried kinnikinnick, rhododendrons and quaking aspens.

Bringing up the blooms

Variegated thyme, begonias and azaleas share a raised L-shaped bed nearly 3 feet deep with three Bob White crab apples,

whose bright fruits attract birds in winter. A soaker hose strung across the surface of the bed makes watering effortless.

Summer haven for house plants

A Texas-sized Neoregelia cruenta and a host of smaller tropical bromeliads move out for an airing in a Houston lath house.

A sloping concrete path that drains excess rain water borders this collection of bromeliads, their pots buried to the rims in mulch.

Holding your own on a slope

Baccharis, a native California ground cover, holds the soil on a sharp poolside slope terraced with Sonoma fieldstone. Two

Monterey cypresses and other drought-resistant shrubs planted above the pool are easily accessible but require little care.

Working to lighten the work load 4

To your friendly neighborhood garden center each year comes new garden gadgetry to cut your weekly work load. And from the commercial nurseries and seed companies come new, easier-to-grow plant varieties. Yet for all the technological and horticultural advances, some basic gardening chores remain unavoidable. Contemplating the most basic chore of all—preparing the ground for planting—a witty gardener and poet named Georgie Starbuck Galbraith penned this couplet:

> The soil conditioner still unmatched
> Is a simple spade with spouse attached.

There are laborsaving tricks, of course, but unless your gardening standards are very lax, or your pocketbook very fat, you will have to invest a certain amount of your own sweat, or your spouse's, in your garden—certainly at the outset. For if you do things properly at the start, your work load later will be much lighter. Plant a tree correctly, and it will be almost care free. Mulch adequately, and you will do less watering and weeding. Read the labels carefully on fertilizer and herbicide containers, then apply the contents properly, and you can not only get the growth you want from the plants you want but will avoid the disasters that come from misuse.

Cast a wary eye on alleged allies in your garden struggles. Ladybug beetles will consume aphids and mealy bugs, and they can be bought in quantity and released in your garden. But they can also depart from your garden suddenly, especially with a breeze to help carry them away. Earthworms, those diggers revered by so many gardeners, will help churn up your soil for you. But they are freeloaders. They do not make poor soil rich. Rather, they seek out soil already rich and crumbly, and their ability to turn over the earth is vastly exaggerated—an amount about equal to each worm's weight each day. One worm would take 100 years to dig as much soil

A carpet of gravel 6 inches deep inhibits weeds and retains moisture in an urban garden, while setting off gray lamb's ears, a prostrate juniper, a lacy-leaved Japanese maple and a container of petunias.

as you can move in an hour with a spading fork. So expect to be pretty much on your own in preparing the soil for the long-term health of your trees, shrubs and ground covers.

In conditioning any soil, the key is to give it good texture, what gardeners (and farmers) call "tilth." This means it should be sufficiently open and porous so that plant roots can spread freely. In a seeming paradox, the soil must be moisture retentive enough to tide plants safely over passing dry spells yet sufficiently well-drained so roots do not become waterlogged. Even plants that "like their feet wet," as the nurserymen say, will drown in standing water.

GAUGING THE DRAIN   Drainage, in gardening language, does not refer to water runoff from the surface but rather the seepage of water through the soil. This is easy enough to gauge. Dig a hole a couple of feet deep and fill it with water. Let the hole drain, then refill. If the water level then drops more slowly than about an inch every 45 minutes, and especially if some water remains in the hole overnight, you have a problem. That particular area of your garden, at least, is poorly drained. If, on the other hand, the water disappears from the hole so fast it seems to be sucked out, you have the opposite problem: drainage that is too fast.

Sometimes there is no cure for persistent sogginess—a sogginess too much even for plants that prefer damp soil—other than putting in subsurface tile drains. This is usually a costly business and, at the very least, hard work. But for most drainage problems—both with heavy clay soils that hold water too long and light sandy soils that leak like sieves—the solution is to mix in a liberal amount of organic matter such as leaf mold, compost, peat moss or decayed sawdust. The treatment is the same for both extremes of soil. Even if you do not have a drainage problem at all, it is almost impossible to overdo the addition of such organic matter.

A good proportion is 1 part organic matter to 2 parts garden loam. If you are planting a border of small shrubs or perennials, or ground cover like pachysandra or ivy, spread 2 or 3 inches of peat moss or leaf mold on the ground and dig it in thoroughly with a spading fork. Break up clods of earth with the back of the fork as you go. For an area large enough to make you weary just looking at it, rent a rotary power tiller to do the digging.

PRACTICAL PEAT MOSS   Of the several kinds of organic matter good for soil conditioning, finely chopped peat moss is one of the best, the easiest to use (so long as it is damp enough not to be dusty) and available at virtually every garden center. Homemade compost is at least as good and cheaper too, but it does require that you build and maintain a compost pile. Composting is not hard work, but it is a bother. Garden wastes must be hauled to one place, layered with soil, spread with a fertilizer to stimulate the decomposition process, watered occasionally and turned over regularly. The end product, however, is a superb soil conditioner, called "black gold" by many gardeners.

For composting in limited quantities there is a shortcut. Dump the materials you are composting into a polyethylene bag, the largest you can find. Add a shovelful of soil and a handful of 5-10-5 fertilizer. Wet the mass down and tie the top of the bag tightly. Leave the bag in the sun, flopping it around occasionally and opening it to the air every two weeks, and in eight to 12 weeks the bag will be filled with humus ready to use. Another small-scale composting method is to do it on the spot. Pile dead leaves, grass clipping or other organic materials on your flower beds or vegetable garden in the fall, sprinkle with a decomposing mixture (available at garden stores), and give the material a few turns now and then during the winter months. Rain and snow will keep the pile moist and in the spring you can spade or fork the decomposed material directly into the soil as you prepare it for planting.

In planting larger shrubs or trees, the work of digging the individual holes can be eased by using either a flat-bladed, square-ended spade or a round-pointed digging shovel (but the shovel's blade should be set at less of an angle to the handle than that of the all-purpose loading shovel more commonly sold in hardware stores). Excavate a generous hole to give the roots plenty of room to grow. The hole should be at least twice as wide and deep as the root ball. Apply the old nurseryman's adage—dig a $10 hole for each $5 tree, perhaps amended nowadays to a $20 hole for each $10 tree.

As you dig, place the dark, rich topsoil in one pile and the lighter subsoil in another, mixing organic matter with both piles. Piling everything on a square of heavy plastic film or an old canvas dropcloth makes for easier and neater mixing. Fill the bottom 6 inches of the hole with the topsoil mix, firm it with your foot, and set the tree or shrub in the hole, adding or subtracting topsoil mix below the root ball until the crown of the plant—where roots join the stem—is level with the top of the hole. Shovel in more topsoil mix until the hole is about three-quarters full, fill the hole with water, let it soak in and then shovel in the remaining soil mix as needed, making a dike of earth 2 inches high to form a saucer around the top. Fill this with water and you are done.

While you pause to mop your brow, soothe yourself with the thought that this planting effort is a one-time operation that does not need to be repeated, and one that will pay off in easier maintenance later. You can skimp a bit with a few of the all-but-indestructible

SIMPLIFIED SEEDBEDS

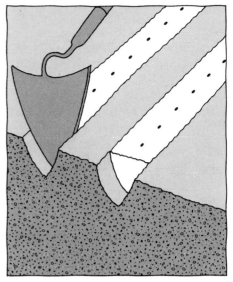

Seedlings are easier to weed and thin if seeds are sown in a vermiculite-filled trench. The light planting medium also gives a high rate of germination, since sprouting seeds can readily push through it. To prepare the trench, make a furrow 1 inch deep and 1 inch wide, using a trowel or pointed hoe. Fill the furrow with vermiculite; then dampen it with water. Make a second shallow furrow down the center of the vermiculite and sow the seeds in it. Cover with a fine layer of vermiculite and mist lightly.

A ONE-TIME OPERATION

shrubs—hydrangeas, spireas, forsythias, mock oranges, privets and deutzias, for example—but most shrubs, including all the evergreens, need the same tender handling you would give a tree. But you will not have to fertilize in initial tree or shrub planting if your soil is rich or if you have added leaf mold or compost, which supplies some nutrients. Many gardeners give such plants an extra boost anyway, by adding a couple of handfuls of fertilizer to the soil mix—a slow-acting organic type like bone meal or cottonseed meal.

A PIPELINE TO HEALTH   While no tree or shrub will flourish in a soil or climate for which it is not suited, methods have been developed by nurserymen that can help your plants over their critical first season or two in problem locations. In very dry climates, nurserymen sometimes grow their seedlings in deep cylinders of cardboard or plastic, to train the roots to reach down toward water after transplanting. You can use cardboard tubes similarly when planting trees or shrubs in the hard, inhospitable soil of a neglected city garden. Put two or three tubes, filled with fine gravel, into the ground vertically alongside the root ball as you plant. When the cardboard rots away, porous "pipes" of gravel remain to carry water or liquid fertilizer down to the plant's roots. In very sandy soil where watering quickly leaches out the nutrients, stuff rock wool—the kind used for home insulation—into the bottom of the planting hole.

To establish woody plants in difficult-to-drain wet soil, try another old trick called mounding-up. Pile soil a foot or two above ground level and plant your tree or shrub in the raised earth. The mound keeps the roots from drowning as they are getting started, and gradually they will help soak up the wetness around them. (The Irish have been doing this for centuries with seed potatoes, laying them on the ground and digging a little soil on both sides to cover; "lazy banks," the Irish call this planting method.) For a steep embankment, where small plants such as ground covers risk being washed out before they get their roots anchored properly, buy erosion netting from a garden supply store, or use burlap if you have it, peg it down and plant through it.

SOLUTION FOR A SCALPING   If you are dealing with truly exhausted soil—or as sometimes happens in new developments, with a plot where the good topsoil has been "scalped" off and sold elsewhere—your only solution may be to buy new topsoil. An intractable, rubble-filled lot may need up to 6 inches of topsoil to get a good assortment of shrubs established; in new developments, builders usually spread at least 3 inches before seeding a lawn. One 5-cubic-yard truckload of topsoil will cover 400 square feet of garden (20 by 20 feet) to a depth of 4 inches or 270 square feet (about 16 by 17 feet) to a depth of 6 inches. The cost per load will vary depending on the local availability of topsoil—in most places such a load costs about as much as three or four large bags of lawn fertilizer—and it will take about an hour to spread it evenly.

Any plants newly set in a garden, as well as those that have been growing there for years, benefit if the soil around them is covered with a protective material—a mulch. Mulching is probably the single most valuable technique of the low-upkeep gardener. It may not be quite a miracle solution to all gardening problems, but it does save a great deal of work. By shielding the soil from the sun, a layer of bark, wood chips, hay or other organic matter slows moisture loss, thus reducing watering chores—and the cost of the water itself—by as much as half. By blocking sunlight, mulch also prevents weed seeds from sprouting. Some gardeners claim that mulch eliminates 90 per cent of the labor of weeding. The few weeds that do struggle up will not be well anchored and can be easily pulled.

By keeping soil moist and crumbly, mulching cuts down on the need for surface watering, thereby helping prevent erosion, since it breaks the force of hoses or heavy rains and slows runoff from a slope; at the same time it prevents mud from being splashed onto plant foliage, reducing the spread of fungus spores and infectious bacteria from the soil.

Not the least of mulching's benefits is that it stabilizes soil temperature and insulates against extremes of heat and cold. During a hot summer the soil under a layer of mulch may be 30 degrees cooler than unmulched soil. During a cold winter, mulching protects roots from injury by keeping the soil temperature constant, especially in the absence of an insulating blanket of snow. In early spring it helps minimize the damage of alternate thaws and freezes that may heave smaller plants from the ground and injure their roots.

Many organic mulches decompose slowly, reducing the need for fertilizing as they add nutrients to the soil. They must, however, be periodically renewed with more material spread on top. Selected with an eye to color and texture, a mulch can also aid in garden design—making a unifying background for plants and providing a carpet that permits you to walk around the garden after a rain without compacting the soil or tracking mud.

To choose a mulch for your needs, you will have to weigh effectiveness as a soil-protecting agent, availability, ease of application, appearance, durability and cost. Organic mulches, composed of various kinds of vegetable matter, often the by-products of farming and industry, are likely to be the cheapest—if you live near a source, though some such sources may be rare, not to say exotic. For instance, cocoa-bean hulls, from cocoa and chocolate factories, are

A SAUCER FOR A SHRUB

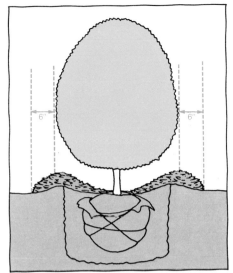

To reduce the watering and weeding needed by a newly planted shrub or tree, make a saucer of soil at the plant's base and fill it with a mulch such as wood chips, pine needles or straw. Spread the mulch 2 inches thick around the perimeter of the saucer, tapering it to less than an inch near the center. Leave a clear circle, 8 inches wide, around the trunk to prevent rot and discourage rodents and borers. As the plant grows, expand the saucer, keeping it at least 6 inches beyond the spread of the branches.

IN THE MATTER OF MULCH

easily handled, do not blow or burn easily, and disintegrate into a well-balanced fertilizer. When fresh they have a chocolate odor, which gradually disappears. They are often mixed with sawdust and applied in a 2- to 3-inch layer. Because they have a strong potash content and a tendency to heat up, they should not be used around rhododendrons or azaleas. Spent hops from breweries, heavy to haul unless dried, make an inexpensive, moisture-conserving mulch that will last about two years before disintegrating. The strong odor disappears in a few weeks, but the hops may heat up in warm weather and should be kept several inches from stems of shrubs and young trees. (Any organic mulch may promote fungus and rot if it is piled against plant crowns and stems.)

FROM SHELLS TO SEAWEED

Peanut shells are often used as mulch in the South and ground corn cobs are available in many rural areas, though not everyone considers them ornamental. Tobacco stems are coarse enough to admit moisture and air, have some insecticidal properties and add nitrogen to the soil when they decompose. Sugar-cane stalks, also coarse, are water-retentive and disintegrate into excellent humus. Buckwheat hulls, fine, fluffy and black, take two years to decompose but may be scattered by wind. Seaweed, used in coastal areas, disintegrates slowly and is high in potash content.

Cheaper yet are the products of your own garden, which cost nothing but the labor of collecting them. Grass clippings make an adequate mulch, but if applied too thickly they will pack into a dense, mildewy mat that heats up and gives off an odor of decay. Spread them in a layer no more than 2 inches thick or mix the clippings with a coarser organic material like leaves.

(continued on page 79)

Joining forces with the land

When this garden was still part of a New Jersey swamp, water from underground springs ran beneath dense thickets of honeysuckle and poison ivy. The soil, extremely acid from centuries of decaying leaves and pine needles, was at best soggy and at worst inundated by water.

Rather than fight the swamp with bulldozers and truckloads of soil and gravel fill, the owners decided to turn their land into a sanctuary for plants that thrive in a wet, acid environment. They removed the poison ivy and honeysuckle, replacing them with less aggressive native plants like ferns, azaleas and cranberries, rescuing many from nearby areas soon to be developed. They channeled underground springs into the lowest section to form a bog garden. Paths were made with wood chips and pine needles.

The result is a luxuriant woodland garden that is as enchanting to look at as it is easy to maintain. Nature does most of the work, providing plenty of moisture, rich soil and abundant leaf mulch to keep the plants glistening with healthy flowers and foliage.

A ring of osmunda ferns catches reflected sunlight in the bog area of this woodland garden that is actually a front yard.

Brightening the bog

From the wet, spongy soil of this bog garden sprouts a breathtaking array of plants—ferns, cranberries, primroses, mosses, swamp azaleas, Japanese irises and dozens of others. All of them need a moist environment to thrive, and once they have become established in the ground, many need very little additional care. To reduce weeding, the gardener mulches the soil with oak leaves and pine needles; then he steps back and watches the plants flourish.

Japanese primrose blossoms rise from a bed enriched with damp sphagnum moss; the low ground cover at left is a cranberry.

The frilly flowers of Japanese iris, backed by red astilbe, marsh marigolds and masses of cardinal flowers, brighten a creek bank.

A feathery ground cover of moss, so dense it needs little weeding, parts slightly to hint at an underground spring.

Leaves by themselves, nature's own mulch, will protect the soil and enrich it with humus when they decompose. To keep large leaves from blowing about or packing down into a dense, slimy mat that sheds water like shingles, first let leaves rot partially in a compost pile or collect them in the bag of your mower so they will be well chopped. Smaller, crisper leaves that will not mat can be raked directly onto plant beds to a depth of about 3 or 4 inches. Oak leaves and pine needles both increase the acidity of the soil as they disintegrate and for this reason make good mulches for azaleas, rhododendrons, camellias, and other acid-loving plants. Pine needles, fine and loose-textured, readily admit air and water to plant roots. Applied in a layer 2 to 3 inches thick, they last three or four years before they need replenishing. If after several years you find the needles have turned the soil too acid for some plants—causing their leaves to begin to yellow—you can correct this condition with ground limestone watered into the soil through the needle mulch.

Good mulches can also be made from the woody parts of plants. If you have accumulated a pile of dead twigs and branches, you can rent a power shredder, feed the debris into it, and produce your own supply of uniform wood-chip mulch. Spread the chips around plants in a layer 2 to 3 inches deep. They may look raw at first but they will weather to an unobtrusive gray or brown. Like any wood-based mulch, they will draw nitrogen-fixing bacteria from the soil as they decompose, so spread a high-nitrogen fertilizer on the ground—any lawn fertilizer will do—before putting the chips in place.

DEADWOOD MULCH

Wood chips, as well as sawdust and wood shavings, can often be purchased at tree-repair companies and lumber mills. Wood shavings blow around and may create a fire hazard but are useful in moist climates and sheltered locations. Sawdust, like chips and shavings, will weather to a darker color. Apply it no more than 2 inches deep to keep it from caking into an impervious crust. Try too to get a coarse grade.

Tree bark, widely available in garden centers, where it is sold in chunks or shreds and packaged according to size, is one of the best and most decorative of all mulches. For landscaping, it is well worth its relatively higher price. Bark mulch may come from any kind of tree, but the reddish-brown chips of fir, pine and hemlock are the most common and redwood is the most durable. Peat moss, also found at garden centers, is far less satisfactory as a mulch, although it is a superb soil conditioner. Finely chopped peat moss can crust over into a hard, rain-shedding mat, which deprives roots of moisture and air. To avoid this, buy only the coarse, chunky type (often labeled "poultry grade" because it is used in chicken coops).

THE BEST IN BARK

Favorite mulches among vegetable gardeners are hay and straw, whose praises were so loudly sung by Ruth Stout in her breezy and very personal gardening books, *How to Have a Green Thumb Without an Aching Back* and *Gardening Without Work.* For gardeners who do not mind a rustic look, hay mulch can be used around ornamental plants, but Miss Stout demonstrated its best use in a 45-by-50-foot vegetable garden adjoining her rustic cottage in Redding Ridge, Connecticut. There, she would take hay cut from the nearby meadows and pile it 8 inches deep onto the ground each spring. She would then plant through it, spreading the hay just enough for the seeds to sprout. The hay mulch, gradually matting down as the growing season progressed, not only kept the soil moist but also worked its way into the ground to produce a dark, rich humus layer that was sheer delight for a gardener to pick up.

NONORGANIC MULCHES

Vegetable gardening is likewise the most suitable place to use such nonorganic mulches as black plastic polyethylene film, aluminum foil, roofing felt and plastic-coated papers. They provide insulation, suppress weeds and last almost indefinitely. But they do not contribute nutrients or texture to the soil and are most unattractive.

Perhaps the most useful function of a sheet mulch is in serving as a hidden membrane to smother weeds and permit a thinner and therefore less expensive layer of decorative mulch on top. Stretch out the material, punch holes about 6 inches apart to let water and air through, then cover with a decorative mulch. You can even use old newspapers as the membrane; by the time they disintegrate they will have smothered any existing weeds. With or without a membrane, the decorative inorganic mulches—gravel, crushed rock, washed and rounded river stones, beach pebbles, broken shells—can be both pleasing and useful in a low-maintenance garden.

Whatever mulch you use, apply only enough to shade the soil and keep down weeds. Mulch that is too thick may smother plant roots. If it does not, the roots will grow up into the mulch itself, then suffer whenever the mulch dries out under hot summer sun. Coarse materials, being more porous, can be applied in thicker layers than the fine, easily compacted types. With any moisture-retentive organic material, leave space around plant stems to prevent rot.

WHEN TO MULCH

To do the most good, a spring mulch should be laid down before growth starts, weed seeds germinate, and the sun begins to dry the soil. A winter mulch should be placed around plants susceptible to winter damage before the ground has become deeply frozen. Low-maintenance gardeners interested in simplifying things, however, can simply choose a good all-purpose mulch and keep it on their plant beds all year long.

Well-mulched, your garden will need less water. And by watering properly, you will have to water less often. One good soaking is better than two or three light sprinklings; in fact, these sprinklings can do more harm than good. They encourage roots to grow close to the surface—where they are vulnerable to heat, dry spells and uprooting winds—rather than growing deeper.

With all plants, the cardinal rule of watering is: do it as infrequently as possible, but when you do, apply enough to soak the soil all the way down to the plants' root zone, which will range from 2 to 6 inches below ground level in the case of lawn grass to a foot or more for shrubs and trees. (Trees have deep taproots but their feeder roots are usually fairly close to the surface.) To gauge water penetration you can use a hollow-tubed soil probe, which brings up a core of earth for examination, or a tensiometer, which measures moisture levels electrically. Or you can simply experiment by turning on a sprinkler for an hour in various parts of the garden and then digging holes to see how far down the soil is wet. A rule of thumb is that the average garden needs one inch of water each week during the growing season, either from rainfall or the garden hose. To gauge the time it takes your watering system to distribute that amount—and it will probably be longer than you think—set out a tin can or any wide-mouthed container under the spray, with a mark at the 1-inch level. Then, the next time you go a week without rain, you will know how long to run the sprinkler.

Common sense will tell you that watering should not be done at high noon on a hot, parching day, especially if there is a wind. Do it

WHEN TO WATER

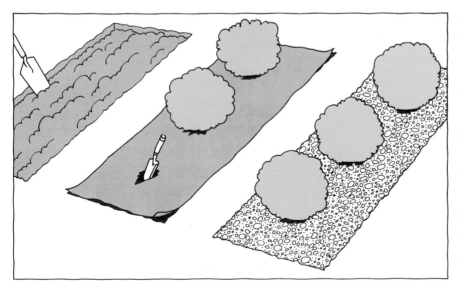

PLANTING THROUGH PLASTIC

A long-lasting mulch to eliminate weeds and conserve moisture can be made of black polyethylene film. Use it on shrubs or perennial beds, but not for plants that spread from underground runners. Prepare the soil, dampen it, then unroll the plastic film over the bed and anchor it. For small plants, use a bulb planter to cut through the plastic and carve planting holes in the soil beneath. For larger plants, cut the plastic with a knife or trowel. Set each plant in a hole, leaving a slight depression to catch water. Poke small holes at 12-inch intervals for rain to trickle through. Cover the plastic with wood chips or gravel.

morning or evening, preferably the latter, for then the plants have all night to absorb the water, with a minimum of loss by evaporation.

For more reasons than just financial, the built-in underground watering systems described in Chapter 3 (*page 56*) may not fit your needs. Your plot may be too small, or the terrain so irregular that as one Virginia nurseryman put it, "you will be drowning some plants and missing others entirely." But there are other ways you can avoid tramping around the garden with hose in hand and feet wet. There are oscillating and turret-type sprinklers that can be adjusted to cover precise areas; traveling sprinklers that slowly move around a track made by the hose itself, reeling up and turning themselves off when they hit the tap; timers that can be preset for automatic shutoff; aboveground sprinkler systems that can be attached at intervals along an ordinary garden hose; bubbler heads, soaking hoses and misting hoses.

Do not overlook ways to make more effective use of natural moisture. Where rainfall is scanty, use stone mulch around trees and shrubs; dew will condense on the stones and seep into the soil. Planting on the north face of a slope also helps.

A SAVING SPRAY

To counteract the drying action of wind, which is particularly damaging to evergreens in cold-winter climates where icy blasts will burn the needles and leaves, use an antitranspirant spray. This spray deposits a thin plastic coating that helps conserve moisture for 4 to 6 months. The same spray will help protect evergreen shrubs in summer if you have to be away. Just before you leave, give them a thorough watering, then spray on the antitranspirant. Some nurserymen use the spray in transplanting as a matter of course, to help keep plants from wilting. If you are buying a live Christmas tree, with the idea of planting it outdoors after the holidays, give it an antitranspirant spray too, so it does not dry out in the house.

Fertilizing, yet another regular chore, is feeding, and as with humans, plant feeding can be overdone. A novice learned this when he bought a suburban property dominated by a magnificent white pine 40 feet tall. Concerned about keeping this priceless asset in top condition, he asked an expert how often he should feed the tree. The expert answered with a question of his own: how much more do you want the tree to grow?

FAIR FEEDING

The reply is a good guide for most other plantings as well. With a well-prepared bed, an organic mulch and enough water, most trees, shrubs and woody vines will need little fertilizing, which not only may be unnecessary but may do the plants harm. Nitrogen, the main growth element in all fertilizers and the first of the three figures listed on fertilizer labels, can promote abundant foliage—but

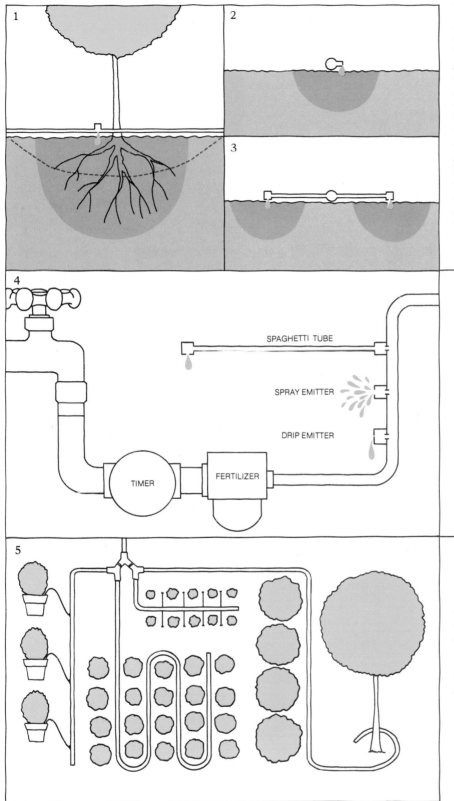

WATERING DROP BY DROP

A drip irrigation system is one of the most efficient ways to water plants. Consisting of a network of flexible polyethylene pipes and emitters, it delivers water slowly to a plant. Although the network soaks a much deeper area around the plant's roots than would a hose or conventional sprinkler, it uses one-quarter to one-half less water. The emitters (1), which plug directly into the main pipeline (2) or into spaghetti-like tubes extending from the pipeline (3), can direct water to any location in the garden. Weeding is reduced because water reaches only the targeted plants.

Drip irrigation systems are marketed under many brand names and can be bought at garden supply stores. They hook up to any outdoor faucet (4). Accessories that automatically shut the system off or inject fertilizer into the water are also available. The emitters drip water through tiny holes at predetermined rates that range from $\frac{1}{2}$ to 4 gallons per hour. Some emitters have caps that can be adjusted for a fine or coarse spray. Both can be attached to spaghetti tubes cut to any convenient length.

The pipes and emitters can be laid out to fit any garden design, directing water to potted plants, vegetable and flower beds, hedges and foundation plantings, or trees, with little puddling or runoff (5). Installed permanently under a layer of mulch, they eliminate the need to haul sprinklers and hoses through the garden. For large gardens, coupling joints can be used to connect two or more systems to a single faucet.

often at the expense of flowers and fruits. (The story is told of one gardener who gave his tomatoes a liberal feeding of lawn fertilizer, high in nitrogen, and then wondered why he had such beautiful tomato plants—but without any fruit.) Moreover, overfed plants may grow out of bounds, requiring pruning, and the tender new shoots may be susceptible to winter damage.

FRIENDLY PHOSPHORUS

The second fertilizer element, phosphorus, is more beneficial, helping to develop strong roots and stems and good leaf and flower color. A fertilizer with a high-phosphorus content is best for general use on permanent plantings in a low-upkeep garden. Bone meal, for example, is roughly 20 to 25 per cent phosphoric acid.

The third main fertilizer ingredient, potassium or potash, gives plants vigor and aids them in resisting disease. An easy way of supplementing potash is to scatter wood ashes from your fireplace around your plants.

If you choose to use a general-purpose chemical fertilizer, select one that is rich in phosphorus but with some potassium and nitrogen, such as a formula marked 10-20-10 or 5-10-5, and apply a somewhat smaller amount than the label calls for.

To reduce the number of applications to a minimum, the best all-around fertilizer is one that releases its nutrients slowly over a period of months or even years. This occurs with most natural organic fertilizers, including bone meal, cottonseed meal, blood meal, fish meal, rotted manure and dried sewage sludge. They are not as concentrated as chemical fertilizers but they keep working longer. (If you use manure, make sure it is thoroughly rotted or buy it in dried, bagged form; fresh manure can quickly burn plants.)

PEPPING UP PLANTS

If a plant begins to look undernourished, you can give it a boost with a chemical fertilizer. A typical 5-10-5 formula should be used in roughly the following proportions (figuring one pound of fertilizer as equal to a pint in volume): for deciduous trees, 2 to 4 pounds for each inch of trunk diameter, measured chest high; for evergreen trees, 2 pounds per inch; for most evergreen and deciduous shrubs, 3 to 6 pounds per 100 square feet of bed, or no more than a half cup for an individual shrub 4 or 5 feet high. Acid-loving shrubs such as azaleas are best fed with a special formula that is made for them, or with a slow-acting, acidifying organic fertilizer like cottonseed meal, about a cupful for a 4- to 5-foot shrub. For trees, fertilizer spikes that you drive into the ground around the drip line are a laborsaver, and release their nutrients over a longer period. But they are not the cheapest way of fertilizing.

An exception to the general rule about take-it-easy fertilizing is a newly planted ground cover, which may seem to take an inordinate amount of time to transform itself from a collection of lonely, spaced-out plantlets into a solid, lush green blanket. To speed up foliage growth, use a chemical fertilizer with a high-nitrogen content, applying it in spring so the succulent new growth thus stimulated will have a chance to harden before winter arrives.

Lawns are another special case, since they must be fed regularly to keep the grass plants growing under the unnatural conditions of repeated mowing. Grass needs a high-nitrogen fertilizer to stimulate leaf growth; typical formulas are 30-5-8, 10-6-4, 22-8-4 and 17-4-4. To save work, set your mower blades to cut at 2 inches or higher, particularly in the heat of midsummer. Taller grass will shade the soil more effectively, cutting down on watering, and the grass will be better able to survive dry spells and competing weeds.

With grass as with other plants, observe a few easy-gardening precautions to avoid later trouble. Use as little fertilizer as possible to keep growth at a minimum and avoid damaging plants. Do not fertilize in midsummer when soft new growth could be injured by hot, dry spells. The best time to feed is just before new growth starts in spring or fall. Do not apply concentrated chemical fertilizers when lawns or leaves are wet; the granules stick to the foliage and may cause chemical burns. Water immediately after fertilizing; this will wash granules off the grass or leaves and get the fertilizer down to the roots where it can do some good. Never use a combination fertilizer and weed killer—or any herbicide, for that matter—under or near the drip line of a tree or shrub; while doing its job of killing weeds it may leach down and sicken the tree or shrub as well.

The basic thing to remember about controlling weeds is that any soil that has been cultivated but not planted is an open invitation to weeds. "Open ground is like a great, vacant apartment house, with everyone trying to move in at the same time," says one landscape architect. "Once the apartments are occupied, the shoving stops." Adds Richard Lighty, University of Delaware associate professor of plant science: "The first rule of low maintenance gardening is this: never break more ground than you can cover, either with plants or with mulches."

English gardeners do not even like to leave the ground beneath the surface empty. They prefer scalping weeds to digging them out. Eventually the weed roots die but meanwhile they occupy space and prevent other intruders from moving in. Scalping is a good way of dealing with weeds, and a scuffle hoe, sometimes called a Dutch hoe, does the job better than the ordinary garden hoe. Instead of having a blade set at right angles to the handle for chopping at the weeds, the scuffle hoe has a blade that lies flat on the ground. You push the hoe

A HANDY GARDEN SCOOP

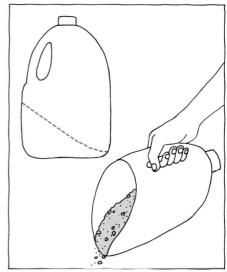

To distribute small amounts of sand, topsoil, grass seed, fertilizer or mulch around the garden, make a scoop from an empty plastic bleach bottle. Cut off the bottom of the bottle at a 45° angle that slants toward the handle. Leave the cap on the bottle to keep the contents from slipping out when the scoop is in use.

A WEEDY SCUFFLE

Tools that make the task tolerable

Proper tools can make the crucial difference between lightening your gardening chores and making them intolerable. For example, a long-handled, round-nosed loading shovel is excellent for moving gravel but hard on the back when used for digging fence-post holes. Similarly, a heavy-duty bow rake does a number of gardening jobs very well, but raking leaves is not one of them; a fan rake of lightweight metal or bamboo will easily collect twice as many leaves as the iron rake, and without scraping holes in your lawn.

Before you invest in any tool, test its weight, balance and grip. Your height, weight and strength will determine what suits you best. If you are a beginning gardener, buy tools one at a time as you need them; as you learn the peculiar requirements of your own garden you can complete your tool collection. Presented here, in groups according to their use, are nine basic tools (illustrated in black on the opposite page) and seven optional tools (green) with which you can tackle such fundamentals as preparing the soil, installing plants, pruning and weeding.

DIGGING AND SHOVELING TOOLS
The best implement for loading and unloading loose material such as gravel, sand or leaf mulch is a scoop-shaped loading shovel with a pointed tip. The blade is set at an angle to the shaft so that when you slide it into a pile of material the blade stays level. But this angle makes the shovel ill-suited for digging. An efficient digging tool has a shallow angle between blade and shaft, so you can exert your weight on it vertically, down through the blade.

A spading fork, square-nosed spade and trowel are basic digging tools, while a transplanting spade—with its narrower blade and round tip—is useful if you will be doing a great deal of transplanting or need deeper holes. The tines of a spading fork are good for turning ground, especially if the soil is rocky, for breaking up clods of earth and for working leaf mold and other soil amendments into the planting bed.

The square-nosed spade's sharp edge makes it an excellent tool for edging, digging straight-sided planting holes, stripping sod or trimming roots on young trees or shrubs. A short D-grip handle gives you control and precision.

Because you will want to step on the top of the blade to push it into the ground, look for a spade with a step-plate or a rolled top edge. For very heavy digging, loosening hard-packed soil and prying up heavy rocks, a pickax is your best bet.

Once the soil is prepared, a trowel is used to dig holes for planting. It is also handy for digging up bulbs or small plants for transplanting. Get one that perfectly fits your hand, preferably one that has a straight shank and a wooden handle in a metal socket that is of a piece with the blade. If you purchase a forged trowel with a metal handle, make certain the end of the handle is capped with a wooden plug or you may find yourself with a palmful of blisters. A trowel with a curved blade is best for most tasks; the curved shape also lets you take up a firm ball of roots when transplanting.

RAKING TOOLS
Because their functions are so different, you should have both a fan-shaped lawn rake and an iron bow rake. The bow rake has strong, curved teeth with which to remove pebbles or clods of earth after a seedbed has been spaded; turned on its back, it is used to level soil. The bow is a kind of shock absorber that gives the rake resilience and durability. The lawn rake is better for sweeping up lawn clippings, leaves and any other light matter, whether on your driveway or lawn; metal rakes are more durable than bamboo ones.

CHOPPING AND CULTIVATING TOOLS
The best all-around hoe for almost any garden chore is an onion hoe, which has a blade 7 inches wide and about 1¾ inches high. It is good for working between rows of small plants; its sharp front edge cuts weeds off at ground level, while its slanted sides make sharp corners that act as small picks.

One of the advantages of a double-edged scuffle hoe is that it works on both the push and the pull. Thus, you can walk backward, cutting off weeds as you go, and not trample the weeds back into the soil.

A pronged cultivator that is light in weight (heavier ones can sink too deeply into the soil and injure roots) is more efficient than a hoe for cultivating in rocky soil, though it is not designed for

deep spading. It combines chopping and pulling motions to break up crusted soil and to pull up weeds.

CUTTING TOOLS
Hand pruning shears are perhaps the most often used garden tool, whether they are the scissors type or the blade-and-anvil type. It is important that you get a pair you can use comfortably. An overall length of 7 or 8 inches is usually adequate. The scissors-type shears will make a neater cut and will not crush tender stems, but the blade-and-anvil type is easier to use, requiring less pressure. In either case, these shears are meant for branches no more than ¾ of an inch in diameter. For thicker branches you will need a pair of lopping shears, which have long handles and short, scissors-type blades. Lopping shears will cut branches up to 1¼ inches in diameter. For heavier limbs, a pruning saw is in order.

CARRYING CARTS
Some sort of wheeled cart is necessary for moving leaves, soil, peat moss and other bulky material from one part of the garden to another. It is also useful as a container in which to mix small batches of concrete or mortar. A metal wheelbarrow has the strength needed for heavy jobs. In addition, a light two-wheeled garden cart is useful for hauling leaves and other garden debris; it is less likely to tip than a wheelbarrow. In both cases, you will need a capacity of 3- to 4-cubic feet.

TOOL CARE
Once you have made your selection, giving your tools proper care will extend their life and make them easier and safer to work with.

Rust is your biggest enemy. After each use, remove any soil that adheres to your tools with rough burlap or a wire brush, then wipe metal parts with an oily rag. Remove any rust that does appear with steel wool and oil. Remove plant gums and resin with kerosene.

Keep edged tools sharp with a flat file; more accidents occur with dull tools than with sharp ones. Oil wooden handles with linseed or vegetable oil, remove splinters with sandpaper, and glue any cracks. Once the tools are cleaned, store them on nails or pegs to prevent accidents and to make them easier to find.

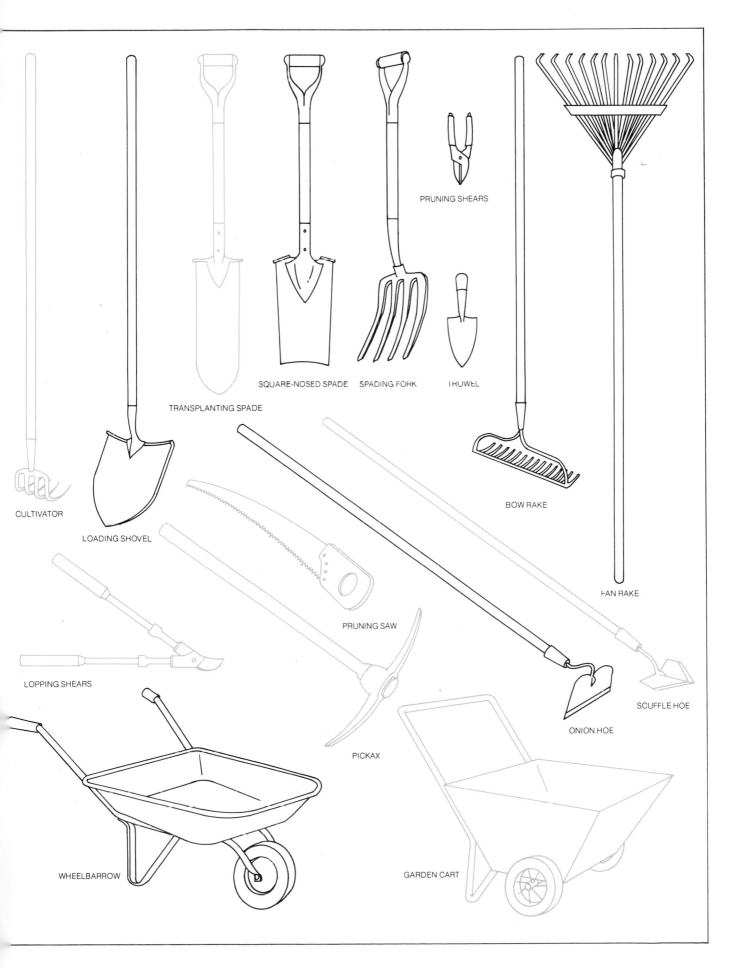

CULTIVATOR

TRANSPLANTING SPADE

SQUARE-NOSED SPADE

SPADING FORK

TROWEL

PRUNING SHEARS

FAN RAKE

BOW RAKE

LOADING SHOVEL

PRUNING SAW

LOPPING SHEARS

SCUFFLE HOE

ONION HOE

PICKAX

WHEELBARROW

GARDEN CART

back and forth to slice the weeds off just below the surface.

Chemical weed killers can make a great contribution to easier gardening if you take care to choose and use them properly. There are two basic sorts of herbicides. Pre-emergence herbicides are preventive chemicals: they keep certain weed seeds from germinating. But they do not affect growing plants. Thus, for instance, you can use a pre-emergence herbicide and plant seedlings immediately thereafter. Postemergence herbicides kill certain weeds that are already growing—and, if you do not watch out, they can kill your good plants too.

CONTROLLED CHEMICALS But in a controlled situation, chemicals have quite legitimate uses. Small tree stumps can be daubed with a brush killer directly after cutting, and the roots will die in place; you will not have to dig them out. Gravel driveways, flagstone walkways, inaccessible ground under decks or porches or hard-to-mow locations can be cleared of all vegetation with judicious use of a soil sterilant. With a special foliage spray, you can rid your lawn of poison ivy. A pre-emergence herbicide can be used on the lawn to prevent crab grass from germinating.

In every case, use the herbicide only as the manufacturer directs. All are potentially dangerous if used indiscriminately. The Arnold Arboretum, at Harvard University, once used a new herbicide to spray poison ivy around the base of a white pine tree. Very little was used, just enough to moisten the foliage of the poison ivy. The bark of the pine was not touched. Yet, in three weeks the white pine and several others nearby, with 6-inch trunks, were clearly dying. The herbicide had been taken into the roots of the poison ivy and from there had spread underground to the tree roots.

LIBERATING THE LAWN But there is no reason you should not use weed killers on your lawn. There you are safe, provided the herbicide does not drift onto flower beds or seep down to contaminate trees or shrubs. A few lawn weeds, such as quack grass, bishop's goutweed and chrysanthemum weed, defy easy eradication. The chemicals that will kill them will kill turf grasses as well. But a broad range of common lawn weeds, including dandelions, crab grass, the various plantains, wild garlic, yarrow, sheep sorrel and many others, can be controlled with selective herbicides that attack undesirable plants without damaging the lawn. The kill ratio may be short of 100 per cent, but in low-maintenance gardening you need to develop a certain tolerance for undesirables that are simply too much work to get rid of.

You should not be tolerant of trash, however. Any garden will be healthier and will present fewer maintenance problems if it is routinely kept neat and clean. Pruning will rarely be necessary if you have wisely chosen and positioned your plants. Properly trained at an early age, shade trees are not likely to need major surgery later. Remove competing leaders of young trees, branches that cross or rub together, and those that make narrow angles with the trunk or are too close to the ground. On any tree or shrub, trim away dead, damaged or diseased branches whenever you see them, cutting close to the trunk to promote healing. Coat large wounds with tree paint. (To simplify that messy job, tree paint comes in spray cans.) At the end of the season, clean debris from beds and borders to eliminate breeding grounds for insects and lurking diseases.

If you do notice some kind of infestation, do not panic. Often, with an insect attack, the worst damage has been done by the time you notice it, and the plant will recover—if not this season, then the next. Take an infested part of the plant to your county agent or to the cooperative extension service for diagnosis, or get out the bug book (every gardener should have one) for a specifically targeted remedy. Plant diseases are harder to cope with than insect infestations and there is no real cure for an already infected plant; the best you can do is to keep a disease from spreading. Dig up the sick plant, along with the mulch around it, and put it in the garbage can.

Finally, a simple matter of scheduling can make your gardening much less burdensome. There is no need to concentrate all of your weekly chores into a single exhausting Saturday or Sunday, or to try to get them all done in the heat of a blistering summer day.

One New Jersey gardener spreads his work load by getting up half-an-hour earlier than usual on a couple of mornings a week during the growing season. He puts in a brisk stint in his garden, then goes to his desk job refreshed—knowing that with another chore out of the way, he will have that much more of his weekend to devote to tennis. A woman in Arizona also does her gardening early in the day; at that time her garden is still inviting, dew-sparkled and cool, in contrast to the enervating 90-degree-plus temperatures of a desert afternoon. Still others escape the heat by planning their work to keep themselves in the shade. Many postpone hoeing and weeding until the cool of the evening.

"A garden shouldn't take you more time than a second cup of coffee after breakfast, or a second drink before dinner," says one experienced Atlanta gardener with spectacular results to show for his efforts. Many gardeners—and not even lazy ones—would consider that morning and night routine too much. But there is a point to what he says. If a garden means anything at all to you, it will be part of your life—and you will work it into your weekly routine not as a chore, but as rest and relaxation.

DEALING WITH PESTS

A RELAXING ROUTINE

An encyclopedia of easy-care plants 5

Happy is the gardener who, with many other calls on his time, has a home landscape filled with plants that pretty much take care of themselves. If your mind is more on boating than on bent grass, or more on travel than tomatoes, selecting a basic framework of such self-sufficient plants will take you a long way toward freeing yourself of incessant gardening chores.

To help you achieve a garden that truly demands only minimum maintenance, the encyclopedia that follows describes plants chosen for their ability to prosper year after year with scant attention. The encyclopedia is devoted entirely to permanent garden plantings; it is divided into six sections covering deciduous trees and shrubs, evergreen trees and shrubs, perennial flowers and ground covers. Within each group, plants have been chosen for their natural immunity to attack by pests and diseases, for neat growth habits that let you put away the pruning shears, for their readiness to accept various types of soil, sun exposure and moisture levels, and for other characteristics that mean less toil for the tender. Traits of individual plants that some gardeners might consider drawbacks, such as exuberant growth that could cause a plant to take up more space than it is welcome to, are also noted. Each plant is keyed to the climate zones where it is most comfortably at home, as shown on the map on page 148.

Within any genus of plants—its general category—different species may vary considerably in the amount of care they require. Hence the selections listed here are often quite precise; you may find old favorites missing because their places have been preempted by others that are a bit less demanding. Since common names can be ambiguous, and often vary regionally, each plant is listed alphabetically within its section by its Latin botanical name to ensure accurate identification at the nursery or in a plant catalogue. Common names are cross-referenced to help you find the plant you seek.

Low-maintenance trees, shrubs, ground covers and perennials are (clockwise from top left): red pine, golden-rain tree, Gold Coast juniper, New England aster, St.-John's-wort, and rose of Sharon.

FIVE-LEAVED ARALIA
Acanthopanax sieboldianus

YELLOW JAPANESE BARBERRY
Berberis thunbergii 'Aurea'

ALPINE JAPANESE QUINCE
Chaenomeles japonica alpina

Deciduous shrubs

ACANTHOPANAX

A. sieboldianus, also called *Aralia pentaphylla* (five-leaved aralia, angelica shrub)

Almost impervious to city smog, pests, shade and drought, five-leaved aralia is a handsome foliage plant that grows in most soils in Zones 4-9. Its fans of glossy green 2-inch leaflets persist long into the autumn, though they eventually turn yellow and drop.

Spines at the base of its leaves make the five-leaved aralia effective in a barrier hedge. Grouped into informal plantings, it requires little pruning. The slim, erect branches grow to heights of 4 to 6 feet. If this shrub becomes too tall or spindly, its stems can be cut back to the ground in early spring and new shoots will replace them.

ALABAMA FOTHERGILLA See *Fothergilla*
ALDER, BLACK See *Ilex*
ALDER BUCKTHORN See *Rhamnus*
ALPINE JAPANESE QUINCE See *Chaenomeles*
ALTHEA, SHRUB See *Hibiscus*
AMERICAN CRANBERRY BUSH See *Viburnum*
AMUR HONEYSUCKLE See *Lonicera*
AMUR PRIVET See *Ligustrum*
ANGELICA SHRUB See *Acanthopanax*
ARALIA See *Acanthopanax*
ARNOLD GIANT FORSYTHIA See *Forsythia*
ARNOLD PROMISE WITCH HAZEL See *Hamamelis*
AZALEA See *Rhododendron*

BARBERRY, JAPANESE See *Berberis*
BAYBERRY See *Myrica*
BEAUTY BUSH See *Kolkwitzia*

BERBERIS

B. thunbergii (Japanese barberry)

Japanese barberry comes close to being a no-maintenance plant throughout Zones 4-10. Easily transplanted, it develops into a dense, well-rounded 4- to 7-foot specimen that needs no pruning. Several shrubs planted 1 to 2 feet apart grow into an effective barrier hedge with short, stiff thorns on the arching branches.

Although some species of barberries have been banned where wheat is a major crop because of the role they play in transmitting black stem rust to wheat, this species is practically pest and disease free. You can plant it and forget it; if you forget it too long, you can cut the out-of-bounds plant back to the ground to rejuvenate it.

Japanese barberry's culture is as easy as its maintenance. Tolerant of dry conditions, it adapts readily to any kind of soil. It develops rapidly in partial shade, although its fall color is best when it is grown in sunny locations. In fall, the small leaves turn the same brilliant red as the ¼-inch berries, which last through the winter. Thornless and dwarf varieties are available, as well as some whose leaves are bright yellow or dull red throughout the growing season.

BIG-LEAVED HYDRANGEA See *Hydrangea*
BILLIARD SPIREA See *Spiraea*
BLACK ALDER See *Ilex*
BORDER FORSYTHIA See *Forsythia*
BRIDAL WREATH See *Spiraea*
BROOM See *Cytisus*
BUCKTHORN, ALDER See *Rhamnus*
BUMALDA SPIREA See *Spiraea*
BURNING BUSH See *Euonymus*

CABBAGE ROSE See *Rosa*
CALIFORNIA PRIVET See *Ligustrum*
CANDLEBERRY See *Myrica*

CHAENOMELES

C. japonica alpina (alpine Japanese quince)

Smallest of the quinces, this dependable shrub thrives in full sun in any good garden soil in Zones 4-8. A dwarf, it seldom grows more than 1½ feet tall, making it useful as a foundation plant or as a rounded, spreading—but rather prickly—ground cover; its branches contain ¼-inch spines. It is covered in spring with bright reddish-orange blossoms, but in cold climates the flower buds may be killed by frost. The greenish-yellow 1¼-inch fruit is good for jellies. In spring the foliage is bronze, turning glossy dark green for the rest of the growing season. The plant is susceptible to San Jose scale.

CHERRY, CORNELIAN See *Cornus*
CHINESE WITCH HAZEL See *Hamamelis*
CLAVEY'S DWARF HONEYSUCKLE See *Lonicera*

CLETHRA

C. alnifolia (summer sweet, sweet pepper bush); *C. alnifolia* 'Rosea' (pink summer sweet)

A native shrub along the eastern coast from Maine to Florida, summer sweet is hardy in Zones 3-10, growing well in full sun or partial shade and flourishing in environments ranging from windy seashores to wet woodlands. In moist, acid soils it may reach 6 feet in height. Dry soils pose the only hazard to this shrub, inhibiting growth and raising susceptibility to red spider mites.

Bushy and erect, summer sweet takes its name from the 3- to 5-inch spikes of tiny white or pale pink flowers whose fragrance perfumes July and August breezes when few other shrubs are in bloom. The shiny green 1½- to 4-inch leaves turn deep yellow to orange in fall.

Summer sweet's tendency to grow in clumps makes it useful in borders. The shrub needs no pruning but its stems can be shortened in early spring.

COMMON PRIVET See *Ligustrum*
COMMON WITCH HAZEL See *Hamamelis*
CORNELIAN CHERRY See *Cornus*

CORNUS

C. alba (Tatarian dogwood); *C. alba* 'Argenteo-marginata' (silver-edged dogwood); *C. alba* 'Sibirica' (Siberian dogwood); *C. mas* (Cornelian cherry); *C. sericea,* also called *C. stolonifera* (red osier dogwood); *C. sericea* 'Flaviramea' (yellow-twigged dogwood)

These shrubby relatives of the popular flowering dogwood tree have their own virtues. They are adaptable to any good garden soil and will grow in full sun or partial shade. They never require pruning unless they are planted to display the brilliant colors of young twigs, in which case they can be thinned in early spring every two or three years or cut to the ground every five years. The shrubby dogwoods are resistant to pests and diseases except for dogwood scurfy scale.

Tatarian dogwood, with its bright red twigs, may reach 9 feet in height if it is left unpruned. It grows rapidly and stands out dramatically against snow, suiting it for specimen planting in Zones 4-10. Silver-edged dogwood grows similarly, in the same zones, and its leaves have white margins. Siberian dogwood, which has coral-red stems, is hardier, growing in Zones 2-10. It grows more slowly and thus is better suited for shrub borders.

PINK SUMMER SWEET
Clethra alnifolia 'Rosea'

SIBERIAN DOGWOOD
Cornus alba 'Sibirica'

CORNELIAN CHERRY
Cornus mas

For climate zones and frost dates, see maps, pages 148-149.

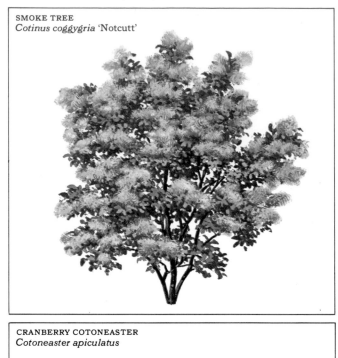

SMOKE TREE
Cotinus coggygria 'Notcutt'

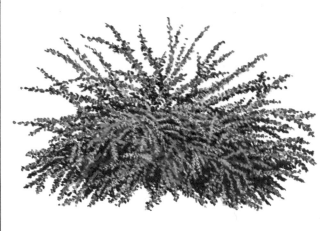

CRANBERRY COTONEASTER
Cotoneaster apiculatus

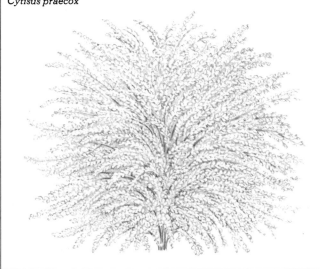

WARMINSTER BROOM
Cytisus praecox

Cornelian cherry will grow 10 to 20 feet tall with a wide spread in Zones 4-8. It is fine for a mixed shrub border or a specimen, and it also can be sheared into a hedge.

Red osier dogwood is fast-growing in wet areas of Zones 2-9 and has coral-red twigs. It rarely grows taller than 6 feet but spreads by underground runners to form wide clumps. Yellow-twigged dogwood grows wide rather than tall and commonly is planted near the red-stemmed Tatarian dogwood for color contrast.

Nearly all dogwoods flower briefly in early spring, and the blooms of the Cornelian cherry are especially prized. After they have flowered, dogwoods produce red or white berries that attract wild birds.

COTINUS
C. coggygria, also called *Rhus cotinus* (smoke tree, smokebush)

This hardy shrub grows in Zones 5-10 in any soil, but it produces its fluffy, smokelike fruit-bearing stalks more profusely in soil that is not fertile than in one rich in humus. In either type of soil, good drainage is essential. In full sun, the smoke tree develops into a rounded shrub 10 to 12 feet high with an equal spread.

The ornamental value of male plants can be disappointing; choose female plants of named varieties that have been propagated for their summer display. These produce quantities of exotic, many-branched 8-inch fruiting stalks feathered with pink or gray hairs that settle among the 2- to 3-inch oval leaves like puffs of smoke. The tiny flowers bloom in early summer. The fruits that follow nestle inconspicuously among the stalks of each long-lasting plume. The blue-green or purple foliage turns yellow to orange in the fall.

COTONEASTER
C. adpressus praecox (early cotoneaster); *C. apiculatus* (cranberry cotoneaster)

Both of these dense, ground-hugging cotoneasters combine ornament with function and are so easy to grow that they are recommended for low-upkeep gardens despite several potential drawbacks. They spread slowly, require little or no pruning and grow in a wide range of climates, from Zones 4-10, in any well-drained soil where they receive full sun or partial shade. While they tolerate dryness, prolonged periods of hot, dry weather opens them to attack by pests such as lace bug and red spider mite. Another weakness is the plants' susceptibility to the fungus called fire blight, which kills leaves in the middle of the growing season.

Early cotoneaster and cranberry cotoneaster both have dark glossy leaves that turn red or orange in the fall, and they bear small red berries that remain on the plant all winter. Early cotoneaster forms compact mounds up to 2 feet tall; cranberry cotoneaster is more erect in habit of growth, with branches that grow 2 to 3 feet tall, then fan out 3 to 5 feet to cover a slope or a low wall.

COTTAGE ROSE See *Rosa*
CRANBERRY BUSH, AMERICAN See *Viburnum*
CRANBERRY COTONEASTER See *Cotoneaster*
CRAPE MYRTLE See *Lagerstroemia*
CUT-LEAVED STEPHANANDRA See *Stephanandra*

CYTISUS
C. kewensis (Kew broom); *C. praecox* (Warminster broom)

Broom thrives in dry, sandy soils rejected by most other plants and actually enriches them by producing nitrogen from root nodules. Given a sunny location, it grows rapidly into pest-free spots of year-round color. Both of the minutely leaved hybrid brooms listed here are covered by small, pale yellow flowers in the spring, and their naked twigs are bright green all winter. Brooms need no pruning, although tall species can be shortened by cutting back stems by two thirds when they have just finished flowering.

A single plant of Kew broom, which is hardy in Zones 6-10, will spread into a dense mat only 6 to 10 inches high but up to 6 feet across. The Warminster broom, which is usually the first of the brooms to flower, is hardy in Zones 5-10. The branches of this bushy, erect shrub, 5 to 6 feet tall, droop under the weight of their flowers.

DEUTZIA
D. gracilis (slender deutzia)

Slender deutzia flourishes in any type of soil, grows in full sun or partial shade and is untroubled by insects or diseases. Its only serious drawback is the susceptibility of its slender, arching stems to frost damage. In Zones 5-9 this rarely presents a maintenance problem, but in the colder winters of Zone 4, early spring pruning of dead stems may be necessary. However, the plant renews itself quickly if cut completely to the ground.

Slender deutzia is a small, compact shrub, 2 to 4 feet high, useful for informal borders or hedges. Its decorative value lies in its spring display of tiny white flowers, blooming in profuse clusters that all but obscure the leaves.

DIERVILLA See *Weigela*
DOGWOOD See *Cornus*
DOUBLEFILE VIBURNUM, MARIES' See *Viburnum*
DWARF WINGED EUONYMUS See *Euonymus*

EARLY COTONEASTER See *Cotoneaster*

EUONYMUS
E. alata (winged euonymus, burning bush), *E. alata* 'Compacta' (dwarf winged euonymus)

Winged euonymus and its dwarf variety are among the easiest of deciduous shrubs to grow; they even appear to be resistant to the destructive euonymus scale that devastates other species in some parts of the country. They are hardy in Zones 3-9, thriving in almost any soil and growing equally well in full sun or partial shade.

Winged euonymus becomes a dense shrub 8 to 9 feet tall. Dwarf winged euonymus reaches a height of only 4 feet in seven years. Its slow growth, rounded shape and great density make it useful as a low-maintenance hedge that needs pruning only once every two or three years.

Both shrubs make a spectacular showing in the fall when their foliage turns blazing scarlet and their seed capsules burst to reveal orange centers. When winter arrives, the stiff branches lined with corky ridges form interesting silhouettes. Inconspicuous yellowish flowers bloom in late spring.

EXBURY AZALEA See *Rhododendron*

FATHER HUGO'S ROSE See *Rosa*
FIVE-LEAVED ARALIA See *Acanthopanax*
FLAME AZALEA See *Rhododendron*

FORSYTHIA
F. 'Arnold Giant' (Arnold Giant forsythia); *F. intermedia* (border forsythia); *F. ovata* (Korean forsythia); *F. suspensa* 'Sieboldii' (Siebold's weeping forsythia)

Yellow forsythia blossoms announce the spring season for

SLENDER DEUTZIA
Deutzia gracilis

DWARF WINGED EUONYMUS
Euonymus alata 'Compacta'

LYNWOOD FORSYTHIA
Forsythia intermedia 'Lynwood'

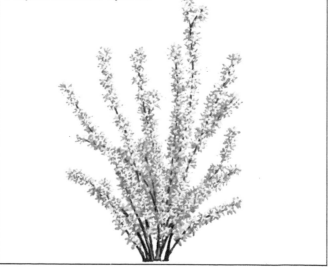

For climate zones and frost dates, see maps, pages 148-149.

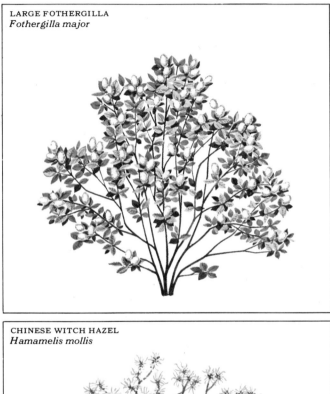

LARGE FOTHERGILLA
Fothergilla major

CHINESE WITCH HAZEL
Hamamelis mollis

many gardeners. They brighten southern landscapes as early as February, and by March and April they have signaled spring's arrival as far north as New England and the Pacific Northwest. Forsythia is popular not only for its early bloom but also for its easy culture. A quick-growing, hardy plant, it thrives in either full sun or partial shade, and tolerates almost any soil and all but the driest sites. This long-lived shrub almost never suffers attack by disease or insects and easily survives the rigors of the city garden.

Some gardeners, however, create a pruning nightmare for themselves by failing to match a forsythia's mature size to the chosen site. Forsythias have graceful, loose, informal shapes and tend to sprawl as wide as they are tall. If they are sited with a thought to their ultimate shape and height, forsythias need only a little annual pruning in spring when flowers fade to remove dead canes or thin crowded ones. The gardener who inherits an overgrown forsythia can cut it 6 inches from the ground in early spring and watch it rejuvenate over two or three years.

Arnold Giant's stiff, upright branches grow to a height of 8 feet in Zones 5-9. The more arching border forsythias grow 6 to 8 feet tall in the same climates. Korean forsythia's flower buds are not as subject to winterkill as those of other species, so it is a good choice for gardens in Zone 4; it also grows 6 to 8 feet tall. Siebold's weeping forsythia, hardy in Zones 5-9, is a spreading plant whose pliant arching branches trail to the ground and root wherever they touch moist soil. This plant grows up to 5 feet tall with branches that trail 10 feet or more along the ground.

FOTHERGILLA

F. major (large fothergilla); *F. monticola* (Alabama fothergilla) (both also called witch alder)

These little-known deciduous shrubs, native to the southeastern United States, grow best in moist, well-drained acid soils and in partial shade or full sun. They are hardy in Zones 5-9, rarely need maintenance, and stage striking displays twice a year. In spring, they are covered with 2-inch-long thimble-shaped flower clusters, made up of tiny white flowers. When fall arrives, the broad 3-inch leaves turn shades of yellow, orange or red; the colors are especially bright where plants have received full sun.

Large fothergilla becomes an upright shrub, 9 feet high, while Alabama fothergilla grows only 6 feet tall, but has a greater spread, with a diameter of 6 to 8 feet. Both shrubs take up to 12 years to reach their full size.

FRAGRANT SNOWBALL See *Viburnum*
FRENCH HYDRANGEA See *Hydrangea*

GARLAND SPIREA See *Spiraea*
GOLDEN PRIVET, VICARY See *Ligustrum*
GOLDEN ROSE OF CHINA See *Rosa*

HAMAMELIS

H. 'Arnold Promise' (Arnold Promise witch hazel); *H. mollis* (Chinese witch hazel); *H. vernalis* (vernal witch hazel); *H. virginiana* (common witch hazel)

Where there is space for these tall and spreading shrubs, witch hazel is a wintertime delight. Its fragrant flowers with bright yellow ribbon-like petals decorate the northern garden in fall or in late winter when no other shrubs bloom. The flowers of the common witch hazel appear on bare twigs in late fall, often as the 4- to 6-inch oval leaves begin to drop. The flowers of the Arnold Promise, vernal and Chinese witch hazels appear in late winter or very early spring. Frosts do not faze these flowers; they open when temperatures are safe and close if the cold becomes too great.

Witch-hazel shrubs will grow in almost any moist, well-drained soil where they receive sun or partial shade; they are even tolerant of dry, polluted urban air. Erect and neat, they rarely need pruning.

Gardeners in Zones 4-9 can grow three of these witch hazels, Arnold Promise, vernal and common. Arnold Promise is a 15-foot hybrid whose winter blossoms are abundant. Vernal witch hazel is a smaller shrub, 6 to 10 feet tall, that is usually the first to flower in late or even midwinter. Common witch hazel grows to 6 to 10 feet. Chinese witch hazel is a 10- to 15-foot shrub hardy only from Zone 5 south.

HARISON'S YELLOW ROSE See *Rosa*

HIBISCUS
H. syriacus (rose of Sharon, shrub althea)
Once its roots are established, the pest-free rose of Sharon requires little pruning or other care. The hardiest hibiscus, it grows in Zones 6-9. It prefers a sunny location in moist but well-drained soil that is enriched with compost or leaf mold, but the shrub will adapt to poor soils, partial shade and the rigors of city gardens.

A young plant under 5 feet tall should be set out in early spring and its roots should be protected with mulch during the first two winters. Further mulching is unnecessary once a plant is well-rooted.

Rose of Sharon's branches grow upright, giving it a slender, 6- to 12-foot silhouette; it becomes broader with age if left unpruned. The 2½- to 4-inch flowers bloom in late summer or early fall; depending on the variety, they may be single or double, and white, pink, red or blue. The dull green 2- to 3-inch leaves do not change color before they drop.

HILLS-OF-SNOW HYDRANGEA See *Hydrangea*
HONEYSUCKLE See *Lonicera*
HORTENSIA See *Hydrangea*
HOUSE HYDRANGEA See *Hydrangea*

HYDRANGEA
H. arborescens 'Grandiflora' (hills-of-snow hydrangea); *H. macrophylla,* also called *H. hortensis, H. opuloides* (big-leaved hydrangea, French hydrangea, hortensia, house hydrangea); *H. paniculata* 'Grandiflora' (peegee hydrangea)

Indifferent to soil, sun and other growing conditions, hydrangeas are popular low-maintenance plants. Long-lasting, showy blooms envelop them from mid- to late summer. Gardeners have little trouble with these coarse-leaved shrubs unless they choose a species that is not hardy in their climate or plant a hydrangea where it does not have enough room to reach its mature size gracefully.

The hills-of-snow hydrangea is a small shrub often used in foundation planting or in borders. It can be grown in Zones 5-10, but severe winters in the northern part of this range may kill unprotected stems. Growing 3 feet tall, it bears 4- to 8-inch rounded clusters of creamy-white flowers.

The big-leaved hydrangea needs the warmer climates of Zones 6-10, since cold winters kill it to the ground. The petals of its rounded 4- to 8-inch flower clusters turn pink or red in alkaline soils, blue in acidic soil. A rampant grower, the big-leaved hydrangea quickly becomes a 3- to 6-foot rounded shrub if not pruned or winterkilled.

The hardiest of the hydrangeas listed is the peegee. In Zones 4-9 it produces erect pyramidal flower clusters 12 to 18 inches tall and up to 1 foot wide. The blossoms last for

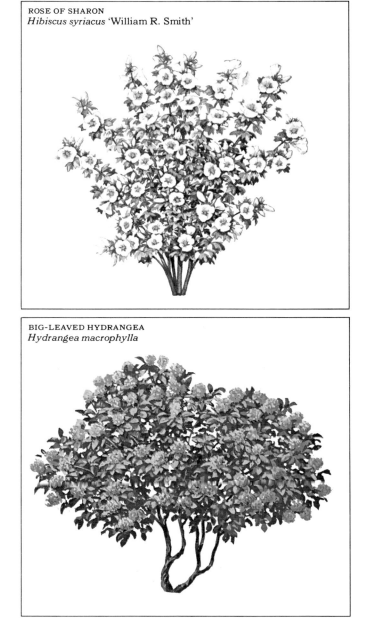

ROSE OF SHARON
Hibiscus syriacus 'William R. Smith'

BIG-LEAVED HYDRANGEA
Hydrangea macrophylla

For climate zones and frost dates, see maps, pages 148-149.

WINTERBERRY
Ilex verticillata

BEAUTY BUSH
Kolkwitzia amabilis

CRAPE MYRTLE
Lagerstroemia indica

weeks, turning from green to white and finally to pink. The peegee hydrangea can grow 3 to 5 feet each growing season and reach 15 to 20 feet in height.

IBOLIUM PRIVET See *Ligustrum*

ILEX
I. verticillata (winterberry, black alder)

Unlike most other members of the holly family, winterberry grows in wet, swampy areas as well as under average garden conditions. In dry soils it is not likely to reach its potential height of 9 or 10 feet. Hardy in Zones 3-8, it thrives in acid soils of average fertility.

Winterberry's ¼-inch red fruits are produced abundantly along the branches. Appearing among the dark green 2-inch leaves before they yellow and drop in the fall, these berries remain on the shrub until Christmas or later. Male and female winterberry plants should be located near each other to ensure fruiting.

JAPANESE BARBERRY See *Berberis*
JAPANESE QUINCE, ALPINE See *Chaenomeles*

KEW BROOM See *Cytisus*

KOLKWITZIA
K. amabilis (beauty bush)

Beauty bush is a care-free shrub. Planted in a sunny or partially shaded location in well-drained soil, it grows 6 to 10 feet tall in Zones 4-9. It has a wide spread which shows to best advantage when planted alone as a specimen shrub.

In late spring, beauty bush bears large sprays of pale to deep pink blossoms that almost obliterate the slender 1- to 3-inch leaves. The flowers last about two weeks and are followed by feathery brown seed pods that remain on the plant after the foliage reddens and drops. The bark of the shrub peels, giving it a shaggy appearance.

KOREAN FORSYTHIA See *Forsythia*
KOREAN RHODODENDRON See *Rhododendron*

LAGERSTROEMIA
L. indica (crape myrtle)

Relatively pest-free crape myrtle provides mid- to late summer bloom in gardens of Zones 7-10 when its large clusters of white to pink, red or purple crinkly flowers tip the end of every branch. Planted in a moist but well-drained soil where it receives full sun, crape myrtle can become 15 to 20 feet tall; smaller varieties are available.

Crape myrtle is susceptible to mildew in humid coastal areas. It needs no pruning, but can be cut back severely in early spring to control its size. At the northern edge of its range, stems may die to the ground each winter but roots survive freezing and new growth appears in the spring and will flower the same year.

LARGE FOTHERGILLA See *Fothergilla*
LEMOINE MOCK ORANGE See *Philadelphus*

LIGUSTRUM
L. amurense (Amur privet); *L. ibolium* (Ibolium privet); *L. obtusifolium regelianum* (Regel privet); *L. ovalifolium* (California privet); *L. vicaryi* (Vicary golden privet); *L. vulgare* (common privet)

Privets have an undeserved reputation as work-making plants due to their popular use in formal hedges. The inexpensive, easy-to-grow and notably hardy privet is practically maintenance-free when used informally. Within their hardiness ranges, the privets thrive in almost any soil if they receive full sun or partial shade. All bear small clusters of white flowers in summer. Fast-growing, strong plants that can tolerate wind, city smog or salt spray, they are seldom plagued by insects or disease. However, the common privet can develop an incurable twig blight; avoid growing it in areas where the blight exists.

Amur and Regel privets grow in Zones 3-9. Amur privet has erect branches, grows 12 to 15 feet tall and is considered the hardiest of all privets. The Regel privet is a smaller shrub, 4 to 5 feet tall, with horizontal or arching branches; it tolerates dry soils. California privet, widely planted because of its fast growth and glossy leaves, becomes about 15 feet tall in Zones 6-9.

Ibolium, Vicary golden and common privets are hardy in Zones 4-9. The glossy-leaved Ibolium privet develops an upright silhouette and grows 12 feet tall. Throughout the summer, the distinctive foliage of the 10- to 12-foot Vicary golden privet is yellow when it is grown in full sun, a bright yellow-green when it is grown in shade. Like the Regel, the common privet grows well in dry locations, becoming a dense, upright shrub up to 15 feet high. California, common and Vicary golden privets, which are naturally deciduous, are almost evergreen in warm regions.

LINDEN VIBURNUM See *Viburnum*

LONICERA
L. maackii (Amur honeysuckle); *L. tatarica* (Tatarian honeysuckle); *L. xylosteoides* 'Clavey's Dwarf' (Clavey's Dwarf honeysuckle)

Hardy deciduous honeysuckle shrubs flourish in almost any soil, and though they grow best in full sun, they will flower and fruit in partial shade. Vigorous and free of insects and disease, honeysuckles bloom profusely in spring or early summer and lure birds to the garden with their flowers and small, bright berries. These upright shrubs need little pruning if they are given space to develop, but they can withstand heavy pruning, making them easy to transplant.

Amur honeysuckle grows 12 to 15 feet tall in Zones 2-9 and has white to yellowish blossoms; it holds its leaves and attractive red berries late into fall. Always trim and tidy, Tatarian honeysuckle grows 8 to 10 feet high in Zones 3-9. Among all North American landscaping shrubs, it is considered one of the hardiest and easiest to grow. It can, however, become leggy if grown in deep shade. It bears white, pink, rose or red flowers followed by red or yellow berries. Clavey's Dwarf honeysuckle is hardy in Zones 4-9 and grows only 3 to 6 feet tall. The small yellowish spring flowers are followed in midsummer by red berries.

MAIDEN'S BLUSH ROSE, GREAT See *Rosa*
MARIES' DOUBLEFILE VIBURNUM See *Viburnum*
MOCK ORANGE See *Philadelphus*

MYRICA
M. pensylvanica, also called *M. caroliniensis* (bayberry, candleberry)

Bayberry, an aromatic plant whose berries have a waxy coating used in candlemaking, thrives in soils that are sandy and low in nutrients. A dune plant that grows wild along the Atlantic coast from Newfoundland to Maryland, it is suited to seaside gardens but also grows well inland. Little or no pruning is needed, since the shrubs are naturally compact.

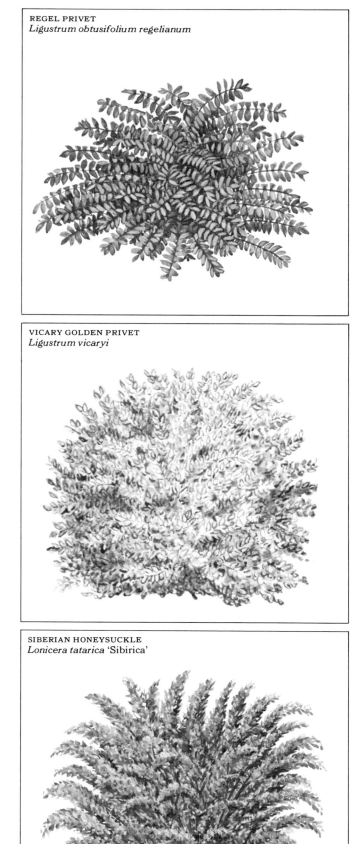

REGEL PRIVET
Ligustrum obtusifolium regelianum

VICARY GOLDEN PRIVET
Ligustrum vicaryi

SIBERIAN HONEYSUCKLE
Lonicera tatarica 'Sibirica'

For climate zones and frost dates, see maps, pages 148-149.

BAYBERRY
Myrica pensylvanica

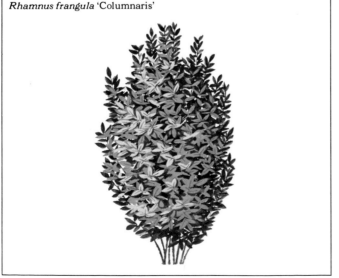

GLACIER MOCK ORANGE
Philadelphus virginalis 'Glacier'

TALLHEDGE ALDER BUCKTHORN
Rhamnus frangula 'Columnaris'

Bayberries need full sun and well-drained acid soil. Hardy in Zones 2-8, they become 8 to 9 feet tall under ideal growing conditions but only 3 to 5 feet in ordinary garden soil. At the southern end of its range, this deciduous shrub may hold its dull green leaves all winter. Male and female plants are needed to produce the pale gray berries, which cling to the plant into the winter, attracting migrating birds.

OLD-FASHIONED WEIGELA See *Weigela*
OSIER DOGWOOD, RED See *Cornus*

PEEGEE HYDRANGEA See *Hydrangea*
PEPPER BUSH, SWEET See *Clethra*

PHILADELPHUS
P. coronarius (sweet mock orange); *P. lemoinei* (Lemoine mock orange); *P. virginalis* (virginalis mock orange)

Wet soils or deep shade are the only growing conditions that limit the vigor of mock oranges. Pests or diseases do not bother them, they require little pruning except when damaged by winter cold in the north and they bloom while quite young. Their ornamental feature is a profusion of fragrant white flowers that lasts for two weeks in early summer.

Sweet mock orange grows 7 to 9 feet tall in Zones 4-9 and does well in dry soils. The Lemoine mock orange hybrids grow 4 to 8 feet tall and are hardy in Zones 5-9. Virginalis mock orange reaches 5 to 8 feet in Zones 5-9; it is usually used at the back of borders since it tends to become leggy and bare at its base. In compensation, its flowers are very fragrant and make beautiful cut-flower sprays. One hybrid, Minnesota Snowflake, is said to withstand temperatures of −30° and to grow without losing its lower branches.

PINK SUMMER SWEET See *Clethra*
PINKSHELL AZALEA See *Rhododendron*
PRIVET See *Ligustrum*
PROVENCE ROSE See *Rosa*

QUINCE, JAPANESE ALPINE See *Chaenomeles*

RED OSIER DOGWOOD See *Cornus*
REGEL PRIVET See *Ligustrum*

RHAMNUS
R. frangula 'Columnaris' (Tallhedge alder buckthorn)

Among alder buckthorn varieties, Tallhedge's 10- to 12-foot height, narrow 4-foot width and rapid growth recommend it where a tall, columnar hedge is desired quickly. A young Tallhedge plant that is only 2 feet tall will develop into a dense shrub 12 feet high in six to eight years. Occasional top shearing can be used to keep them lower and increase their density.

No serious pests or diseases affect the Tallhedge buckthorn, which is hardy in Zones 2-8. It does best in full sun but will grow well in partial shade and in almost any soil, even one that is wet.

RHODODENDRON
R. calendulaceum (flame azalea); *R.* 'Exbury hybrids' (Exbury azalea, Exbury hybrid azalea); *R. mucronulatum* (Korean rhododendron); *R. schlippenbachii* (royal azalea); *R. vaseyi* (pinkshell azalea); *R. viscosum* (swamp azalea)

Where soils are moist and naturally very acid, deciduous azaleas and rhododendrons thrive in partial shade, especially in hot areas, but grow reasonably well in full sun. The species and hybrids listed above need very little pruning and seldom have serious infestations. Their foliage may turn to bright hues in autumn.

Flame azaleas grow 4 to 9 feet tall in Zones 5-8 and occasionally reach 15 feet. Their bright scarlet, orange or yellow clusters of late spring or early summer flowers are long lasting, even in full sun.

The Exbury hybrids, hardy in Zones 5-8, bloom in enormous clusters; 2- to 3-inch individual flowers number as many as 18 to a flower head. Pink, red, orange, yellow and white, they blossom on 4- to 5-foot plants in early summer. Foliage turns red, orange or yellow in autumn.

The Korean rhododendron is one of the earliest azaleas to bloom in Zones 4-8; its pink to purple flowers are susceptible to late frosts. Plant them in a sheltered area to avoid undue exposure. They grow 4 to 6 feet tall.

Royal azaleas tolerate less acid soils in Zones 4-8 than the other species. Growing 6 to 10 feet tall, they bear large, freckled pink flower clusters in the spring; in the fall, leaves may turn orange, yellow and red.

Delicate pinkshell azaleas grow best in the moist soil bordering ponds in Zones 3-8, where they grow 6 to 8 feet tall and flower in late spring to early summer. Low, wet areas in Zones 3-8 suit the late-blooming swamp azalea, which bears extraordinarily fragrant white blossoms tinged with pink in midsummer on branches up to 9 feet tall.

RHUS See *Cotinus*

ROSA

R. alba 'Incarnata' (cottage rose, Great Maiden's Blush rose); *R. centifolia* (cabbage rose, Provence rose); *R. harisonii* (Harison's Yellow rose); *R. hugonis* (Father Hugo's rose, Golden Rose of China); *R. rugosa* (Rugosa rose)

Though most garden roses require intensive care, there are a few exceptions. The five shrub roses listed above are all hardy, vigorous and easy to grow. Compared with such demanding hybrids as the floribundas, grandifloras and teas, these shrub roses need little winter protection, demand little dusting or spraying to combat pests and diseases, require little pruning, and tolerate adverse growing conditions. Their fruits, called hips, attract birds to the garden. For most prolific growth, plant these roses in full sun and well-drained soil supplemented with peat moss, leaf mold or compost.

The cottage rose grows in Zones 4-10. It has outstanding double-petaled pink-tinged white flowers in midsummer on 4- to 6-foot canes. Known as the "Rose of a Hundred Petals," the cabbage rose was one of the first wild roses to be brought under cultivation. In Zones 5-10 it grows 3 to 6 feet tall, 8 feet wide or more, and bears fragrant pink blooms in early summer. Harison's Yellow rose is hardy from Zone 4 south. It is a 5- to 6-foot shrub with 2-inch double-petaled blossoms that appear in early summer. The exquisite yellow flowers of Father Hugo's rose, hardy in Zones 5-10, are among the earliest to bloom, often in late spring. Its arching canes may grow 7 feet tall in spreading clumps.

The extremely hardy Rugosa rose grows in Zones 2-10 and tolerates salt spray. Perhaps the least demanding of cultivated roses, it develops into clumps 5 to 6 feet tall and in time up to 20 feet across. Its purple-red blooms, 2½ to 3½ inches in diameter, appear in late spring and early summer; in fall its hips and foliage are a brilliant orange.

ROSE See *Rosa*
ROSE OF SHARON See *Hibiscus*
ROYAL AZALEA See *Rhododendron*
RUGOSA ROSE See *Rosa*

EXBURY AZALEA
Rhododendron 'Exbury hybrids'

FATHER HUGO'S ROSE
Rosa hugonis

RUGOSA ROSE
Rosa rugosa

For climate zones and frost dates, see maps, pages 148-149.

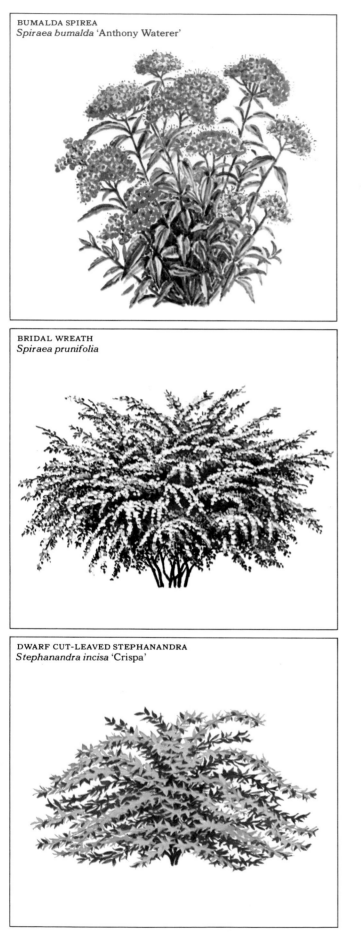

BUMALDA SPIREA
Spiraea bumalda 'Anthony Waterer'

BRIDAL WREATH
Spiraea prunifolia

DWARF CUT-LEAVED STEPHANANDRA
Stephanandra incisa 'Crispa'

SHOE-BUTTON SPIREA See *Spiraea*
SHRUB ALTHEA See *Hibiscus*
SIBERIAN DOGWOOD See *Cornus*
SIEBOLD VIBURNUM See *Viburnum*
SIEBOLD'S WEEPING FORSYTHIA See *Forsythia*
SILVER-EDGED DOGWOOD See *Cornus*
SLENDER DEUTZIA See *Deutzia*
SMOKE TREE See *Cotinus*
SMOKEBUSH See *Cotinus*
SNOWBALL, FRAGRANT See *Viburnum*

SPIRAEA

S. arguta (garland spirea); *S. billiardii* (Billiard spirea); *S. bumalda* 'Anthony Waterer' (Bumalda spirea); *S. prunifolia*, also called *S. prunifolia* 'Plena' (bridal wreath, shoe-button spirea); *S. vanhouttei* (Vanhoutte spirea)

Easy cultivation, a high degree of hardiness and resistance to pests and diseases all make spireas good choices as low-maintenance deciduous shrubs. They thrive in any well-drained soil and will grow in partial shade, although they have more flowers and denser foliage in full sun. They need little pruning except occasional removal of errant shoots at the plant's base or some of the oldest branches.

Spireas are grouped in two categories based on the season of bloom: spring-blooming types with flower clusters spaced along branches and summer-blooming types with flower clusters at the tip of each branch.

Of the spring-blooming types, garland spirea flowers most profusely. Flat clusters of tiny white flowers appear on arching 5- to 6-foot branches in midspring as the leaves unfold. Next to bloom is bridal wreath, which becomes a narrow, erect 7-foot shrub. Its tiny double-petaled flowers resemble ⅜-inch buttons, and unlike most spireas, its red-to-orange fall color is dependable. Similar in size and appearance to garland spirea is Vanhoutte spirea, the most common spirea. The Vanhoutte's foliage may turn orange or red in fall.

Among the summer-blooming spireas, the Billiard forms 4- to 6-foot clumps with each branch tipped by a conical rose-colored flower spike. The Bumalda spirea is a compact 2-foot shrub that bears deep-pink blooms intermittently for several weeks. The Bumalda spirea is hardy in Zones 5-10; the others grow in Zones 4-10.

STEPHANANDRA

S. incisa 'Crispa' (dwarf cut-leaved stephanandra)

Gracefully arching dwarf cut-leaved stephanandra grows in almost any moist soil in full sun or partial shade. The plant stays neat without pruning, needing little care except occasional removal of deadwood.

Because this species of stephanandra roots readily when the tips of its branches touch soil, it is used on steep banks to hold the earth and prevent erosion. The plant grows 2 feet tall and about 4 feet wide, making it useful under low windows, atop walls or in front of taller shrubs.

Dwarf cut-leaved stephanandra is hardy in Zones 5-8, although it is subject to winterkill during severe winters at the northern edge of its range.

SUMMER SWEET See *Clethra*
SWAMP AZALEA See *Rhododendron*
SWEET MOCK ORANGE See *Philadelphus*
SWEET PEPPER BUSH See *Clethra*

TALLHEDGE ALDER BUCKTHORN See *Rhamnus*
TATARIAN DOGWOOD See *Cornus*
TATARIAN HONEYSUCKLE See *Lonicera*

VANHOUTTE SPIREA See *Spiraea*
VERNAL WITCH HAZEL See *Hamamelis*

VIBURNUM

V. carlcephalum (fragrant snowball); *V. dilatatum* (linden viburnum); *V. plicatum tomentosum* 'Mariesii' (Maries' doublefile viburnum); *V. sieboldii* (Siebold viburnum); *V. trilobum,* also called *V. americanum* (American cranberry bush)

The varied viburnums include both evergreen and deciduous plants, ranging from low shrubs to treelike forms, all noted for extreme hardiness and easy care. The five deciduous species listed above are especially pest resistant. These thrive in moist, well-drained fertile soil, in full sun or partial shade. Planted where they have space to reach their mature size without crowding, they need little pruning. All five are ornamental, with conspicuous clusters of white flowers in late spring or early summer followed by red, blue or black fruits. Their foliage turns a rich burnished red in fall.

Fragrant snowball and linden viburnum both may grow to 9 feet in Zones 5-9. The round 4- to 5-inch flower clusters of the fragrant snowball appear in late spring, blooming before the flat but equally large clusters of the linden viburnum. With a soft shine on its foliage, a fragrant snowball shows to good advantage as a specimen plant. Linden viburnum is noteworthy for its profusion of red berries in autumn.

Gardeners in Zones 4-9 can plant two viburnums with distinctive shapes. Maries' doublefile viburnum has widely spreading horizontal branches and grows up to 9 feet tall. Siebold viburnum has lustrous, crinkly leaves on upright branches, growing 6 to 10 feet tall.

The American cranberry bush is among the hardiest of the viburnums. It reaches 8 to 12 feet in Zones 2-9 and grows best at the northern end of this range. Its edible red fruits are too tart for birds but make excellent jams and jellies.

VICARY GOLDEN PRIVET See *Ligustrum*
VIRGINALIS MOCK ORANGE See *Philadelphus*

WARMINSTER BROOM See *Cytisus*
WEEPING FORSYTHIA, SIEBOLD'S See *Forsythia*

WEIGELA

W. florida, also called *W. rosea, Diervilla florida* (old-fashioned weigela); *W.* hybrids (hybrid weigela)

Gracefully arching weigela shrubs are notably pest-free and easy to cultivate in almost any well-drained soil; they thrive in full sun but tolerate partial shade. The only maintenance they need is an easy pruning, when flowers fade, to clean out dead stems and thin dense branches. Though they are hardy from Zone 5 south, weigelas are recommended as easy-garden plants no farther north than Zone 6. Widespreading weigelas need space, up to 6 to 8 feet, to show themselves to their best advantage, a requirement that may rule them out of a small garden.

Weigelas bloom from late spring to early summer, bearing long-lasting clusters of flower funnels in shades of white, pink, purple, rose or red. Old-fashioned weigelas grow 6 to 9 feet tall; hybrids can reach 12 feet, and both mature rapidly.

WINGED EUONYMUS See *Euonymus*
WINTERBERRY See *Ilex*
WITCH ALDER See *Fothergilla*
WITCH HAZEL See *Hamamelis*

YELLOW-TWIGGED DOGWOOD See *Cornus*

FRAGRANT SNOWBALL
Viburnum carlcephalum

MARIES' DOUBLEFILE VIBURNUM
Viburnum plicatum tomentosum 'Mariesii'

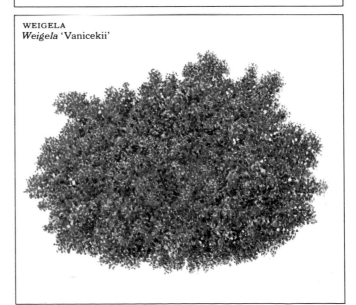

WEIGELA
Weigela 'Vanicekii'

For climate zones and frost dates, see maps, pages 148-149.

GLOSSY ABELIA
Abelia grandiflora

VARIEGATED JAPANESE AUCUBA
Aucuba japonica 'Picturata'

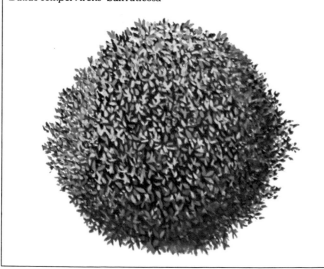

COMMON DWARF BOX
Buxus sempervirens 'Suffruticosa'

Evergreen shrubs

ABELIA

A. 'Edward Goucher' (Edward Goucher abelia, pink abelia); *A. grandiflora* (glossy abelia)

The summer-flowering abelias, which bloom when most flowering shrubs have long since shed their blossoms, are exceedingly easy to grow. They adapt to full sun or partial shade and tolerate any well-drained soil, although they do best in an acid soil enriched with leaf mold or peat moss. The plants are rarely bothered by pests or diseases and will grow in Zones 6-10, though they may die back to the ground if the temperature falls to zero. Winter-damaged plants recover rapidly, usually blossoming again by midsummer.

Abelias have long, arching branches and need plenty of room; both kinds listed here form bushy plants 3 to 5 feet high and equally wide. They are good background plants but may also be used as single specimens. Edward Goucher abelia has pink-purple blossoms; glossy abelia has pale pink blossoms. On both species, young foliage is bronze, turning to shiny dark green in summer and back to bronze in fall.

ANDROMEDA See *Pieris*

AUCUBA

A. japonica (Japanese aucuba)

Although it is not hardy north of Zone 7 except in sheltered locations, Japanese aucuba is one of few broad-leaved evergreens that will thrive in polluted city air. It does best in a moist, well-drained soil, although established plants can even survive drought. Japanese aucuba grows rapidly but rarely needs pruning to keep it shapely. Its large leaves remain attractive year round unless the plants get too much summer sun, in which case the leaves are likely to burn.

Japanese aucubas come in many varieties; some remain compact at 2 to 3 feet, others grow as high as 15 feet in 10 years. Their glossy leaves are usually dark green, but there are several variegated forms in which the leaves are spotted or blotched with yellow. The flowers are inconspicuous but female plants bear decorative, long-lasting red berries in winter if male plants are nearby.

BIGLEAF WINTER CREEPER See *Euonymus*
BITTERSWEET, EVERGREEN See *Euonymus*
BOX, LITTLELEAF See *Buxus*
BOXWOOD See *Buxus*
BURFORD HOLLY See *Ilex*

BUXUS

B. microphylla (littleleaf box, boxwood); *B. sempervirens* 'Suffruticosa' (common dwarf box, English dwarf box, European dwarf box, edging box)

Slow-growing and long-lived, box is an oldtime landscaping favorite, its mounds of dense evergreen foliage prospering whether left alone or sheared into formal hedges. The boxes tolerate full sun or partial shade and grow in almost any well-drained moist soil, but they do best in soils enriched with peat moss or leaf mold. Boxes are hardy in Zones 6-9, littleleaf box being better suited for the colder areas of Zone 6, while common dwarf box can be planted safely only from the southern fringes of Zone 6 southward. The low-growing types listed here are more resistant than full-sized boxes to boxwood leaf miners, which attack the undersides of leaves and make blister-like swellings.

Littleleaf boxwood grows very slowly to 3 to 4 feet tall and spreads 2 to 3 feet; common dwarf box, also slow-growing, will reach a height and spread of 3 feet in about 25 years.

CAMELLIA

C. japonica (common camellia)

The easiest camellia species to grow is the common camellia. It tolerates a wider range of growing conditions than is generally known. The plants adapt well to the rigors of urban life and require little pruning if young plants are located where they can grow to mature size without crowding.

Camellias grow best in humid areas of Zones 7-9 in partial shade where soil is moist but well drained and slightly acid. Some varieties will grow and bloom in full sun and adjust to low humidity, though their growth will be slower and their foliage lighter.

Varieties of common camellias bear 2- to 5-inch waxy pink, red, white or variegated blossoms from late fall to early spring. There are single and multi-petaled forms, all with glossy, leathery dark green leaves. Some common camellias sprawl while others are erect, but all grow slowly, reaching up to 10 feet in 10 to 15 years.

CHAMAECYPARIS

C. obtusa 'Compacta' (compact hinoki false cypress); *C. obtusa* 'Gracilis' (slender hinoki false cypress); *C. obtusa* 'Nana' (dwarf hinoki false cypress); *C. obtusa* 'Pygmaea' (pygmy hinoki false cypress)

These compact evergreens are ideal for easy shrub borders and rock gardens. As slow-growing shrubs, they seldom need pruning. They will grow in sun or partial shade and tolerate almost any well-drained soil, although they grow best when they are given full sun and moist, rich soil. Hardy in Zones 4-8, they flourish where the air is cool and moist and are rarely infested by pests. Their scalelike foliage stays bright green throughout the year.

All false cypresses need shelter from drying winter wind. Compact hinoki false cypress, an extremely slow-growing variety, forms a broad cone about 3 feet tall; an occasional plant may become 7 feet tall and 8 feet wide in about 40 years. Slender hinoki false cypress, a faster-growing type, makes narrower cones that rarely surpass 6 feet in height. *C. obtusa* Nana, a dwarf, seldom exceeds 2 feet in height and breadth; it is often confused with the faster growing *C. obtusa* Nana Gracilis, which reaches a maximum height of about 6 feet. Pygmy hinoki false cypress, another dwarf, seldom grows more than 2 feet tall and 3 feet wide.

CHERRY LAUREL See *Prunus*
CHINESE PRIVET See *Ligustrum*
COMMON DWARF BOX See *Buxus*
COMPACT HINOKI FALSE CYPRESS See
    Chamaecyparis
CYPRESS, FALSE See *Chamaecyparis*

DROOPING LEUCOTHOË See *Leucothoë*
DWARF BOX See *Buxus*
DWARF HINOKI FALSE CYPRESS See *Chamaecyparis*

EDGING BOX See *Buxus*
EDWARD GOUCHER ABELIA See *Abelia*

ELAEAGNUS

E. pungens (thorny elaeagnus, silverberry)

Extremely adaptable, the thorny elaeagnus grows in sand or loam, where the soil is either dry or moist, and in full sun or partial shade. This evergreen shrub can weather extremes of heat and wind, is readily transplanted and is rarely attacked by insects. Add to this its lack of pruning requirements and it becomes ideal for Zones 7-10 of the South.

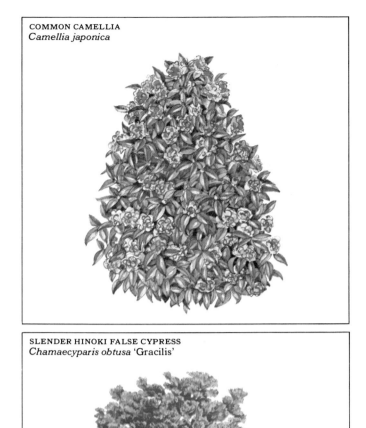

COMMON CAMELLIA
Camellia japonica

SLENDER HINOKI FALSE CYPRESS
Chamaecyparis obtusa 'Gracilis'

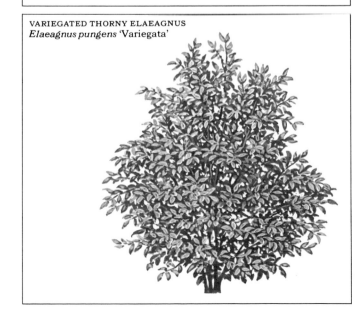

VARIEGATED THORNY ELAEAGNUS
Elaeagnus pungens 'Variegata'

For climate zones and frost dates, see maps, pages 148-149.

Thorny elaeagnus grows rapidly, developing a height and spread of 8 to 12 feet in about 10 years. While grown chiefly for the winter appearance of its wavy-edged 1½- to 4-inch leaves, in fall it bears inconspicuous but very fragrant white flowers that are followed by tiny red berries in the spring. There are varieties with silver or gold leaf edges; *E. pungens* Variegata has yellowish-white leaf edges. Variegated forms are slightly more subject to damage from cold and wind.

ENGLISH LAUREL See *Prunus*
ENGLISH YEW, SPREADING See *Taxus*

EUONYMUS
E. fortunei 'Vegeta' (bigleaf winter creeper, evergreen bittersweet)

One of the easiest of ornamental shrubs to grow, bigleaf winter creeper thrives in full sun or partial shade and in almost any soil, wet or dry. Hardy in Zones 5-8, this tough evergreen naturally rambles to form sprawling horizontal bushes or it will climb a few feet up a support by means of clinging rootlets. If its glossy leaves die during a severe winter at the northern end of its growing range, new ones take their place by early spring. The plant is showy in fall when it is covered with fleshy orange to red berries. Susceptibility to euonymus scale is its only serious problem; if pesticides are ineffective the plant must be cut back to the ground to produce healthy new growth.

The fast-growing bigleaf winter creeper usually reaches 4 feet in height with a spread equally as wide in about 8 to 10 years. Among the hardiest types of *E. fortunei* varieties are the Emerald strains, which are exceptionally tolerant of air pollution; they include Emerald Charm, 4 to 5 feet tall with an 18-inch spread; Emerald Pride, 4 to 5 feet tall; Emerald Gaiety, a drought-resistant form that grows 4 to 5 feet tall with white-edged leaves; Emerald 'n Gold, 4 feet tall with yellow-edged leaves; and the dwarf Emerald Cushion that grows 15 to 18 inches tall and 3 feet across.

EVERGREEN BITTERSWEET See *Euonymus*

FALSE CYPRESS See *Chamaecyparis*
FALSE HOLLY See *Osmanthus*

GLOSSY ABELIA See *Abelia*
GLOSSY PRIVET See *Ligustrum*
GOLD COAST JUNIPER See *Juniperus*
GOLDEN PFITZER JUNIPER See *Juniperus*
GOUCHER ABELIA, EDWARD See *Abelia*

HEAVENLY BAMBOO See *Nandina*
HEMLOCK See *Tsuga*
HICKS' YEW See *Taxus*
HINOKI FALSE CYPRESS See *Chamaecyparis*
HOLLY See *Ilex*
HOLLY, FALSE See *Osmanthus*
HOLLY GRAPE See *Mahonia*
HOLLY OSMANTHUS See *Osmanthus*
HOLLYWOOD JUNIPER See *Juniperus*

ILEX
I. cornuta 'Burfordii' (Burford holly); *I. crenata* 'Convexa' (convexleaf Japanese holly); *I. glabra* (inkberry); *I. pedunculosa* (long-stalked holly)

Red-berried English and American hollies with their jagged leaves have made holly one of the best-known evergreen shrubs. Several other evergreen hollies are also noteworthy

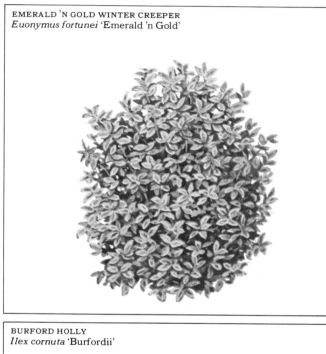

EMERALD 'N GOLD WINTER CREEPER
Euonymus fortunei 'Emerald 'n Gold'

BURFORD HOLLY
Ilex cornuta 'Burfordii'

for pest-resistance and undemanding growing characteristics.

In addition to red-berried species, there are hollies with black, yellow or orange fruits nestled among glossy leaves that can be smooth edged and oval as well as scalloped and spiny. Most species require both male and female plants for berry production; females should be within 100 feet of a male and they should be planted in a ratio of roughly one male to ten females. A few female species will produce berries without pollination and are called self-fertile.

All of the hollies listed here are naturally graceful in shape and require little pruning; clipping a few branches for holiday decorating easily satisfies the shrubs' pruning needs. They grow well in full sun or partial shade, given a well-drained, slightly acid soil. In summer, hollies grow best if their roots are kept moist, but they withstand winter cold better if their root systems are somewhat dry.

Burford holly is a self-fertile variety that is considered one of the best hollies to grow in Zones 7-9. Its large orange-to-red winter berries are surrounded by glossy, nearly spineless leaves. The Burford holly may grow 6 to 10 feet tall in about six years in the South. Dazzler is a compact, slower-growing Burford holly that produces red berries; the variety D'Or bears yellow fruits.

Convexleaf holly, also hardy in Zones 6-9, rarely grows taller than 4 feet in 10 years but spreads 6 feet or more across, making it a good choice for planting below a window. Because its small black berries are hardly visible, both male and female plants are equally ornamental. The Heller Japanese holly, *I. crenata* Helleri, has ½-inch-long leaves and grows slowly into a dense shrub 3 feet wide.

Inkberry is the hardiest evergreen holly, surviving temperatures down to -30° in partial shade in Zones 4-9. Unlike most hollies, this species spreads by underground stems so it does well along sandy seashores. *I. glabra* Compacta, a slow-growing compact variety of inkberry, usually remains less than 4 feet tall.

Long-stalked holly bears its bright red berries on long stems like cherries. Hardy in Zones 6-9, it develops into a narrow, conical treelike shrub that becomes 10 to 15 feet tall in 10 years. Its oval, spineless leaves resemble the foliage of the mountain laurel.

INKBERRY See *Ilex*

JAPANESE ANDROMEDA See *Pieris*
JAPANESE AUCUBA See *Aucuba*
JAPANESE HOLLY, CONVEXLEAF See *Ilex*
JAPANESE PITTOSPORUM See *Pittosporum*
JAPANESE PRIVET See *Ligustrum*
JAPANESE SKIMMIA See *Skimmia*
JAPANESE YEW, UPRIGHT See *Taxus*
JUNIPER See *Juniperus*

JUNIPERUS
J. chinensis aurea 'Gold Coast' (Gold Coast juniper); *J. chinensis* 'Pfitzeriana Aurea' (golden Pfitzer juniper); *J. chinensis* 'Torulosa' (Hollywood juniper); *J. communis* 'Depressa' (prostrate juniper)

If a juniper gets plenty of sun and is planted in well-drained soil, it will grow almost anywhere. Some varieties of this hardy shrub will tolerate partial shade, and many will grow even in dry, rocky locations. Some junipers grow only an inch or so in a season and others shoot up at the rate of 12 inches or more, but all are easy to keep at a desired height for many years with only light pruning. Insect pests and juniper rust can be controlled with pesticides. If male and

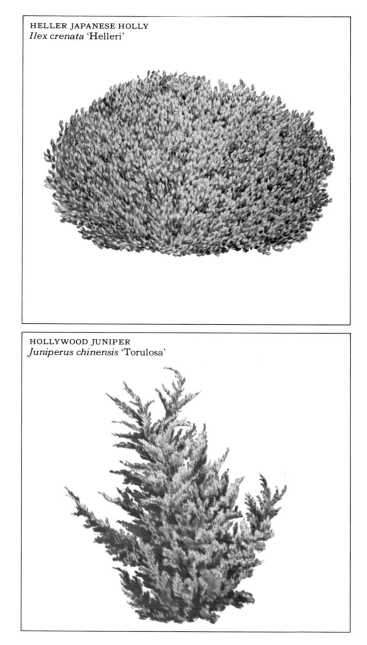

HELLER JAPANESE HOLLY
Ilex crenata 'Helleri'

HOLLYWOOD JUNIPER
Juniperus chinensis 'Torulosa'

For climate zones and frost dates, see maps, pages 148-149.

107

MOUNTAIN LAUREL
Kalmia latifolia

DROOPING LEUCOTHOË
Leucothoë fontanesiana

SUWANEE RIVER PRIVET
Ligustrum japonicum 'Suwanee River'

female plants are grown close together, the females will bear silvery berries.

Gold Coast juniper, hardy in Zones 4-9, keeps its soft-textured gold foliage year round, and spreads in mounds 2 to 3 feet tall and up to 5 feet wide. The golden Pfitzer juniper, also hardy in Zones 4-9, is a compact shrub that rarely grows more than 3 feet tall and 5 feet wide; its gold-tinged foliage turns yellow-green in fall and winter. Hollywood juniper, hardy in Zones 7-9, has twisted, picturesque branches that emerge from a conical shape up to 15 feet tall. Prostrate juniper is a relatively low-growing variety, rarely exceeding 3 or 4 feet in height but reaching a diameter of 15 to 20 feet in about 15 years. It does well in dry, gravelly soil and is hardy in Zones 2-9.

KALMIA

K. latifolia (mountain laurel)

In the shade of towering trees or on the north side of a high wall, mountain laurel thrives and blooms without pruning or removal of spent flowers. Hardy in Zones 5-9, these evergreen shrubs will adjust to full sun if the soil is kept moist. Mountain laurel needs an acid soil. Maintain a permanent 2- to 3-inch mulch of wood chips, oak leaves or ground bark under the shrub to keep the soil moist and cool. During the winter, the leaves are sometimes browned by the wind. They may also be discolored by leaf-spot disease. Slow growing, mountain laurel reaches about 6 feet in height and width in 10 years. Its clusters of cuplike white or pink blossoms cover the dark, glossy foliage in late spring.

LAUREL, CHERRY See *Prunus*
LAUREL, ENGLISH See *Prunus*
LAUREL, MOUNTAIN See *Kalmia*
LEATHERLEAF MAHONIA See *Mahonia*
LEATHER-LEAVED HOLLY GRAPE See *Mahonia*

LEUCOTHOË

L. fontanesiana, also called *L. catesbaei, L. walteri* (drooping leucothoë)

Drooping leucothoë flowers very freely in shade. In areas of Zones 5-9 where soils are moist and acid, its low, spreading branches, which bear dense foliage, will hide foundations or fill in at the base of an old shrub or tree. It is rarely troubled by pests or diseases. The only care it requires is the removal of old canes to ground level every few years in spring. In extremely cold weather, the plant's upper leaves may drop or discolor, requiring some additional pruning.

Drooping leucothoë grows to a height of 3 to 5 feet in about 5 years, then spreads slowly outward by means of underground runners. Dark, lustrous green leaves on curving reddish stems turn bronze in winter. The leaves of the Girard's Rainbow variety emerge red or pink, then become variegated with shades of yellow, green and copper. In the spring, clusters of tiny white flowers dangle from the lower sides of the shrub's arching canes.

LIGUSTRUM

L. japonicum (Japanese privet, wax-leaf privet); *L. lucidum* (glossy privet, Chinese privet)

Fast-growing privets flourish in either shade or sun and in almost any kind of soil in Zones 7-10. These evergreen shrubs are relatively pest free and will tolerate drought and neglect. They can be used as tall windbreaks that have clusters of white flowers in summer and in fall blue-black berries that attract birds. Cutting out some older branches will prevent the plant from becoming leggy and bare at the base. Old plants cut to within 10 to 12 inches of the ground in early spring quickly revive.

Japanese privet will attain heights of 6 to 15 feet in about six years. The Suwannee River hybrid, which resists cold exceptionally well, reaches its mature height of 6 feet in six to eight years. Glossy privet (which, despite its name, has leaves that are less shiny than those of the Japanese privet) can grow 30 feet tall in southern regions.

LITTLELEAF BOX See *Buxus*
LONG-STALKED HOLLY See *Ilex*

MAHONIA
M. aquifolium (Oregon holly grape, Oregon grape); *M. bealei* (leather-leaved holly grape, leatherleaf mahonia)

Holly grapes are resilient shrubs that will tolerate a wide range of well-drained soils, although they do best in moist ground. The spiky, holly-like leaves of the Oregon holly grape turn bronze in winter, while the leather-leaved holly grape remains green year round. Both species prefer partial shade but will adapt to full sun except in hot, dry regions; the Oregon species will grow in deep shade as well. Holly grapes are rarely bothered by pests and their rather sprawling habit responds well to pruning.

Oregon holly grape, which usually grows 3 or 4 feet tall in as many years, is hardy in Zones 5-9. If given shelter from wind in winter, it can survive brief cold spells down to −10°. The less hardy leather-leaved holly grape can reach 8 to 10 feet in height, and its large leaves, flowers and fruit make it a handsome plant. Both species bear clusters of bright yellow flowers in spring, followed by grapelike blue berries that can be made into jelly.

MOUNTAIN ANDROMEDA See *Pieris*
MOUNTAIN LAUREL See *Kalmia*

NANDINA
N. domestica (nandina, heavenly bamboo, sacred bamboo)

In gardens of the southern and western United States, nandina thrives in full sun or partial shade in almost any moist soil, but it grows best in earth enriched with organic matter. Hardy in Zones 7-10, this shrub is evergreen in southern areas; at the north edge of its range, leaves drop in the fall. Nandina requires little pruning; if old stems are cut to the ground in early spring, however, the plant quickly sends up new shoots and will be more shapely.

The ornamental foliage of the nandina changes from pinkish to bronze in early spring to dark green by summer, then to vivid red in late fall. Its red berries last from fall well into winter. Slow-growing, the shrub reaches a height of 2½ to 6 feet in about three to six years; it is a good choice for planting against foundations or in borders for winter color.

NERIUM
N. oleander (oleander, rosebay)

Oleander is a tough warm-climate evergreen that can resist drought, wind, heat, air pollution and salt spray. It will grow in almost any soil in sun or partial shade but does best in moist, well-drained soil enriched with peat moss or leaf mold. Hardy only in Zones 8-10, these shrubs benefit from occasional pruning for thicker growth; otherwise they need little care once they are established. Plants may be damaged by cold weather or become leggy as they age, but either difficulty can be corrected by cutting damaged or old stems to the ground in spring. New shoots grow quickly.

The oleander is an outstanding ornamental with bamboo-

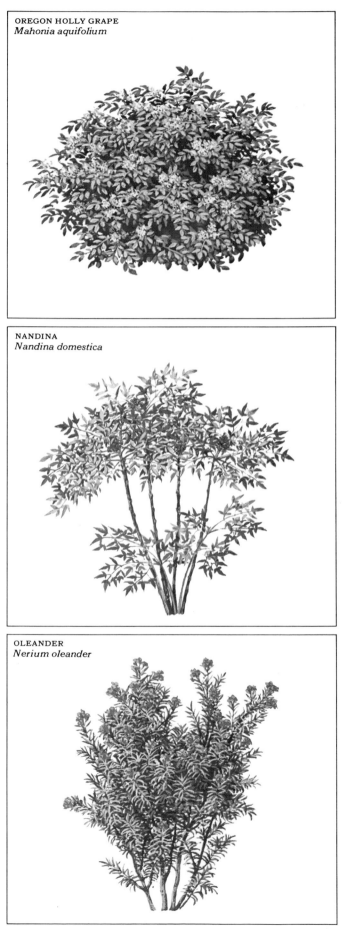

OREGON HOLLY GRAPE
Mahonia aquifolium

NANDINA
Nandina domestica

OLEANDER
Nerium oleander

For climate zones and frost dates, see maps, pages 148-149.

HOLLY OSMANTHUS
Osmanthus heterophyllus

JAPANESE ANDROMEDA
Pieris japonica

JAPANESE PITTOSPORUM
Pittosporum tobira

like foliage that remains green all year; it bears large, fragrant clusters of pink, red or white flowers from late spring into fall. It is effective either planted alone or grouped into a windbreak or informal hedge. A rapid grower, it forms narrow columns 8 to 12 feet tall in about six to eight years; oleanders may reach a height of 20 feet. All parts of the plant are poisonous if they are eaten.

OLEANDER See *Nerium*
OREGON GRAPE See *Mahonia*
OREGON HOLLY GRAPE See *Mahonia*

OSMANTHUS
O. heterophyllus, also called *O. aquifolium, O. ilicifolius* (holly osmanthus, false holly)

A naturally shapely shrub, holly osmanthus requires no pruning and is rarely troubled by pests. It thrives in full sun or partial shade and grows best in well-drained moist soil supplemented with peat moss or leaf mold. If grown in partial shade, it will tolerate drier soils. Hardy in Zones 7-10, holly osmanthus retains its glossy, spiny dark green foliage all year. In fall it is covered with tiny, fragrant greenish-white flowers that are followed by blue-black berries.

This evergreen is good as a border plant or natural hedge. If grown in the open as a specimen plant it forms a round shrub that may reach a height of 15 feet in 10 years, but it may be kept 5 or 6 feet tall by pruning at any season. Some varieties have leaves edged in yellow or white.

PFITZER JUNIPER, GOLDEN See *Juniperus*

PIERIS
P. floribunda (mountain andromeda); *P. japonica* (Japanese andromeda)

Andromedas are easy broad-leaved evergreens whose naturally graceful growth habit requires little pruning. They thrive in moist, acid soil in partial shade, but they will tolerate full sun. Attractive throughout the year, the plants bear flower clusters in spring that resemble lilies of the valley; new flower buds for the following year appear in summer and decorate the plants through fall and winter. Andromedas need shelter from strong winter winds in the northern part of their range.

Mountain andromeda, hardy in Zones 5-8, bears upright, pyramid-shaped white flower clusters. It is untroubled by pests and grows slowly, reaching 2 to 3 feet in height with an equal spread in about five years; it grows slowly to about 6 feet tall if left unpruned. Japanese andromeda, hardy in Zones 6-8, bears its white flowers in drooping clusters. New leaves unfold a glossy bronze in spring, turning green in summer. The shrub does well in humid areas but the leaves are damaged by severe cold. The species may be attacked by lace bugs, which can be controlled with a pesticide. Japanese andromeda grows up to 9 feet tall but compact varieties stay between 4 and 6 feet.

PINK ABELIA See *Abelia*

PITTOSPORUM
P. tobira (Japanese pittosporum)

Japanese pittosporum flourishes in almost any soil and can withstand heat, wind and salty air in a mild climate. It will even survive drought once it is established, though it prefers moist, well-drained soil. It thrives in full sun or partial shade in Zones 8-10. It is not bothered by pests and needs little pruning. Japanese pittosporum is an excellent plant for informal hedges and can also be sheared for a formal hedge. In spring this evergreen shrub is covered with clusters of creamy white flowers that smell like orange blossoms. Its thick, leathery leaves form a dense symmetrical mound, 6 to 10 feet tall and equally wide, in about 10 years.

PRIVET See *Ligustrum*
PROSTRATE JUNIPER See *Juniperus*

PRUNUS
P. laurocerasus (cherry laurel, English laurel)

Fast-growing and virtually pest free, cherry laurel is well suited for use in unpruned windbreaks and hedges in Zones 6-10 and can also be sheared for a formal effect. It can tolerate salty sea air, full sun or partial shade and its broad, glossy leaves remain green year round. It prefers moist, well-drained soil enriched with peat moss or leaf mold. In northern sections, shrubs need to be sheltered from wind.

Cherry laurel forms a broad mound 10 feet tall in about six years, reaching a maximum height of 25 to 30 feet in the South. Two especially hardy varieties are Schipka cherry laurel, which reaches a height of 4 to 6 feet in four years, and Zabel cherry laurel, which may grow 3 to 5 feet tall and 5 to 8 feet wide in five years. Cherry laurel produces small white flowers in late spring or early summer, followed by black berries that attract birds.

PYGMY HINOKI FALSE CYPRESS See *Chamaecyparis*

ROSEBAY See *Nerium*

SACRED BAMBOO See *Nandina*
SARGENT'S WEEPING HEMLOCK See *Tsuga*
SILVERBERRY See *Elaeagnus*

SKIMMIA
S. japonica (Japanese skimmia)

In Zones 7 and 8, Japanese skimmia is a good choice for a low-maintenance garden because it tolerates neglect. It is not susceptible to diseases or pests and its shiny evergreen leaves are attractive all year. It requires partial shade and grows best in moist, acid soil enriched with peat moss or leaf mold. The species never needs pruning, though its foliage is often cut for use in indoor arrangements. Showy scarlet berries appear on female plants in fall and often remain through winter into May or June, when clusters of tiny white flowers bloom. Male plants must be planted near females to ensure pollination. The slow-growing Japanese skimmia takes four years or more to form well-branched mounds 2 to 4 feet tall and 3 to 6 feet wide; it rarely grows much larger.

SLENDER HINOKI FALSE CYPRESS See
Chamaecyparis
SPREADING ENGLISH YEW See *Taxus*

TAXUS
T. baccata 'Repandens' (spreading English yew); *T. cuspidata* 'Capitata' (upright Japanese yew); *T. media* 'Hicksii' (Hicks yew)

Yews, planted by the millions in the northern two thirds of the United States, are among the most versatile and easy to grow of all narrow-leaved evergreens. They will thrive in almost any kind of light from partial shade to full sun and will adjust to almost any well-drained soil. They grow best in slightly acid soil. They require no pruning, but they will tolerate severe shearing and can be kept small indefinitely if

SCHIPKA CHERRY LAUREL
Prunus laurocerasus 'Schipkaensis'

JAPANESE SKIMMIA
Skimmia japonica

HICKS YEW
Taxus media 'Hicksii'

SARGENT'S WEEPING HEMLOCK
Tsuga canadensis 'Pendula'

BLOODLEAF JAPANESE MAPLE
Acer palmatum 'Atropurpureum'

that is desired. They resist most pests and diseases and can be transplanted easily.

Yews have been cultivated since the days of the Greeks for their deep green foliage. Female plants bear bright red berries if a male is growing nearby. Yews vary widely in size and shape, depending on the variety, suiting them to almost any use in the low-maintenance garden. Spreading English yew, hardy in Zones 6-8, forms a mass 3 to 5 feet wide and 1 to 4 feet tall. This variety is suited to rock gardens and low foundation plantings. Upright Japanese yew, hardy in Zones 4-6, grows in a pyramid shape that generally remains under 15 feet. Hicks yew, which is also hardy in Zones 4-6, forms a column with upward-reaching branches that reaches a height of 20 feet in 15 to 20 years. Hicks yew is most often used in a windbreak or informal hedge and can be kept as low as 2 feet with periodic pruning.

THORNY ELAEAGNUS See *Elaeagnus*

TSUGA
T. canadensis 'Pendula' (Sargent's weeping hemlock)

Naturally graceful, Sargent's weeping hemlock is a lush, spreading evergreen shrub with soft pendulous branches that require no pruning. The plant is relatively free of pests. It can tolerate temperatures down to $-30°$ and will flourish on the shady north side of a house where very few other shrubs will grow; yet it adjusts to full sun in all but the southern sections of Zones 4-6. Although it will survive in sandy or rocky locations, Sargent's weeping hemlock grows best in cool, moist, acid soil. It does not tolerate drying winter winds or urban pollution.

This slow-growing shrub spreads to a width almost twice its height. In most gardens it rarely exceeds 6 feet in height and 10 feet in breadth, though in ideal locations it may reach a height of 15 feet and a width of 40 feet in 25 to 50 years. The plant is suited for use in rock gardens or as a dramatic lawn accent where its low branches have room to spread.

UPRIGHT JAPANESE YEW See *Taxus*

WAX-LEAF PRIVET See *Ligustrum*
WEEPING HEMLOCK, SARGENT'S See *Tsuga*
WINTER CREEPER, BIGLEAF See *Euonymus*

YEW See *Taxus*

Deciduous trees

ACANTHOPANAX See *Kalopanax*

ACER
A. ginnala (Amur maple); *A. palmatum* 'Atropurpureum' (bloodleaf Japanese maple); *A. platanoides* (Norway maple); *A. saccharum* (sugar maple, rock maple)

Long favorites as lawn or street shade trees, most maples will grow in moist or dry soil, in full sunlight or partial shade, and suffer little damage from insects. The species listed here are structurally strong, with branch patterns capable of withstanding heavy wind and the weight of ice and snow. Maple trees may be infected by a fungus disease that can be recognized by wilted foliage; the disease can be controlled in its early stages by pruning.

Amur maple is a rapid-growing, shrubby, cold-resistant tree whose range extends from Zone 7 to the northern areas of Zone 2. It is useful in screen plantings or as a specimen, and has fragrant tiny white flowers in spring, red winged seeds in summer and vivid scarlet, yellow or orange leaves in the fall. A 5- to 6-foot tree reaches its ultimate height of 20 feet in five to seven years.

The bloodleaf is the only variety of Japanese maple whose foliage retains its red-purple color from spring through fall. To be sure of getting this depth of color, select grafted trees from a local nursery when they are in leaf. It grows in Zones 6-8, and is one of the hardiest of the Japanese maples, but late frosts may damage new growth, necessitating pruning. A 4- to 5-foot tree becomes 15 feet tall and equally wide in about ten years. It grows best in partial shade and moist soil.

The Norway maple grows quickly and survives in polluted city air or on wind-swept salt-sprayed seacoasts; it is hardy in Zones 3-8. In spring it bears tiny yellow flowers; its foliage turns yellow in the fall. Different varieties suit different requirements: *A. platanoides* Globosum seldom grows more than 18 feet tall but has a 20- to 30-foot spread; it stays below most utility lines. *A. platanoides* Erectum is a tall tree for a constricted space; it grows up to 30 feet tall but is only 6 feet wide.

The stately, slow-growing sugar maple tolerates severe winter weather but is not a good city tree; its shallow roots are damaged by ice-melting chemicals used on streets. It grows in Zones 3-8 and is noted for fall foliage in brilliant shades of red, orange and yellow. This species also has two varieties that are tall and narrow, *A. saccharum* Columnare and *A. saccharum* Monumentale; their height is 50 to 60 feet although they are only about 12 feet wide.

AMERICAN BEECH See *Fagus*
AMERICAN YELLOWWOOD See *Cladrastis*
AMUR CORK TREE See *Phellodendron*
AMUR MAPLE See *Acer*
ARALIA, CASTOR See *Kalopanax*
ARNOLD CRAB APPLE See *Malus*
ASH See *Fraxinus*
ASH, KOREAN MOUNTAIN See *Sorbus*

BEECH See *Fagus*

BETULA
B. papyrifera (canoe birch, paper birch, white birch)
Although the natural range of the canoe birch is the northern United States and southern Canada, it adapts to colder and warmer temperatures, growing anywhere in Zones 2-7. A fast-growing, short-lived tree, it requires full sun and does best in moist, sandy or average garden soil. Of all birch species this one is the most resistant to borers. Its branches are stronger than those of other birch species and resist the weight of snow and ice.

The canoe birch will reach 60 to 75 feet in 60 years, with a spread equal to about half its height. Its shiny green leaves sparkle and quiver in summer winds, then turn yellow in the fall, and its bare white single or multiple trunks and delicately patterned branches present a beautiful contrast against a clump of evergreens.

BIRCH See *Betula*
BLACK GUM See *Nyssa*
BLACK TUPELO See *Nyssa*
BLOODLEAF JAPANESE MAPLE See *Acer*
BRADFORD PEAR See *Pyrus*

CALLERY PEAR, BRADFORD See *Pyrus*
CANOE BIRCH See *Betula*
CASTOR ARALIA See *Kalopanax*

NORWAY MAPLE
Acer platanoides

CANOE BIRCH
Betula papyrifera

For climate zones and frost dates, see maps, pages 148-149.

KATSURA TREE
Cercidiphyllum japonicum

EASTERN REDBUD
Cercis canadensis

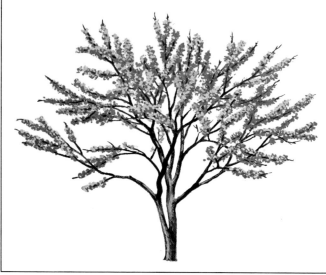

YELLOWWOOD
Cladrastis lutea

CERCIDIPHYLLUM
C. japonicum (katsura tree)

The broadly spreading katsura tree has particular value in easy gardens: its heart-shaped leaves attract no insect pests whatsoever and the loose arrangement of its foliage permits air to circulate freely through the crown. It does best in full sun and moist, well-drained soil and is hardy in Zones 4-9. In Zones 7-9, however, it needs some protection from the sun.

The katsura tree grows rapidly to a height of about 25 feet and ultimately becomes 40 to 60 feet tall. It is valued as both a shade tree and an ornamental. The leaves, tinged with red when new, turn green as they mature, and in the fall vary in hue from yellow to scarlet.

CERCIS
C. canadensis (eastern redbud)

The redbuds are native American trees that need little care once they are established, although the deep root system demands that they be planted in deep, moist, well-drained soil. They thrive in sun or partial shade and in acid or alkaline soil. The eastern redbud, especially recommended, is hardy over most of the United States, from Zones 5-9. It grows rapidly when young, eventually reaching a height of 25 to 35 feet. In the open, it spreads to as much as 20 feet, but in shaded, woodland situations it spreads less and grows taller. It produces clusters of purple-pink flowers in early spring before the leaves appear, but there is also a white variety, *C. canadensis alba*. The leaves of the redbud are glossy and heart shaped and turn yellow in autumn.

CHINESE SCHOLAR TREE See *Sophora*

CLADRASTIS
C. lutea, also called *C. tinctoria* (yellowwood, American yellowwood)

A tall straight trunk, broadly spreading branches and deep nonintrusive roots make the yellowwood an ideal garden shade tree; its roots threaten neither plants nor patio pavement. It is hardy in Zones 4-9 and does best in full sun and a moist, well-drained soil but will tolerate heat and dry conditions if the soil is deep enough to accommodate its long roots. In dry soils, however, it should be watered when young. Yellowwood is relatively free of pests and diseases and it seldom needs any attention when mature, although its zigzagging branches may need thinning to lessen wind damage. The tree bleeds if pruned in any season other than summer.

Yellowwood, at maturity, is 30 to 50 feet tall and may spread to as much as 25 feet. Its broad, graceful shape is annually clothed in bright green leaves, and every two or three years it produces fragrant wisteria-like clusters of white flowers. The leaves turn orange to yellow in the fall; in the winter the yellowwood displays the angular patterns of its branches and smooth light-gray bark.

CORNUS
C. florida (flowering dogwood); *C. florida* 'Rubra' (pink flowering dogwood); *C. kousa* (Kousa dogwood, Japanese dogwood)

The small, beautiful dogwood tree lends itself to woodland settings or to city gardens with limited space and can be planted in full sun or in partial shade. Hardy in Zones 5-9, it does best in cool climates and moist, well-drained acid soils but will tolerate a variety of soils if they are mulched to keep them moist in a dry season. Dogwoods are slow to heal if injured. In droughts they may be damaged by bark borers, and petal blight can be a problem in areas of high humidity.

Flowering dogwood, which is hardy in Zones 5-9, grows 15 to 30 feet high and has a spread of 15 to 20 feet. Its white or pink blossoms appear in spring, before the leaves, along the tops of the horizontal branches. Bright red berries follow. In autumn, the green foliage turns deep red. The Kousa dogwood (Zones 6-9) flowers about a month later than *C. florida,* after the leaves have appeared. Its blossoms are white and its large fruits strawberry red; its leaves turn red in the fall. It grows 15 to 25 feet tall and wide.

CORK TREE, AMUR See *Phellodendron*

CORYLUS
C. colurna (Turkish filbert, Turkish hazel)

An excellent tree for dry areas, the Turkish filbert will remain green and vigorous after other trees begin losing their leaves for want of moisture. Hardy from Zone 5 southward, this species of *Corylus* grows best in well-drained deep alkaline soil. Although it bears edible nuts, its chief appeal for many gardeners is ornamental. It forms a dense pyramid up to 75 feet high. The bark on mature trees resembles that of the cork tree, and in spring the male flowers, growing in separate clusters from the female blossoms on the same tree, create a display of golden yellow catkins.

CRAB APPLE See *Malus*
CUCUMBER TREE See *Magnolia*

DAVIDIA
D. involucrata (dove tree)

This import from western China looks fragile but is not. It does best in garden soil that has been supplemented with humus, and benefits from the partial shade of other deciduous trees, though it will tolerate full sun if it is given extra watering during dry periods. It is generally free of pests and diseases. The tree's hardiness range is Zones 6-8, and although it blooms erratically, it seems to grow best in areas where winters are cold.

The dove tree has ascending branches, loosely pyramidal, that spread outward to a distance that may equal the tree's height. Once it is established, it grows at the rate of about a foot a year, a 4- to 5-foot tree reaching a height of 15 feet in 10 to 12 years, with a mature height of 50 to 60 feet. The flowers appear every third or fourth spring. Each bloom consists of a red-and-white ball-shaped cluster of stamens supported by two large fluttering white bracts of unequal size, one on each side, that suggest the wings of a dove. The blossoms last for about two weeks and are followed by an inedible pear-shaped green fruit.

DOGWOOD See *Cornus*
DOROTHEA CRAB APPLE See *Malus*
DOVE TREE See *Davidia*

EASTERN REDBUD See *Cercis*
EUROPEAN BEECH See *Fagus*

FAGUS
F. grandifolia (American beech, red beech, white beech); *F. sylvatica* (European beech)

Beeches are grown widely in American gardens throughout Zones 4-8. Though slow to mature, they are so long-lived they seldom need replacing. These majestic trees adapt to less-than-perfect growing conditions but do best in full sun and a well-drained, slightly acid soil. The one thing they must have is space: the branches of a beech can sometimes

PINK FLOWERING DOGWOOD
Cornus florida 'Rubra'

TURKISH FILBERT
Corylus colurna

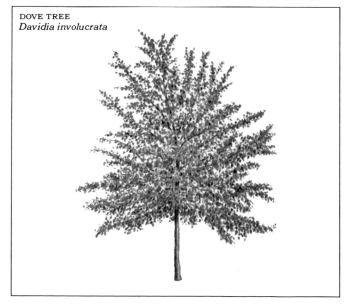

DOVE TREE
Davidia involucrata

For climate zones and frost dates, see maps, pages 148-149.

EUROPEAN BEECH
Fagus sylvatica

FRANKLINIA
Franklinia alatamaha

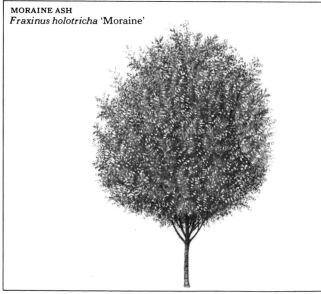

MORAINE ASH
Fraxinus holotricha 'Moraine'

spread 50 to 60 feet in diameter. For this reason they are generally grown as single specimens, although in the wild they are found in splendid groves. The foliage of the beech is pest free and its nuts are eagerly sought by squirrels and birds, taking care of that cleanup problem. The tree's shallow root system and dense foliage prevent any other plants from growing beneath it, but this is not a serious drawback since the lower branches generally dip to touch the ground, hiding the bare soil under them.

When they are mature, American beeches are 70 to 90 feet tall, although some may reach 140 feet and live 400 years. They have a dense, rounded canopy, green leaves that turn golden-bronze in the fall, and smooth silvery-gray bark. European beeches, which are more graceful than the American species, come in many varieties, some with pendulous or weeping branches and deeply cut fernlike leaves. Their bark is darker gray than that of the American species, and their shape is more pyramidal.

FILBERT, TURKISH See *Corylus*
FLOWERING DOGWOOD See *Cornus*
FRANKLIN TREE See *Franklinia*

FRANKLINIA

F. alatamaha, also called *Gordonia alatamaha* (franklinia, gordonia, Franklin tree)

The small, graceful franklinia, prized as an ornamental in Southern gardens, does well in moist, well-drained acid soil and may be planted in partial shade, although its autumn color will be brighter and it will bear more flowers if it is grown in full sun. It is hardy as far north as Zone 6 and may be grown throughout the South except in the southernmost part of Zone 9.

Franklinia becomes 15 to 20 feet tall in about 10 years in the South; in the North, it matures in 10 years and seldom grows more than 6 to 10 feet tall. It bears fragrant, camellia-like white flowers that bloom in early fall, simultaneously with the onset of the tree's red and orange fall foliage. All franklinias are descendants of wild plants found in Georgia in 1765 and named for Benjamin Franklin; the tree has not been found growing wild since then.

FRAXINUS

F. americana (white ash); *F. holotricha* 'Moraine' (Moraine ash); *F. pennsylvanica lanceolata* 'Marshall's Seedless' (Marshall's Seedless ash)

The white ash tree is so common in most parts of the United States that in some areas it is regarded as a weed. It is hardy in Zones 3-8 and grows well in full sun and many kinds of soil, although a deep, well-drained soil is best. An 8- to 10-foot white ash sapling will become a 25-foot tree in five to eight years.

Grass grows well in the ash's filtered shade. Pests and diseases seldom affect it, and its leaves crumble conveniently when they fall, disappearing into the lawn so that little raking is needed. The tree's one drawback is its winged seeds, which blow over the lawn and garden and sprout; seedlings can be avoided by planting one of the specially propagated seedless males.

The stately white ash reaches a height of 70 to 90 feet with a rounded spreading canopy up to 50 feet wide. Its autumn color depends on the variety: of two outstanding male seedless types, Autumn Purple turns deep purple and Rosehill becomes bronzy red. The Moraine ash (Zones 5-8) seldom exceeds a height of 35 feet and is more oval in shape than the white ash; its canopy is barely 20 feet across and its leaves turn pale yellow in the fall. Marshall's Seedless ash (Zones 3-9) has a pyramidal shape, reaches a height of 50 to 60 feet, and its autumn leaves are yellow.

GINKGO
G. biloba (ginkgo, maidenhair tree)

The ancient ginkgo, on earth for 150 million years, has excellent resistance to the smoke and fumes of the city. The tree is immune to all pests and diseases, so it never needs spraying. In the fall, its leaves turn bright yellow, then drop all at one time, sometimes in a single day, making life easy for the gardener who wants to rake only once. The tree needs no pruning.

The ginkgo requires sun but it tolerates virtually any well-drained soil in Zones 4-9. During its gawky 20-year adolescence the tree has long, asymmetrical, ascending branches. At maturity a tree will stand up to 80 feet tall with a 40-foot spread and thus is suitable only for large yards. There are several varieties that have a narrow, columnar shape at maturity and are used in street plantings.

The ginkgo is a stately tree. Its branches flare out in a wide, picturesque way. Its 1- to 4-inch bright green leaves are fan shaped with wavy edges and cleft centers. Both male and female trees flower, but only male trees should be planted; female trees produce a fleshy fruit with a repulsive odor.

GLEDITSIA
G. triacanthos inermis (thornless honey locust)

The thornless honey locust is transplanted with ease; even large ones can be moved with proper equipment, making the species a good choice for gardeners who do not want to nurse a seedling tree. Fast growing, a 6- to 8-foot thornless honey locust will become 20 to 25 feet tall in five or six years.

The thornless honey locust grows in full sun in Zones 4-9. It will tolerate almost any well-drained soil, even alkaline, and the deep roots withstand drought. The feathery leaves cast a filtered shade, making gardening easy under the tree. In autumn, leaves dry and crumble as they fall, eliminating raking. An established tree rarely needs pruning.

Mature height for a thornless honey locust varies from 35 to 70 feet, depending on the variety chosen, and the tree spreads as it grows, sometimes fanning out as wide as it is tall. The leaves turn yellow early in the fall and as the tree ages, its trunk and branches turn dark gray to black, providing an elegant contrast against snow. When choosing a honey locust, buy one of the thornless and seedless cultivars such as Moraine since others brandish thorns up to 4 inches long and drop messy seed pods.

GOLDEN-RAIN TREE See *Koelreuteria*
GORDONIA See *Franklinia*
GUM, BLACK See *Nyssa*
GUM, SOUR See *Nyssa*
GUM, SWEET See *Liquidambar*

HAZEL, TURKISH See *Corylus*
HONEY LOCUST, THORNLESS See *Gleditsia*

JAPANESE DOGWOOD See *Cornus*
JAPANESE MAPLE, BLOODLEAF See *Acer*
JAPANESE PAGODA TREE See *Sophora*

KALOPANAX
K. pictus, also called *K. septemlabus, Acanthopanax ricinifolius* (castor aralia)

This sturdy shade tree with huge maple-shaped leaves

GINKGO
Ginkgo biloba

MORAINE THORNLESS HONEY LOCUST
Gleditsia triacanthos inermis 'Moraine'

CASTOR ARALIA
Kalopanax pictus

For climate zones and frost dates, see maps, pages 148-149.

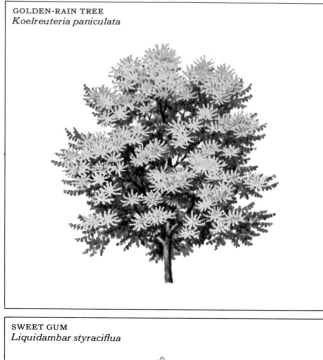

GOLDEN-RAIN TREE
Koelreuteria paniculata

SWEET GUM
Liquidambar styraciflua

TULIP TREE
Liriodendron tulipifera

grows in almost any moist, well-drained soil. It is hardy in Zones 4-8 and does best in full sun but must be planted in soil deep enough to accommodate the tree's long roots. Pests and diseases seldom trouble it, and it keeps its rounded shape without pruning. Its one drawback is the ½-inch thorns that grow along the branches of the young tree, but these disappear as the tree ages.

The castor aralia grows fairly rapidly, a 6- to 8-foot tree becoming 20 feet tall in seven to nine years and eventually attaining a height of 60 to 80 feet with a nearly equal spread. The shiny dark green leaves turn dull red in the fall and are 7 to 14 inches across. Small clusters of tiny white blossoms appear in midsummer, to be followed by black berries which are quickly eaten by birds.

KATSURA TREE See *Cercidiphyllum*

KOELREUTERIA

K. paniculata (golden-rain tree)

The golden-rain tree needs little care even in the polluted air of city gardens. It will grow in almost any well-drained soil, even alkaline, and established trees are drought resistant. The tree resists pests and diseases, and it does not require pruning. Fairly fast-growing, a 6- to 8-foot tree will reach 20 feet in five or six years. The species grows well in Zones 6-9, but too much shade will make its foliage sparse.

A mature golden-rain tree is about 30 to 40 feet tall, with a flat-topped spread almost as wide. Its compound leaves, which are 8 to 15 inches long, are reddish when they unfold, then turn blue-green. In early summer the tree produces airy clusters of yellow flowers that almost cover it. The thousands of petals floating to the ground, like a golden rain, give the tree its common name. The flowers are followed by balloon-like seed pods that turn from green to pink to brown and cling to the tree into winter.

KOREAN MOUNTAIN ASH See *Sorbus*
KOUSA DOGWOOD See *Cornus*

LAUREL OAK, NORTHERN See *Quercus*
LEMOINE PURPLE CRAB APPLE See *Malus*
LINDEN, LITTLE-LEAF See *Tilia*

LIQUIDAMBAR

L. styraciflua (sweet gum)

The sweet gum is especially good for planting in wet areas of Zones 5-9. It is remarkably resistant to pests and diseases, except in the mid-Atlantic states where it is subject to sweet-gum blight. It can stand occasional flooding; in fact, it prefers soil that is continually moist, making it a good choice for riverbanks and areas of heavy rain. It also will tolerate drier soils. In ideal conditions—deep, loamy, acid soil—a 10- to 12-foot tree may become 25 to 30 feet tall in about seven years. Any pruning that a young tree requires should be done in winter. Once it is established, the sweet gum needs little attention.

The broad, symmetrical pyramids of sweet gums average 60 to 70 feet tall at maturity. The leaves resemble five-pointed stars; in fall, their crimson, orange and yellow color display rivals that of the maples and lasts up to six weeks. Inconspicuous yellowish-green flowers develop into burrlike seed balls that drop in fall and winter.

LIRIODENDRON

L. tulipifera (tulip tree, tulip poplar, yellow poplar)

One of the largest trees in the eastern regions of North

America, the tulip tree is a good choice for a sunny location in a big yard. It is easy to transplant, grows fast in Zones 5-9 and tolerates extremes of heat and cold. The tulip tree grows best in moist, well-drained soil that is deep enough to accommodate the tree's long roots. It is not seriously affected by pests or diseases. Mature trees rarely require pruning.

In the open, the tulip tree has wide-spreading branches that bend toward the earth. The tallest grow to 150 feet, but more commonly the trees are 70 to 90 feet tall with a spread of 35 to 40 feet. The 2½- to 5-inch leaves are light green as they unfold in spring, then turn shiny deep green in summer; in autumn they become a clear golden yellow that is sometimes flecked with brown. The tree bears greenish-yellow 2-inch tulip-shaped flowers, but generally not until the tree is 10 to 20 years old. The blossoms are followed by 2- to 3-inch conical seed capsules that cling to the branches after the leaves have fallen.

LITTLE-LEAF LINDEN See *Tilia*
LOCUST, THORNLESS HONEY See *Gleditsia*

MAGNOLIA

M. acuminata (cucumber tree); *M. acuminata cordata* (yellow cucumber tree); *M. loebneri* 'Merrill' (Merrill magnolia); *M. stellata* (star magnolia)

Deciduous magnolias are less finicky than their southern-belle image suggests. They are fast growing in full sun or partial shade and are adaptable to many different types of gardens, according to the size of the species chosen. The coarse leaves resist leaf-eating insects and the trees tolerate the fumes and dust of city gardens. They grow best in moist, acid soil, supplemented with peat moss or leaf mold.

Magnolias are cherished for their spring flowers. These dramatic early spring blossoms, commonly appearing even before the leaves, are as much as 6 inches in diameter. They may be yellow, white, pink or reddish. The blooms are succeeded by green cucumber-like fruits that turn red in the fall and open to reveal pea-sized, bright red seeds.

The cucumber tree is one of the fastest growing of the magnolias and needs plenty of space; it eventually becomes 90 feet tall in Zones 4-9. A handsome shade tree, it bears leaves up to 10 inches long.

Shrublike with leaves 3 to 6 inches long, the yellow cucumber tree is a less hardy smaller edition of the cucumber tree. It thrives in Zones 5-9, growing about 30 feet tall. Resplendent when standing alone, the hybrid Merrill magnolia is pyramidal in shape and fast growing in Zones 5-9. It may grow 30 feet tall and has large white flowers.

The star magnolia grows in Zones 5-9. The fragrant white flowers may be killed by late frost in the northern part of its range. Dense and often shrublike, with several trunks, it grows 15 to 20 feet tall.

MAIDENHAIR TREE See *Ginkgo*

MALUS

M. arnoldiana (Arnold crab apple); *M. baccata* (Siberian crab apple); *M.* 'Dorothea' (Dorothea crab apple); *M. purpurea* 'Lemoinei' (Lemoine purple crab apple)

Among flowering trees, crab apples are the easiest to grow and the most resistant to winter cold. Low-maintenance gardeners should choose carefully from among the hundreds of varieties available, however. Some, including those listed above, bear a profusion of fragrant pink, white or red blossoms and colorful fruits annually, but others bear only in alternate years. With minimal care, crab apples can give

CUCUMBER TREE
Magnolia acuminata

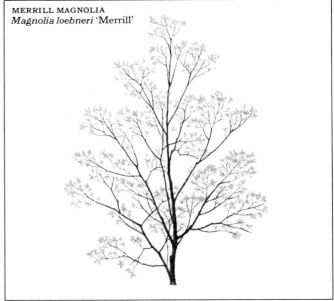

MERRILL MAGNOLIA
Magnolia loebneri 'Merrill'

ARNOLD CRAB APPLE
Malus arnoldiana

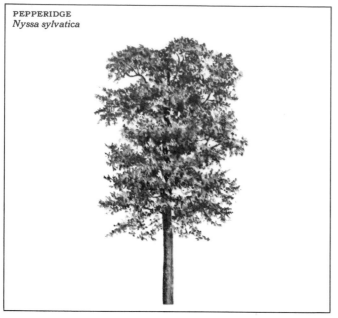

PEPPERIDGE
Nyssa sylvatica

SORREL TREE
Oxydendrum aboreum

AMUR CORK TREE
Phellodendron amurense

almost year-round pleasure, from the first explosion of spring flowers through the bright red or yellow ornamental fruits that will draw birds to the fall garden.

Crab apples grow best in full sunlight and moist, well-drained, slightly acid soil. They grow quickly and are most easily cared for when planted singly or in small groups. An annual spraying will ensure freedom from most diseases. The Arnold crab apple grows 12 to 20 feet tall in Zones 3-8, while the Siberian crab apple grows 35 to 50 feet tall in Zones 2-8. Both the Dorothea crab apple and the Lemoine purple crab apple reach heights of 20 to 25 feet in Zones 3-8.

MAPLE See *Acer*
MARSHALL'S SEEDLESS ASH See *Fraxinus*
MERRILL MAGNOLIA See *Magnolia*
MORAINE ASH See *Fraxinus*
MOUNTAIN ASH, KOREAN See *Sorbus*

NORWAY MAPLE See *Acer*

NYSSA
N. sylvatica (pepperidge, black tupelo, black gum, sour gum)

The pepperidge is an adaptable tree that is very ornamental. With dense, glossy green foliage that turns vivid orange and scarlet in the fall, it grows in Zones 4-9, tolerating extremes of temperature and urban pollution. It grows best in full sun and moist, acid soil, but it will also tolerate partial shade or boggy sites. It even succeeds in seaside gardens if it is protected from the wind. It is difficult to transplant; small specimens should be moved in early spring.

Once established, a pepperidge grows at a moderate rate. A 5-foot tree may reach 20 feet in 10 to 15 years, usually attaining a height of 30 to 50 feet. An occasional tree may reach 90 feet. Pruning is rarely necessary, and the pepperidge is virtually pest free. If male and female trees are grown near each other, the female will bear clusters of inconspicuous ½-inch dark blue fruits in midsummer. These are attractive to birds but will stain a terrace.

OAK See *Quercus*

OXYDENDRUM
O. arboreum (sorrel tree, sourwood)

Planted in moist, well-drained acid soil supplemented with peat moss or leaf mold, the sorrel tree will enhance a garden throughout the year. It grows in Zones 5-8. The sorrel tree, which may have a single trunk or multiple trunks, is slow-growing, seldom exceeding 25 feet in height. It almost never needs pruning and is rarely attacked by pests or diseases.

In summer, the tree bears pendulous clusters of tiny bell-shaped white flowers, followed in fall by grayish seed pods that cling to the tree into winter. The tree's lustrous leathery leaves turn a brilliant scarlet in the fall, and even the bleakest winter landscape is animated by the patterns of its pyramidal silhouette. The sorrel tree's flowers and fall color are at their best if the tree is grown in full sunlight, but it will tolerate partial shade.

PAGODA TREE, JAPANESE See *Sophora*
PAPER BIRCH See *Betula*
PEAR, BRADFORD See *Pyrus*
PEPPERIDGE See *Nyssa*

PHELLODENDRON
P. amurense (Amur cork tree)

Tolerant of harsh urban conditions, the Amur cork tree

will adapt to almost any soil in full sun in Zones 3-8. It is easy to establish, easy to transplant and virtually pest free. An 8- to 10-foot-tall Amur cork tree may reach 20 feet in five to seven years, with an eventual height of 30 to 50 feet. These trees rarely need pruning.

The Amur cork tree's wide-branching growth habit and deeply ridged bark make it outstanding in winter gardens. Its dark green leaves turn yellow and drop in a short period of time in the fall, revealing the tree's form and texture. Lawn grasses grow well beneath its filtered shade in summer. Female trees bear small black berries that attract migrating birds in the fall, but the fruits stain terraces.

PIN OAK See *Quercus*
POPLAR, TULIP See *Liriodendron*
POPLAR, YELLOW See *Liriodendron*
PURPLE CRAB APPLE, LEMOINE See *Malus*

PYRUS
P. calleryana 'Bradford' (Bradford pear, Bradford Callery pear)

For the most part, pear trees should be shunned by the low-maintenance gardener. One exception is a spectacular hybrid variety, Bradford; though its fruit is inedible, it is resistant to fire blight, a common pear-tree disease that kills branches and is difficult to control. It is also thornless, unlike the species. A hardy tree, the Bradford pear grows in Zones 3-9 in almost any garden soil. It needs full sun. The Bradford pear tolerates air pollution and needs pruning only to remove lower branches of young trees when headroom is desired.

A mature Bradford pear grows up to 50 feet tall and spreads 30 to 50 feet. It is pyramidal when young but assumes a more rounded shape as it matures. Clusters of white flowers appear in spring before the leaves unfold. The flowers are followed by pea-sized, rust-colored fruits that are hidden by the leaves and eventually eaten by birds. The 1½- to 3-inch leaves cling late into the fall, turning deep red to scarlet with a look of polished leather.

QUERCUS
Q. alba (white oak); *Q. imbricaria* (shingle oak, northern laurel oak); *Q. palustris* (pin oak); *Q. phellos* (willow oak); *Q. rubra,* also called *Q. borealis* (red oak)

At home in slightly acid soil and full sun, the long-lived deciduous oaks are suitable for any garden of appreciable size. Their strong, wide-spreading branches resist damage from wind or ice and their filtered shade and the acid quality of their decayed leaves provides a receptive environment for many smaller plants. Fall colors of many oaks are red, and the dead leaves may cling late to the branches, adding muted color to winter gardens. Different species grow at different rates, but most soon become too massive for small lots.

The imposing white oak reaches 50 to 80 feet in height and sometimes develops an even broader spread. In Zones 3-9, an 8- to 10-foot white oak will become 20 to 25 feet tall in 10 or 12 years, with a broad, rounded crown whose leaves turn purplish-red in the fall. The shingle oak, which is symmetrical in form, makes a handsome ornamental tree that is also useful as a windbreak or tall hedge, since its lower branches sweep the ground. In Zones 6-8, an 8- to 10-foot shingle oak grows to a height of 20 to 25 feet in 10 or 12 years, eventually reaching more than 50 feet and developing an equal spread. The long, smooth-edged leaves, red when they are unfolding, soon become shiny dark green and in the fall turn rich yellow to russet.

The pin oak grows best in moist, well-drained soil but will

BRADFORD PEAR
Pyrus calleryana 'Bradford'

WHITE OAK
Quercus alba

WILLOW OAK
Quercus phellos

tolerate wetter conditions. It is hardy in Zones 3-9 and grows rapidly, an 8- to 10-foot tree reaching 20 to 25 feet in five or six years. At maturity it is 60 to 70 feet tall with a 25- to 40-foot spread. The upper branches of the pin oak ascend, the middle branches are horizontal, and the lower branches may sweep the ground. Its graceful branching structure makes the pin oak a beautiful specimen tree in winter and summer alike. The leaves turn bronze to red in the fall. The willow oak, another rapid grower that thrives in most soils and is impervious to city conditions, is less hardy; it grows only in Zones 6-8. Smaller than most oaks, an 8- to 10-foot tree will become 20 to 25 feet tall in five or six years, and will eventually reach a height of 40 to 60 feet with a 30- to 40-foot spread. Its narrow, pointed willow-like leaves are bright green in summer, turning yellow in autumn.

Another fast-growing oak species, the red oak, tolerates poor soils and the polluted atmosphere of cities. In Zones 3-9, an 8- to 10-foot tree will reach 20 feet in five or six years, with an ultimate height of 75 feet. The red oak is pyramidal when it is young, but with age its canopy becomes broader and more rounded in outline. The pointed, deeply lobed leaves turn red in the autumn.

RED BEECH See *Fagus*
RED OAK See *Quercus*
REDBUD, EASTERN See *Cercis*
ROCK MAPLE See *Acer*

SCHOLAR TREE, CHINESE See *Sophora*
SHINGLE OAK See *Quercus*
SIBERIAN CRAB APPLE See *Malus*

SOPHORA

S. japonica (Japanese pagoda tree, Chinese scholar tree)

The Japanese pagoda tree was traditionally used in temple gardens in the Orient. It grows best in moist, well-drained soil deep enough to accommodate its long root structure, though it will tolerate other kinds of soil, and can survive drought. The tree does well in polluted air, and it resists pests. It grows in Zones 5-8.

In full sun, this outstanding shade tree grows as much as 20 feet in eight to ten years. Eventually it reaches 50 to 75 feet tall with an equal spread. Without pruning, the Japanese pagoda tree grows in a symmetrical round shape, but most gardeners prune to provide headroom beneath the drooping lower branches.

In late summer, when most trees have finished flowering, the Japanese pagoda tree is covered with erect, 10- to 15-inch-tall clusters of tiny yellowish to cream-colored flowers. The blossoms last about a month and are followed by 3- to 4-inch yellowish pods that persist into winter. The tree does not bloom until it is more than 15 to 20 years old, but its lustrous, feathery leaves make it a handsome garden specimen in the meantime.

SORBUS

S. alnifolia (Korean mountain ash)

A year-round beauty, the Korean mountain ash is pest free; it is the only mountain ash that is resistant to borers. It thrives in full sun and in any well-drained soil in Zones 4-8 and requires little pruning, growing rapidly without training into a handsome specimen tree. Only heavily polluted air impedes its growth.

Korean mountain ash is cone shaped when it is young but becomes rounded in maturity and provides dense shade. It may grow eventually to 50 feet in height. In early summer it

JAPANESE PAGODA TREE
Sophora japonica

KOREAN MOUNTAIN ASH
Sorbus alnifolia

bears clusters of small white flowers, which mature into bright orange-to-red berries. These remain on the branches into the winter unless they are eaten by squirrels and birds. Unlike other mountain ashes, the Korean species has simple rather than compound leaves; they turn shades of scarlet and orange in the fall. The smooth gray beechlike bark is very attractive in winter.

SORREL TREE See *Oxydendrum*
SOUR GUM See *Nyssa*
SOURWOOD See *Oxydendrum*
STAR MAGNOLIA See *Magnolia*
SUGAR MAPLE See *Acer*
SWEET GUM See *Liquidambar*

THORNLESS HONEY LOCUST See *Gleditsia*

TILIA

T. cordata (little-leaf linden)

A very satisfactory tree for small gardens and city streets, the little-leaf linden grows slowly but provides dense shade. An 8- to 10-foot tree may become 20 feet tall in five years, eventually growing 50 to 70 feet tall with a spread of half its height. It will grow in any good soil in Zones 3-8, though it does best in moist, well-drained soil that is deep enough to accommodate its long roots. It adapts to either full sun or partial shade and requires little pruning.

A mature little-leaf linden is compact and pyramidal with branches that dip at the ends. The heart-shaped leaves grow 1½ to 3 inches long and turn yellow in the fall in cold regions; in warm areas they stay green until they are killed by frost. The clusters of small yellow flowers in summer are deliciously fragrant and attract bees. Small, pealike fruits stay on the tree well into the winter.

TULIP POPLAR See *Liriodendron*
TULIP TREE See *Liriodendron*
TUPELO, BLACK See *Nyssa*
TURKISH FILBERT See *Corylus*
TURKISH HAZEL See *Corylus*

WHITE ASH See *Fraxinus*
WHITE BEECH See *Fagus*
WHITE BIRCH See *Betula*
WHITE OAK See *Quercus*
WILLOW OAK See *Quercus*

YELLOW POPLAR See *Liriodendron*
YELLOWWOOD See *Cladrastis*

Evergreen trees

ABIES

A. concolor (white fir, Colorado fir, concolor fir)

Of all the fir trees, the white fir is the most care free. It resists urban dirt and pollution, and although it grows best in cool, moist climates it is able to withstand periods of heat and drought. Like most fir trees it resists pests and diseases except in warm climates, where it may be attacked by spider mites. It grows in Zones 3-6, in full sun and a moist, well-drained acid soil.

With its symmetrical shape, fragrant blue-green needles and reliable growth of 1½ to 2 feet a year, the white fir is an excellent landscape tree. When young it may grow somewhat unevenly, but after six to eight years it becomes pyramidal. In 30 to 60 years this tree may become 50 or 60 feet tall.

LITTLE-LEAF LINDEN
Tilia cordata

WHITE FIR
Abies concolor

For climate zones and frost dates, see maps, pages 148-149.

BLUE ATLAS CEDAR
Cedrus atlantica 'Glauca'

DEODAR CEDAR
Cedrus deodara

ALBERTA SPRUCE, DWARF See *Picea*
AMERICAN HOLLY See *Ilex*
ARBORVITAE See *Thuja*
ATLAS CEDAR, BLUE See *Cedrus*
AUSTRIAN PINE See *Pinus*

BLACK PINE See *Pinus*
BLUE ATLAS CEDAR See *Cedrus*
BLUE COLUMN JUNIPER See *Juniperus*
BULL BAY See *Magnolia*
BURK'S RED CEDAR See *Juniperus*

CANADA HEMLOCK See *Tsuga*
CANAERT RED CEDAR See *Juniperus*
CAROLINA HEMLOCK See *Tsuga*
CEDAR See *Cedrus*
CEDAR OF LEBANON See *Cedrus*
CEDAR, OREGON See *Chamaecyparis*
CEDAR, PORT ORFORD See *Chamaecyparis*
CEDAR, RED See *Juniperus*
CEDAR, WESTERN RED See *Thuja*

CEDRUS

C. atlantica 'Glauca' (blue Atlas cedar); *C. deodara* (deodar cedar); *C. libani* (cedar of Lebanon)

The tall cedars need every little attention, flourishing in full sun and in almost any well-drained soil, but they must be given adequate space, not only because of their size but also for an appreciation of their decorative shape. On broad lawns they can become magnificent showpieces. Conical when it is young, the cedar usually spreads as it ages, eventually reaching a height of more than 100 feet and a width of 40 to 60 feet. Cedars are famous for their aromatic wood and are admired for the large cones that take two years to mature.

The blue Atlas cedar, hardier than most cedars, grows in Zones 6-9 at a rate of 18 inches or more a year when young. Until it is about six years old its branches look rather straggly, but the mature blue Atlas has wide-spreading open branches and a flattish top. Its light blue-green needles often sparkle with a silvery sheen, and it is considered among the most beautiful of evergreens.

The deodar cedar grows 18 to 24 inches a year when young, eventually forming a shapely pyramid with graceful branches that bend down at the tips and long blue-green needles. It grows in Zones 7-9 and does especially well in southern heat. The dark green cedar of Lebanon grows slowly at a rate of about 1 foot a year to become a many-tiered open pyramid, formal in appearance and durable and hardy in character. It grows in Zones 5-9, but at the northernmost limits it should be planted on a warm south-facing slope.

CHAMAECYPARIS

C. lawsoniana (Lawson's false cypress, Port Orford cedar, Oregon cedar); *C. obtusa* (hinoki false cypress)

Both of these ornamental false cypresses and their varieties are naturally shapely, so they seldom need pruning. They are virtually free of pests and diseases, doing well in any location where the air and ground are moist and the soil is well drained and slightly acid. They do not grow well in hot, dry sites, in air that is chemically polluted, or in locations exposed to strong winds.

Lawson's false cypress, hardy in Zones 6-9, forms a dense, soft pyramid that reaches about 20 feet in height in as many years and has a spread of 5 to 7 feet. Its ultimate height is 60 to 70 feet. Varieties of Lawson's false cypress range in foliage color from silver or gray to blue or green. Fletcheri is blue and feathery; it reaches its mature height of 12 to 20 feet in about 15 years. Stewartii has yellow tips in spring that turn dark green later in the year. It grows into a broad, 20- to 30-foot-tall pyramid in about 25 to 30 years.

Hinoki false cypress, Zones 4-9, grows slowly into a 40- to 50-foot-tall cone and may ultimately reach a height of about 90 feet. Its branches droop slightly at their tips and the foliage is glossy dark green. The variety Crippsii grows 20 to 30 feet tall in 25 years. Its foliage is yellow when new, becoming dark green later in the year.

CHINESE JUNIPER See *Juniperus*
CHRYSOLARIX See *Pseudolarix*
COLORADO FIR See *Abies*
COLORADO SPRUCE, MOERHEIM See *Picea*
COLUMN JUNIPER, BLUE See *Juniperus*
COLUMNAR GIANT ARBORVITAE See *Thuja*
CONCOLOR FIR See *Abies*

DEODAR CEDAR See *Cedrus*
DOUGLAS FIR See *Pseudotsuga*
DOUGLAS SPRUCE See *Pseudotsuga*
DWARF ALBERTA SPRUCE See *Picea*

EASTERN RED CEDAR See *Juniperus*
ENGLISH HOLLY See *Ilex*

FALSE CYPRESS See *Chamaecyparis*
FIR See *Abies*
FIR, DOUGLAS See *Pseudotsuga*
FIR, RED See *Pseudotsuga*

GIANT ARBORVITAE See *Thuja*
GOLDEN LARCH See *Pseudolarix*

HEMLOCK See *Tsuga*
HINOKI FALSE CYPRESS See *Chamaecyparis*
HOLLY See *Ilex*

ILEX
I. aquifolium (English holly); *I. opaca* (American holly)

Of all ornamental evergreens, hollies are among the few that can withstand polluted urban conditions, and the American holly adapts readily to the natural hardships of an exposed seaside location. In sun or partial shade, they flourish in almost any well-drained soil, but they bear more fruit in full sun and moist, slightly acid soil. These shapely plants seldom need pruning and are rarely bothered by pests except the holly leaf miner. At the northern edge of their growing areas, the trees need shelter from winter wind and sun. These two hollies should not be planted where there are prolonged hot, dry spells. A female holly will have berries only if a male tree is within 100 feet of it; in large plantings, at least one male is necessary for every 10 females.

The red winter berries of English and American hollies have made them popular ornamentals, but their glossy green leaves are attractive year round. English holly, hardy in Zones 6-9, becomes a tall pyramidal tree; it may reach a height of 70 feet in 100 years. American holly, hardy in Zones 5-9, grows as a broad pyramid to a height of 8 to 15 feet in 10 to 15 years, reaching a maximum height of 40 to 50 feet. From the many varieties of American and English holly, gardeners should select those that have been successfully grown under local conditions for several years.

JUNIPER See *Juniperus*

For climate zones and frost dates, see maps, pages 148-149.

LAWSON'S FALSE CYPRESS
Chamaecyparis lawsoniana

AMERICAN HOLLY
Ilex opaca

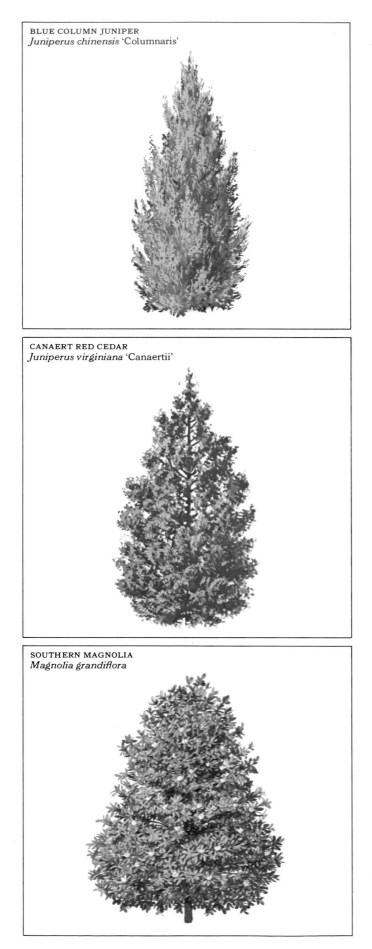

BLUE COLUMN JUNIPER
Juniperus chinensis 'Columnaris'

CANAERT RED CEDAR
Juniperus virginiana 'Canaertii'

SOUTHERN MAGNOLIA
Magnolia grandiflora

JUNIPERUS

J. chinensis (Chinese juniper), *J. chinensis* 'Columnaris' (blue column juniper), *J. chinensis* 'Keteleeri' (Keteleer juniper), *J. chinensis* 'Mas'; *J. virginiana* (eastern red cedar), *J. virginiana* 'Burkii' (Burk's red cedar), *J. virginiana* 'Canaertii' (Canaert red cedar), *J. virginiana* 'Glauca' (silver red cedar)

Nothing seems to discourage the tough, handsome junipers. They grow in almost every climate zone in the United States and Canada, and in any soil—rocky or sandy, acid or alkaline. Wind does not affect them, and neither do drought, smog or salt spray. In fact, the only thing likely to create problems for them is a fungus they may pick up if planted near apple trees, hawthorns or cotoneasters. Called cedar-apple rust, it may cause unsightly juniper galls.

Junipers range in size from creeping ground covers to 90-foot tall columnar trees. The columnar types grow so slowly that it is seldom necessary to prune them to hold their dimensions in check. Juniper's foliage stays on the plant year round but may lighten in winter. Female plants bear ornamental gray-blue berries in fall and winter. To be sure of getting berries, buy junipers when the plant is in fruit and be sure to plant a male juniper nearby. Junipers are excellent specimen trees and are often used for windbreaks.

All the varieties of Chinese juniper listed here are more commonly grown by nurserymen in the United States than the original Chinese species. Blue column juniper, which has dense blue-green foliage, is a narrow cone-shaped tree that reaches a height of 15 to 20 feet in about 20 years. Keteleer juniper has bright green foliage and large, light blue berries; it has a broad conical form that spreads open gracefully, growing 20 feet or more in 30 years. *J. chinensis* Mas, one of the best columnar varieties, grows to 30 feet but bears no fruit. Chinese junipers are hardy in Zones 4-9.

Among American junipers, the eastern red cedar and its variants have darker foliage and slightly smaller berries than the Chinese junipers. Hardy in Zones 2-9, this native tree is naturally columnar but may broaden with age. The original species reaches up to 75 feet in height and in good soil may live for as long as 100 years; in winter its foliage turns brownish. Burk's red cedar is a 30-foot tree with gray-blue foliage that turns purplish in winter. Canaert red cedar, a 20- to 30-foot tree, remains dark green throughout the winter and bears masses of pale blue berries. Silver red cedar grows 15 to 20 feet tall, with foliage that changes from bright blue-gray in spring to blue-green in summer.

KETELEER JUNIPER See *Juniperus*

LARCH, GOLDEN See *Pseudolarix*
LAWSON'S FALSE CYPRESS See *Chamaecyparis*
LIVE OAK See *Quercus*

MAGNOLIA

M. grandiflora (southern magnolia, bull bay)

The stately southern magnolia's tough, leathery evergreen leaves are resistant to pests and urban pollution, but its bark is too easily injured for it to be used as a street tree. A magnolia needs plenty of room; at its mature height it is a towering pyramid 90 feet tall with a spread of 45 feet. But the tree takes 75 to 100 years to reach that size. The fragrant 8- to 10-inch waxy white flowers blossom in spring and summer, or in regions where the weather is consistently warm, practically all year round.

A magnolia prospers in deep, moist, acid soil and full sun, but will grow with as little as three hours of direct sunlight a day. It is hardy in Zones 7-9, but in the northernmost part of

Zone 7 it should be sheltered from the wind. In planting and transplanting, handle a magnolia with care; its thick fleshy roots decay when bruised or broken and should be encased in a large ball of earth when the tree is moved. The safest time to plant is in the spring, just before growth begins.

NORWAY PINE See *Pinus*

OAK, LIVE See *Quercus*
OREGON CEDAR See *Chamaecyparis*

PICEA
P. glauca 'Conica' (dwarf Alberta spruce, dwarf white spruce); *P. omorika* (Serbian spruce); *P. pungens* 'Moerheimii' (Moerheim Colorado spruce)

Among the most rugged of evergreens, spruces withstand extreme winter cold. The trees maintain their symmetrical cone shape without pruning, and the needles cling to the trees for six to eight years. Spruces require full sun and do best in moist, well-drained soil but will adapt to light, dry soils if watered when young, until their roots are established. Handsomest in their youth, spruces tend to lose their lower branches as they mature, so the trees may become less attractive in later years.

The dwarf Alberta spruce, Zones 2-7, is a compact conical plant that grows only 1 to 4 inches a year, eventually reaching a height of 7 to 10 feet in 15 to 20 years. Its extremely dense green foliage makes it an excellent hedge. It is also handsome as a formal specimen tree. In a southern exposure the foliage of this spruce may be burned by a combination of winter sun and wind.

The Serbian spruce, Zones 4-7, has a narrow, tapered pyramidal shape with graceful pendant branches that move in the wind, disclosing the dark green needles' whitish undersurfaces. Serbian spruce grows slowly to a height of 50 or 60 feet after 60 years but is only 15 feet wide at the base; it may ultimately become 90 feet tall.

Moerheim Colorado spruce, Zones 2-7, of broader conical shape, has needles that are a striking blue. It is the best suited of the spruces to urban locations, for it resists pollutants. At maturity, in 35 to 50 years, it may attain a height of 50 feet, but it is at its best for the first half of its life and may need to be removed before it reaches full size.

PINE See *Pinus*
PINE, UMBRELLA See *Sciadopitys*

PINUS
P. cembra (Swiss stone pine); *P. nigra*, also called *P. austriaca* (Austrian pine, black pine); *P. resinosa* (red pine, Norway pine); *P. strobus* (eastern white pine, Weymouth pine); *P. sylvestris* (Scotch pine)

There is a pine tree for just about every part of North America, for pines grow in warm climates or cold, in sandy or clay soil, in pure air, polluted air or salty sea spray. As a group they are hardy in Zones 2-7, and the ornamental species listed here generally resist the pests and diseases that may attack other pines. All pines should be grown in full sun; otherwise they may become thin and straggly.

The Swiss stone pine matures slowly and is excellent for formal plantings and small gardens. Very narrow and conical in its youth, with dense, dark blue-green foliage, it becomes round-topped and less uniform after it reaches its mature height of 25 feet in 25 to 30 years. The sturdy Austrian pine grows only in Zones 4-8; it withstands urban pollution, salt spray, wind, drought or heat and adapts to either alkaline or

For climate zones and frost dates, see maps, pages 148-149.

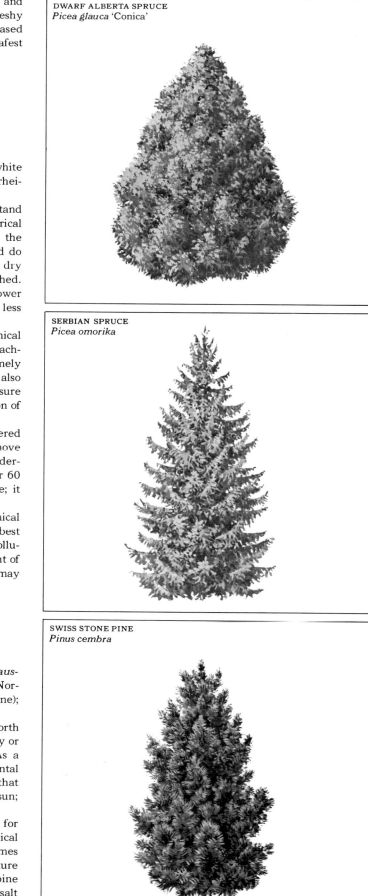

DWARF ALBERTA SPRUCE
Picea glauca 'Conica'

SERBIAN SPRUCE
Picea omorika

SWISS STONE PINE
Pinus cembra

RED PINE
Pinus resinosa

GOLDEN LARCH
Pseudolarix amabilis

DOUGLAS FIR
Pseudotsuga menziesii

acid soil. A symmetrical cone shape when young, it grows rapidly, developing an open, rounded shape at maturity, when it is 20 to 30 years old and 35 to 50 feet tall. It is useful in a windbreak or screen planting.

The stately red pine will grow in poor soil and does best in sandy ground; it tolerates both wet and dry soil conditions. Growing rapidly, as much as two feet a year when young, the red pine may become 50 feet tall after 25 or 30 years. Its reddish-brown bark and its wide-spreading branches hung with lustrous, dark green needles make it a colorful accent plant in a winter garden.

The eastern white pine, often considered the most beautiful of the American pines, tolerates partial shade but needs sandy soil and should be sheltered from winter winds. It does not do well south of Zone 7. Easily transplanted, the eastern white pine is a valuable specimen or background tree because of its soft blue-green color. It grows rapidly, about 2 feet a year, and develops an open rounded shape at maturity, when it is 25 to 40 years old and 50 to 75 feet tall.

The Scotch pine, also a rapid-growing tree, does well in either wet or dry soil and is hardy in Zones 2-8. With its stiff, gray- or blue-green needles, orange-brown bark and crooked wind-swept shape, it is a striking feature of any landscape. When it is mature, at 35 to 60 years, the Scotch pine stands from 40 to 70 feet tall.

PORT ORFORD CEDAR See *Chamaecyparis*

PSEUDOLARIX
P. amabilis, also called *P. kaempferi, Chrysolarix amabilis* (golden larch)

This curious conifer, whose needles turn golden yellow and drop off in the fall, has no known enemies; it grows untroubled by insects or diseases and may live 100 years. It thrives in a moist, well-drained acid soil in Zones 6 and 7, and should be planted in full sun, sheltered from the wind. The golden larch is not a tree for small gardens. At 70 years it may be only 45 feet tall, but its branch spread will equal its height. Ultimately it may become 120 feet tall.

As a lawn tree, the golden larch in fall is decorative against the dark green of other conifers, and in winter its bare horizontal branches spread across the snowy landscape.

PSEUDOTSUGA
P. menziesii, also called *P. douglasii, P. mucronata, P. taxifolia* (Douglas fir, Douglas spruce, red fir)

The tall, straight Douglas fir, basis of much of the West Coast lumbering industry, is a graceful addition to a large garden. It grows quickly, adding 1 to 2 feet a year in moist, slightly acid well-drained soil, although porous, sandy soil will slow its growth. It thrives in full sun, tolerates dappled shade, and is hardy in Zones 5 and 6. For gardens in the eastern United States it is best to use plants raised in the Rockies, sometimes labeled *P. menziesii glauca;* seedlings from the Pacific seacoast are less hardy.

In cultivation the Douglas fir grows between 40 and 100 feet high in 50 to 75 years. Its shape is broadly conical, with upward curving or pendulous branches, depending on the variety. The needles are short, soft and blue-green; the cones, hanging from the undersides of the branches, may be as much as 4½ inches long.

QUERCUS
Q. virginiana (live oak)

Of the several species of evergreen oak, the live oak adapts best to a wide variation in climate. It grows throughout Zones 8-10, its tough wood seldom damaged by summer storms and unpredictable spells of cold. In the northernmost areas of its range, however, it may be deciduous, losing its shiny, leathery leaves in the autumn. The live oak grows best in moist soil and full sun but it will tolerate partial shade. It eventually attains massive proportions. At its full height of 50 to 60 feet, which it reaches in 35 to 40 years, the spread of its horizontal branches may be wider than the tree is tall and its trunk may be as much as 35 feet around. Because of its size it should only be planted in large gardens.

RED CEDAR See *Juniperus*
RED CEDAR, WESTERN See *Thuja*
RED FIR See *Pseudotsuga*
RED PINE See *Pinus*

SCIADOPITYS
S. verticillata (umbrella pine)

The symmetrical, slow-growing umbrella pine is the epitome of an easy-care lawn tree. It is pest and disease free, requires no pruning, keeps its needles for two or three years, and its lower branches stay full and green. It is hardy in Zones 5-8, growing best in deep, moist, neutral-to-acid soil and in full sun except where the summers are hot; in this case, the tree should be planted where it will be shaded from the intense late-afternoon sun. It should also be planted where there is protection from the wind. The umbrella pine has long, dark green, shiny needles and a pyramidal shape. It grows only 6 inches a year—it takes about 50 years for the tree to become 25 to 30 feet tall.

SCOTCH PINE See *Pinus*
SERBIAN SPRUCE See *Picea*
SILVER RED CEDAR See *Juniperus*
SOUTHERN MAGNOLIA See *Magnolia*
SPRUCE See *Picea*
SPRUCE, DOUGLAS See *Pseudotsuga*
STONE PINE, SWISS See *Pinus*
SWISS STONE PINE See *Pinus*

THUJA
T. plicata (giant arborvitae, western red cedar); *T. plicata* 'Fastigiata' (columnar giant arborvitae)

A long-lived tree that seldom needs pruning, giant arborvitae grows relatively fast into a specimen tree for a large lawn or to form a tall screen. It grows best in full sun, though it tolerates partial shade. Giant arborvitae will flourish in any moist, well-drained soil and thrives in high humidity. Its flat, scalelike needles, unlike those of other arborvitaes, remain green through the winter. Even when it is old, the tree keeps its huge lower branches and never looks thin or unsightly. Giant arborvitae can withstand temperatures down to $-10°$ in Zones 6-8. Trees grown from seeds from the mountains of Montana and Utah are most resistant to winter damage.

The giant arborvitae forms a narrow pyramid that is 50 or more feet tall and about 20 feet wide in 40 to 60 years. The columnar giant arborvitae grows slender and dense; it can be sheared easily as a neat hedge. These trees can be shortened by clipping off top branches.

TSUGA
T. canadensis (Canada hemlock); *T. caroliniana* (Carolina hemlock)

With dipping branches and soft, feather-like dark green needles, both of these hemlock species rank high among attractive, easy-to-grow evergreens. At every stage, they

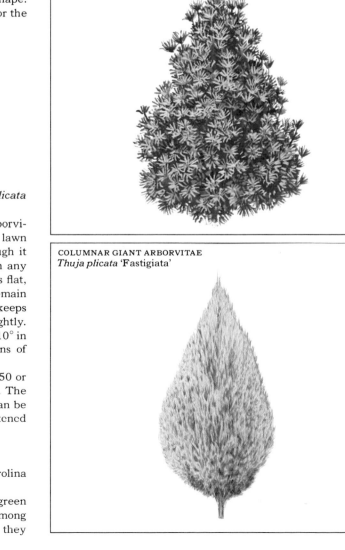

LIVE OAK
Quercus virginiana

UMBRELLA PINE
Sciadopitys verticillata

COLUMNAR GIANT ARBORVITAE
Thuja plicata 'Fastigiata'

For climate zones and frost dates, see maps, pages 148-149.

CAROLINA HEMLOCK
Tsuga caroliniana

WOOLLY YARROW
Achillea tomentosa

AMERICAN COLUMBINE
Aquilegia canadensis

maintain their graceful contours with no pruning. Planted as hedges, they withstand shearing well. They are rarely troubled by pests. They grow well in either full sun or partial shade and prefer a cool, moist, slightly acid soil. Severe wind or winter sun will damage young trees. In their southern areas of growth, they do best in partial shade.

The Canada hemlock, a hardy tree, can withstand temperatures down to $-30°$ in Zones 4-7. This cone-shaped species usually grows 25 to 50 feet tall in 15 to 30 years; its maximum height is 90 feet. Its varieties range in contour from narrow columns and flat globes to low-growing dwarfs. Carolina hemlock, hardy in Zones 4-8, grows well in polluted urban areas where other hemlocks do not. The compact, pyramidal tree becomes 15 to 40 feet tall in 15 to 20 years, reaching a maximum height of up to 70 feet.

UMBRELLA PINE See *Sciadopitys*

WEYMOUTH PINE See *Pinus*
WHITE FIR See *Abies*
WHITE PINE, EASTERN See *Pinus*
WHITE SPRUCE, DWARF See *Picea*

Perennials

ACHILLEA
A. filipendulina, also called *A. eupatorium* (fern-leaved yarrow); *A. millefolium* (common yarrow, milfoil); *A. tomentosa* (woolly yarrow)

Drought-resistant yarrows bloom reliably in poor soil when given a sunny, well-drained position. They are suited to gardens throughout Zones 3-10 where the soil has not been enriched by the addition of organic matter. Most yarrows have fernlike foliage, aromatic when crushed, that is neat and attractive throughout the growing season. The flowers bloom in large, flat-topped clusters in the summer. Yarrow grows so vigorously that plants may need division every three or four years to prevent overcrowding.

Fern-leaved yarrow has strong stalks 4 feet tall that bear 4- to 6-inch yellow flower clusters; it may require staking in a windy area. Common yarrow's foliage stays green almost all winter. This plant grows up to 18 inches tall and forms a dense mat; it is sometimes used as a ground cover and sheared after it blooms. The white flowers appear in 2- to 3-inch clusters. Woolly yarrow's 6- to 12-inch stalks bear fuzzy gray-green foliage and yellow flower clusters up to 2 inches across. It is also sometimes used as a ground cover and sheared. As a border plant it may need division more frequently than other species.

ALUMROOT See *Heuchera*
AMERICAN COLUMBINE See *Aquilegia*

AQUILEGIA
A. caerulea (Rocky Mountain columbine, Colorado columbine); *A canadensis* (American columbine, eastern columbine); *A. hybrida* (hybrid columbine)

The adaptable columbines grow in Zones 4-10 in moist, well-drained soil. Although there is less tendency for plants to dry when they are grown in partial shade, which prolongs the flowering season, columbines will tolerate sun as long as the soil is moist. A columbine's chief disadvantage is that it declines in vigor after about three years and must be replaced; it cannot be renewed by dividing it.

Columbines are suitable for both borders and rock gardens. They bloom from late spring into summer, bearing distinctively spurred one- or two-colored flowers up to 4 inches across. Rocky Mountain columbine has 2- to 3-inch blue-and-white flowers on stems up to 2½ feet tall. American columbine, parent to many modern hybrids, can tolerate dry, sandy soil. It bears flowers with yellow petals and red spurs on 3- to 4-foot stems. Of the numerous hybrids, which produce 3- to 4-inch flowers in a wide color range, the McKana hybrids are favorites; they produce long-spurred flowers on plants up to 3 feet tall.

ASTER

A. frikartii 'Wonder of Staffa' (Wonder of Staffa aster); *A. novae-angliae* (New England aster); *A. novi-belgii* (New York aster)

These three asters are long-lived perennials that flower freely in sunny, well-drained locations. For a wide range of late-summer to early-fall color, asters are more reliable than chrysanthemums because they live longer and are easier to grow. Asters bloom in almost every hue except yellow, and plants range in height from less than a foot to almost 6 feet. Those more than 2 feet high may require staking, but the low-maintenance gardener can do this by placing twiggy tree branches among the young plants to support them; the foliage of mature plants will hide these casual underpinnings.

Most asters require one periodic gardening chore—clumps must be divided every two or three years in spring or fall to retain vigor and maximum flower size. Clumps that are left undivided become crowded, increasing the dampness around their foliage and thus their susceptibility to rust and mildew diseases. One exception is Wonder of Staffa aster, a sturdy hybrid that requires division only every fourth year. It tolerates drier growing conditions than the other two asters listed here, blooms earlier and longer, and has 1½- to 2-foot stems. It is, however, less hardy and less colorful than the New York and New England asters, growing only in Zones 5-8 and producing fragrant 2½-inch flowers in lavender only.

The New England and New York asters, parents of many notable hybrids, are hardy in Zones 4-8. The New England aster offers a more limited color palette than the New York species, but its vigor and ability to reseed itself recommend it for low-maintenance gardens. Ranging from 3 to 5 feet in height, varieties of New England aster bear 1½- to 2-inch flowers from pink to purple among hairy foliage. New York asters offer not only a wide choice of colors but also of sizes. There are 9- to 18-inch dwarfs suitable for rock gardens, edgings or ground covers, up to 3- or 4-foot hybrids useful in borders. New York asters are slightly more susceptible to mildew and rust than the others.

ASTILBE

A. arendsii (astilbe, false spirea); *A. japonica* (Japanese astilbe)

This perennial, hardy in Zones 4-8, rises year after year if it is given the right growing conditions. It blooms most profusely in partial shade and well-drained garden soil if the soil is evenly and constantly moist. Avoid planting it where the soil dries out quickly or where drainage is poor. Astilbe will also grow and flower in full sun if there is enough organic material in the soil to hold moisture. The plant's one drawback is that it rapidly depletes nutrients in the soil and, when undernourished, produces fewer flowers. To remedy this, astilbe must be fertilized and may need to be divided every two or three years in spring or fall. Gardeners who attend to this occasional chore are rewarded by a two-month profusion of plumelike flower clusters up to a foot long in midsummer. Astilbe grows 2 feet high and blooms in shades of white

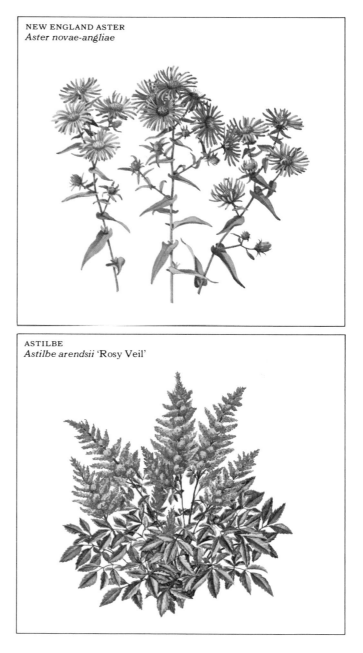

NEW ENGLAND ASTER
Aster novae-angliae

ASTILBE
Astilbe arendsii 'Rosy Veil'

For climate zones and frost dates, see maps, pages 148-149.

through pink, lavender, and red; varieties of Japanese astilbe have white to red flowers.

BACHELOR'S-BUTTON, PERENNIAL See *Centaurea*
BALLOONFLOWER See *Platycodon*
BELLFLOWER, CLUSTERED See *Campanula*
BELLFLOWER, JAPANESE See *Platycodon*
BELLFLOWER, PEACH-LEAVED See *Campanula*
BETONY, WOOLLY See *Stachys*
BLANKETFLOWER See *Gaillardia*
BLEEDING HEART See *Dicentra*
BLOOD-RED CRANE'S-BILL See *Geranium*
BLOOD-RED GERANIUM See *Geranium*
BLUEBELL, TUSSOCK See *Campanula*
BLUET, MOUNTAIN See *Centaurea*

CAMPANULA

C. carpatica (Carpathian harebell, tussock bluebell); *C. glomerata* (clustered bellflower); *C. persicifolia* (peach-leaved bellflower)

While many perennials require division every two or three years to keep them growing vigorously, these bellflowers prefer to be left undisturbed for four or five years. They grow in Zones 4-8 in full sun or partial shade and almost any well-drained garden soil.

The Carpathian harebell forms small, round 4- to 6-inch clumps of foliage; the blue, violet or white flat-cupped flowers rise on wiry stems in summer. The clustered bellflower forms neat 1- to 2-foot mounds of dense foliage in sun, but in shaded locations it tends to spread and become invasive. Clusters of white, blue or purple 1-inch bells appear from late spring until early summer. The peach-leaved bellflower is a particularly durable species—its single-flowered varieties will reseed themselves. It bears 1½-inch white or blue flowers on stems up to 3 feet tall in summer; some hybrids grow even taller and produce larger flowers.

CANDYTUFT, EVERGREEN See *Iberis*
CARPATHIAN HAREBELL See *Campanula*
CAUCASIAN LEOPARD'S-BANE, MISS MASON See *Doronicum*

CENTAUREA

C. cineraria, also called *C. rutifolia, C. candidissima* (dusty miller); *C. montana* (mountain bluet, perennial bachelor's-button)

Well-drained soil and a sunny location satisfy the needs of both of these widely differing centaurea species. Dusty miller is a popular perennial in Zones 9 and 10 and a reliable annual as far north as Zone 4. The gray, fernlike foliage covered with soft white hairs contrasts with its small yellow or purple flowers in summer. Its 12- to 18-inch silver mounds are ideal as edging plants. Grown as a perennial, dusty miller should be divided in the spring about every four years to prevent crowding.

Mountain bluet thrives in Zones 4-8 and bears large, elegant blue flowers that appear earlier than those of most perennials, then continues to bloom into midsummer. Often it produces a second crop of blossoms in autumn. This hardy plant spreads rapidly.

CHINESE PEONY See *Paeonia*
CLUMP SPEEDWELL See *Veronica*
CLUSTERED BELLFLOWER See *Campanula*
COLORADO COLUMBINE See *Aquilegia*
COLUMBINE See *Aquilegia*

CARPATHIAN HAREBELL
Campanula carpatica

MOUNTAIN BLUET
Centaurea montana

COMMON BLEEDING HEART See *Dicentra*
COMMON PEONY See *Paeonia*
COMMON YARROW See *Achillea*
CONEFLOWER, ORANGE See *Rudbeckia*
CORAL-BELLS See *Heuchera*

COREOPSIS
C. auriculata 'Nana' (dwarf eared coreopsis); *C. grandiflora* (big-flowered coreopsis); *C. verticillata* (thread-leaved coreopsis)

The daisy-like coreopsis, which flowers freely through the summer, will thrive even if left untended. Planted in spring or fall, it grows well even in infertile soil in any sunny, well-drained location. Hardy in Zones 4-10, the perennial is extremely easy to propagate by clump division but can be left undisturbed for years. It is not necessary to fertilize coreopsis and the plants do not need staking. All species produce excellent cut flowers.

Dwarf eared coreopsis grows up to 6 inches tall and may be used as a ground cover or as an edging in the front of a border. It bears 2-inch orange-yellow flowers. Big-flowered coreopsis bears a profusion of golden-yellow flowers, 2 to 3 inches across, on bushy plants that reach 3 feet in height. Thread-leaved coreopsis has narrow, finely divided leaves on stems 1 to 2 feet tall and produces yellow blossoms 2 inches in diameter.

CRANE'S-BILL, BLOOD-RED See *Geranium*

DAY LILY See *Hemerocallis*

DICENTRA (DIELYTRA)
D. eximia (fringed bleeding heart, plumed bleeding heart); *D. formosa* (western bleeding heart, Pacific bleeding heart); *D. spectabilis* (common bleeding heart)

The bleeding hearts have simple requirements, the most important of which is a moist, well-drained site where the soil has been enriched with organic matter. These sturdy perennials grow best in partial shade but will tolerate full sun if the soil is kept moist. Bleeding hearts grow in Zones 2-10 except in Florida and along the Gulf Coast; they live as long as 20 years in Zones 2-7 but may live only five years in Zones 8-10 because of the long hot summers. When plants are divided every third or fourth spring, care should be taken not to damage the brittle roots.

These perennials are prized for the heart-shaped flowers which dangle from arching stems and for their fernlike foliage. Fringed bleeding heart, an especially long-blooming species, produces small pink flowers from midspring through autumn. Western bleeding heart has rose-lavender flowers from spring to fall. Hybrids from these two species usually have more abundant flowers that are larger and more vivid in color than either of the parents. The common bleeding heart, a garden favorite for more than a century, bears large pink flowers in late spring. Fringed bleeding heart will seed itself and spread, while the western bleeding heart increases by underground runners.

DIELYTRA See *Dicentra*
DONKEY'S EARS See *Stachys*

DORONICUM
D. cordatum 'Miss Mason,' also called *D. caucasicum* 'Miss Mason' (Miss Mason Caucasian leopard's-bane)

Although most leopard's-bane varieties are a bane to the low-maintenance gardener because they require staking and

BIG-FLOWERED COREOPSIS
Coreopsis grandiflora 'Sunburst'

COMMON BLEEDING HEART
Dicentra spectabilis

MISS MASON CAUCASIAN LEOPARD'S-BANE
Doronicum cordatum 'Miss Mason'

For climate zones and frost dates, see maps, pages 148-149.

BLANKETFLOWER
Gaillardia aristata 'Goblin'

BLOOD-RED CRANE'S-BILL
Geranium sanguineum

drop their foliage in the summer, Miss Mason Caucasian leopard's-bane is an exception. Growing up to 18 inches tall, its mounds of ground-hugging heart-shaped leaves remain on the plant until autumn arrives.

Miss Mason grows in Zones 4-9 except in Florida and along the Gulf Coast. Give it sun or partial shade and plant it in moist but well-drained soil; otherwise its shallow roots may dry. This variety of leopard's-bane spreads by means of creeping underground runners and sometimes seeds itself. When plants become overcrowded, the 2-inch yellow flowers may decrease in size. To prevent this, divide the shallow root mats every two or three years.

DUSTY MILLER See *Centaurea*

EARED COREOPSIS, DWARF See *Coreopsis*
EASTERN COLUMBINE See *Aquilegia*
EVERGREEN CANDYTUFT See *Iberis*

FALSE SPIREA See *Astilbe*
FERN-LEAVED PEONY See *Paeonia*
FERN-LEAVED YARROW See *Achillea*
FRINGED BLEEDING HEART See *Dicentra*
FUNKIA See *Hosta*

GAILLARDIA
G. aristata, also called *G. grandiflora* (blanketflower, gaillardia)

The colorful blanketflower is an exceedingly easy perennial to grow in a low-maintenance garden. It often begins flowering in the same season that its seeds are sown. It is largely pest free and it can survive heat and drought. Blanketflower flourishes in Zones 3-10 and prefers full sun. It thrives and flowers best in most well-drained soils; planting in heavy clay should be avoided.

The hairy foliage of blanketflower grows in mounds that range in height from 8 inches to 3 feet, depending on the variety. The flowers, which may be red, yellow, or red and yellow combined, are 2½ to 4 inches across and rise out of the foliage on slender stems continuously from early summer to frost; the flowers, which resemble daisies, are ideal for cutting for indoor bouquets. Clumps of blanketflower may be divided every two or three years. Tall varieties need staking to keep them from sprawling.

GERANIUM
G. sanguineum (blood-red crane's-bill, blood-red geranium)

The blood-red crane's-bill grows and blooms most profusely in full sun and almost as well in partial shade and is best planted in poor to average soil. In very fertile soil, growth will be rampant and the perennial will need too much cutting back and dividing to qualify as a low-maintenance plant. Planted properly in Zones 4-10, these perennials need little maintenance and are relatively pest free. They should remain undisturbed for at least four years and can grow much longer without needing division.

Blood-red crane's-bill forms dense mounds of deeply lobed green foliage that becomes bright red in the autumn. The mounds grow 12 inches tall and have a spread of 24 inches. The plants flower throughout the summer; the 1- to 2-inch flowers are red-purple. Prostratum is an excellent dwarf variety whose attractive foliage forms a dense mound that is 4 to 6 inches high and 18 inches across. Its bright pink flowers blossom throughout the summer.

HAREBELL, CARPATHIAN See *Campanula*

HEMEROCALLIS

H. fulva 'Europa' (tawny day lily, orange day lily)

Able to adapt to a wide range of conditions, day lilies are among the most indestructible of garden perennials. They are never troubled by pests. They tolerate poor soil but bloom best in well-drained garden soil enriched with leaf mold or peat moss. Very fertile soil, however, may encourage foliage growth at the expense of flowers. Planted in full sun or partial shade in Zones 3-10, they require no maintenance. In areas with hot summers, afternoon shade is desirable. Although day lilies can survive indefinitely without division, plants will flower best if they are divided every four to six years in spring or fall.

Hundreds of hybrids are available, offering the lily-like flowers in a great range of colors and sizes and blooming times from May to October. The bright green arching foliage can be confined to loose open clumps or allowed to spread as a ground cover, especially useful for erosion control on banks. The tawny day lily is the variety most commonly seen in gardens, its orange-red flowers sometimes blooming at a height up to 5 feet. *H.* Primrose Mascotte forms clumps of foliage with pale yellow flowers that make an attractive foreground planting. It grows to about 20 inches in height.

HEUCHERA

H. sanguinea (coral-bells, alumroot)

Long-lasting ground-hugging plants able to grow in either full sun or partial shade, coral-bells are a good choice for borders or rock gardens. Except for the removal of faded flower stalks to prolong flowering, they require maintenance infrequently. They do not spread, and they need dividing only every four to six years. Coral-bells bloom from late spring through late summer, and their rounded evergreen leaves remain attractive all year long. Plants do best in moist, well-drained soil enriched with organic matter, with their crowns set 1 inch below the soil level. To ensure that the roots become established, coral-bells should be planted in spring. In the north they should be mulched in winter to keep the plants from heaving if the ground freezes. Their crowns may have to be pushed back into the soil in spring.

These perennials grow throughout Zones 4-10 except in Florida and along the Gulf Coast. They have mounds of foliage 4 to 6 inches high with flower stalks 1 to 2 feet tall. These produce hundreds of ¼-inch flowers in colors ranging from pure white to brilliant red, depending upon the variety.

HOSTA (FUNKIA)

H. plantaginca, also called *H. subcordata grandiflora* (fragrant plantain lily)

Needing almost no maintenance, hostas provide striking accents of lush foliage from spring to autumn frost in Zones 3-9. Although they grow best in partial shade, some species tolerate full sun to deep shade. Moist, well-drained soil enriched with leaf mold or peat moss is best, but hostas grow in a wide range of soils. Divisions planted in early spring can be left undisturbed indefinitely. Hostas are useful in perennial beds, in borders or as ground covers. They are also planted singly because of their attractive radial symmetry.

Fragrant plantain lily has bright greenish-yellow leaves 1 foot long and 6 inches wide, growing in mounds 1½ feet tall. The fragrant white flowers are borne on stalks that rise above the leaves in late summer and early autumn. There are over two hundred varieties of hosta to choose among. Leaves, which may be variegated, come in many shades of green and range up to a foot or more in length and breadth. Flowers come in white, blue and purple.

DWARF HYPERION DAY LILY
Hemerocallis 'Primrose Mascotte'

CORAL-BELLS
Heuchera sanguinea

PLANTAIN LILY
Hosta 'Royal Standard'

For climate zones and frost dates, see maps, pages 148-149.

EVERGREEN CANDYTUFT
Iberis sempervirens

RUSSELL HYBRID LUPINE
Lupinus 'Russell Hybrids'

CHINESE PEONY
Paeonia lactiflora 'Philippe Rivoire'

HUNGARIAN SPEEDWELL See *Veronica*

IBERIS
I. sempervirens (evergreen candytuft)

A low-maintenance edging plant able to grow in full sun or partial shade, evergreen candytuft needs well-drained soil; the plants may die if the soil is too wet in winter. This long-lived perennial is hardy in Zones 3-10, but in cold areas its small, narrow leaves may need to be protected with evergreen boughs. It resists the ill effects of air pollution. Useful in front of flower beds, as foundation plantings and in rock gardens, evergreen candytuft grows in mounds 6 to 9 inches tall that spread in an irregular circle up to 2 feet in diameter. From spring to early summer the plant is covered with flat clusters of small white flowers. After these blossoms fade, shearing off the old stems at least halfway encourages new growth and prevents the clumps from becoming woody and open. A second period of bloom in the fall sometimes occurs in southern regions.

JAPANESE ASTILBE See *Astilbe*
JAPANESE BELLFLOWER See *Platycodon*

LAMB'S EARS See *Stachys*
LEOPARD'S-BANE, CAUCASIAN See *Doronicum*
LILY, PLANTAIN See *Hosta*
LIVE-FOREVER See *Sedum*
LUPINE See *Lupinus*

LUPINUS
L. 'Russell Hybrids' (Russell hybrid lupine)

The rather particular requirements of Russell hybrid lupines include moist, well-drained, slightly acid soil, full sun or partial shade, and summers that are consistently cool and humid. Given these conditions, the plants will reward the gardener from late spring to midsummer with a grand display of flowers. Flower spikes 2½ to 3½ feet tall stand erect above 2-foot-tall clumps of deeply divided leaves. The large pealike flowers may be white, red, pink, yellow or blue, and some are bicolored. Since their flowering season is relatively short, they are best used at the back of a bed.

Lupines grow in Zones 4-7 and in West Coast sections of Zones 8 and 9. Where summer temperatures rise above 85°, mulch the soil to keep it as moist and cool as possible. If necessary, use insecticide to control the large lupine aphid, which can deform flower spikes.

MARIES' BALLOONFLOWER See *Platycodon*
MILFOIL See *Achillea*
MOUNTAIN BLUET See *Centaurea*

NEW ENGLAND ASTER See *Aster*
NEW YORK ASTER See *Aster*

ORIENTAL POPPY See *Papaver*

PACIFIC BLEEDING HEART See *Dicentra*

PAEONIA
P. lactiflora, also called *P. albiflora* (Chinese peony); *P. officinalis* (common peony); *P. tenuifolia* (fern-leaved peony)

Peonies survive winter temperatures of −40° and seem to thrive on neglect; they have been known to flourish untended in the same place for 30 years or more. Their blossoms are full and fragrant; their neat, glossy foliage stays green until frost; and their roots thrive in almost any well-drained soil, though a slightly acid one is best. They grow best in full sun but will tolerate partial shade. They are hardy in Zones 3-8 and in the West Coast area of Zone 9.

Peonies are used as accent plants, as hedges or in beds, and they make good cut flowers. They should be planted carefully with their crown buds no more than 2 inches below the soil level; they may not flower if planted deeper. Do not be alarmed by the ants that appear on the flower buds; they are harmless and actually aid the plant's flowering.

June-blooming Chinese peonies produce single or double white, pink or red blossoms up to 6 inches wide. Common peonies bloom in late May with single or double blossoms 4 inches across in the same colors. Fern-leaved peonies have dense, deeply cut foliage and the 3½-inch crimson flowers bloom in late May. A desirable garden variety is the double-flowered *P. tenuifolia* Flore-pleno.

PAPAVER
P. orientale (Oriental poppy)

June-blooming Oriental poppies grow in Zones 3-8 and in cool parts of Zone 9. They need full sun and a light, sandy, well-drained garden soil. Wet soil, especially in winter, will kill them. Seldom bothered by pests or diseases, Oriental poppies require only that the flowers of larger varieties be staked. These graceful, open plants produce brilliantly colored tissue-like blossoms 6 to 12 inches across on stems 2 to 4 feet tall. By midsummer the flowers fade and the coarse, hairy foliage dies back to the ground, so Oriental poppies should be planted among other perennials that will fill in the gaps. In fall new foliage appears and remains through the winter. Division every five years in late summer is recommended. Newly planted Oriental poppies will not flower until the second year. Mulch new plants during their first winter around, but not over, the foliage.

PEACH-LEAVED BELLFLOWER See *Campanula*
PEONY See *Paeonia*
PLANTAIN LILY See *Hosta*

PLATYCODON
P. grandiflorus 'Mariesii' (Maries' balloonflower, Japanese bellflower)

Thriving for more than 20 years if left undisturbed, Maries' balloonflower needs only light, well-drained soil to flourish. No maintenance is necessary; pests and diseases are rarely a problem. The plant is hardy in Zones 3-10 except in Florida and along the Gulf Coast. This violet-blue-flowered variety, unlike others of the same color, can adapt to partial shade, but it grows best in full sun. Its height of 12 to 18 inches eliminates the need for the staking required by taller varieties. To avoid root rot, Maries' balloonflower should not be planted in wet soil. Since plants do not begin growing until late spring, they should be marked so they will not be dug up inadvertently during early cultivation.

Each plant grows slowly, eventually forming a clump 1½ feet wide. Clumps do not spread and should not be divided. The 2- to 3-inch star-shaped flowers appear all summer.

PLUMED BLEEDING HEART See *Dicentra*
POLYANTHUS PRIMROSE See *Primula*
POPPY, ORIENTAL See *Papaver*
PRIMROSE, POLYANTHUS See *Primula*

PRIMULA
P. polyantha (polyanthus primrose)

Easiest of the primroses to grow, polyanthus thrives in

ORIENTAL POPPY
Papaver orientale

MARIES' BALLOONFLOWER
Platycodon grandiflorus 'Mariesii'

POLYANTHUS PRIMROSE
Primula polyantha

For climate zones and frost dates, see maps, pages 148-149.

RUDBECKIA
Rudbeckia fulgida 'Goldsturm'

SHOWY STONECROP
Sedum spectabile 'Meteor'

partial shade in moist, well-drained slightly acid soil that is supplemented with organic matter such as leaf mold. A hybrid, the polyanthus primrose has flowers in a wide range of solid and variegated colors; they appear in midspring. These primroses can be grown in Zones 3-8 if given a summer mulch in dry areas to keep the soil cool. In winter, cover plants with a light, airy mulch such as evergreen boughs to help prevent alternate thawing and freezing of the ground. Clumps may be divided every three or four years.

The oblong, roughly textured leaves of the polyanthus primrose grow in ground-hugging rosettes. Flowers appear in rounded clusters at the tops of 6- to 12-inch stalks. The plants are attractive when massed along partially shaded walks or the banks of streams.

ROCKY MOUNTAIN COLUMBINE See *Aquilegia*

RUDBECKIA
R. fulgida 'Goldsturm' (rudbeckia, orange coneflower)
One of the hardiest and most colorful of the rudbeckias, the Goldsturm variety is a spreading plant that flourishes in Zones 3-10 in full sun; it will also tolerate partial shade, although it does not flower as freely. This perennial not only maintains its vivid color in all but the driest of garden soils— provided the soils are well drained—but it is also more tolerant of moist soil than other rudbeckia varieties. Rarely invaded by pests or diseases, it requires no maintenance other than the division of clumps every four or five years. These plants create a bright, informal effect in a border or in a meadow garden.

With rough-textured foliage growing in open clumps, this rudbeckia bears many large, deep golden yellow daisy-like blossoms with dark brown centers on erect stems 2 feet tall. Flowers bloom from midsummer to midfall. They are excellent for cutting.

RUSSELL HYBRID LUPINE See *Lupinus*

SEDUM
S. spectabile (showy stonecrop, live-forever, sedum)
The most ornamental of the sedums is also one of the toughest. Showy stonecrop grows in almost any soil, provided it is well drained. Thriving in either full sun or partial shade, it tolerates dry conditions and is rarely bothered by pests or diseases. It is a plant known for its durability and it can be left undisturbed for years; division is used only for propagation. Showy stonecrop can be grown in Zones 3-10. It is best displayed in clumps of one to three plants near the front of borders or in rock gardens.

This perennial does not spread but grows slowly to form a dense gray-green mound of foliage 18 inches tall and equally wide. From late summer through late fall, 3- to 4-inch clusters of tiny rose-pink flowers appear. The flowers of different varieties may be white or tones of pink or red.

SPEEDWELL See *Veronica*
SPIKE SPEEDWELL See *Veronica*
SPIREA, FALSE See *Astilbe*

STACHYS
S. byzantina, also called *S. olympica, S. lanata* (lamb's ears, woolly betony, donkey's ears)
Easily grown in almost any well-drained soil, lamb's ears thrives in full sun. This woolly silvery green ground-hugging perennial is rarely attacked by pests or diseases and grows throughout Zones 3-10 except in Florida and along the Gulf

Coast. Chiefly used as an edging plant, it can become invasive if the soil is fertile. Ordinarily the clumps require division only every three or four years. Faded flower spikes must be removed to keep the plants blooming from early summer until frost.

Lamb's ears has tongue-shaped leaves that are densely covered with soft, woolly white hairs. The plants grow in clumps that become 2 to 3 feet in diameter but are only 12 to 18 inches tall. Spikes of pinkish-purple flowers rise up to 1½ feet in midsummer.

STONECROP, SHOWY See *Sedum*

TAWNY DAY LILY See *Hemerocallis*
THREAD-LEAVED COREOPSIS See *Coreopsis*
TUSSOCK BLUEBELL See *Campanula*

VERONICA
V. incana (woolly speedwell); *V. latifolia* (Hungarian speedwell); *V. longifolia,* also called *V. maritima* (clump speedwell); *V. spicata* 'Minuet' (spike speedwell)

The many varieties of speedwell provide low-maintenance flowers throughout the summer. Relatively free of pests and diseases, speedwells grow in full sun or partial shade in almost any soil provided it is well drained; good drainage is especially important during the winter. Speedwells can be grown in Zones 3-10 except in Florida and along the Gulf Coast. Upright stems form open clumps that should be divided after three or four years of flowering.

Speedwell can be planted as a single specimen or massed in groups. Most species grow from 1 to 2 feet tall and bear long spikes of densely packed small blue flowers. Woolly speedwell has silvery stems and leaves and, from early to midsummer, bears light-blue flowers. A variety of Hungarian speedwell, Crater Lake Blue, produces deep blue flowers. Some varieties of clump speedwell have white, lilac or blue flowers from midsummer to fall. Spike speedwell Minuet flowers all summer.

WESTERN BLEEDING HEART See *Dicentra*
WONDER OF STAFFA ASTER See *Aster*
WOOLLY BETONY See *Stachys*
WOOLLY SPEEDWELL See *Veronica*
WOOLLY YARROW See *Achillea*

YARROW See *Achillea*

Ground covers
AARONSBEARD ST.-JOHN'S-WORT See *Hypericum*
AFRICAN DAISY, TRAILING See *Osteospermum*

AJUGA
A. reptans (bugleweed, carpet bugle, ajuga)

As a low ground cover, bugleweed requires no special care except a very light raking to whisk away any dead leaves that fall on it. It grows in either full sun or shade; thrives in rich, moist soil but does not require it, and spreads rapidly by surface runners. The plant chokes out weeds but is shallow rooted enough to grow in rock crevices.

Bugleweed bears flat rosettes of glossy leaves, each 2 to 4 inches long. The foliage, which may be bronze, purple, deep green or variegated cream and green, depending on the variety, turns reddish-bronze in the fall. In the southern part of its range, Zones 8-10, the leaves stay bronze all winter. In the north, Zones 4-7, they drop off in winter but the plant

LAMB'S EARS
Stachys byzantina

SPIKE SPEEDWELL
Veronica spicata 'Minuet'

BUGLEWEED
Ajuga reptans

For climate zones and frost dates, see maps, pages 148-149.

BEARBERRY
Arctostaphylos uva-ursi

SWEET WOODRUFF
Asperula odorata

LILY OF THE VALLEY
Convallaria majalis

survives temperatures as low as −10°. Spikes bearing blue, rosy purple or white blossoms poke up 4 to 6 inches above the foliage in spring.

ARCHANGEL, YELLOW VARIEGATED See *Lamium*

ARCTOSTAPHYLOS
A. uva-ursi (bearberry, kinnikinnick)

Bearberry, a native evergreen, grows best in soil that is not especially rich and makes an excellent low-maintenance ground cover for rocky or sandy sites. Growing wild on sand dunes and mountainsides, bearberry withstands wind and drought. It can be cultivated in Zones 2-7, and while it benefits from mulching for weed control when young, it can be virtually forgotten once established. A low, slow-growing shrub, bearberry never needs pruning and grows well in full sun or partial shade. It is difficult to transplant unless it has been grown in a container.

Mature bearberry stands 6 to 12 inches tall with trailing branches that root as they creep up to 15 feet along the ground. The plant's leathery, shiny leaves are dark green and about an inch long. In autumn they turn bronze. Pinkish flowers, tiny and bell-like, bloom in spring, followed by red berries that attract birds.

ASPERULA
A. odorata, also called *Galium odoratum* (sweet woodruff)

Few summer ground covers are easier to grow than sweet woodruff, especially in the shade of a rhododendron shrub or among the shallow roots of a maple tree. This aromatic perennial grows 6 to 8 inches high in Zones 4-9 except in Florida. It spreads rapidly, given shade and a moist, humus-rich, acid soil. Though it dies back to the ground each fall, sweet woodruff renews itself easily in the spring. It never needs dividing, but new plants can be started by dividing clumps in spring or early fall.

Mature beds of sweet woodruff are thick and green. Star-like whorls of eight 1- to 2-inch leaves ascend around unusual square stems. Clusters of tiny white flowers blossom through spring and early summer. Dried leaves and stems have the fragrance of newly cut hay.

BABY WINTER CREEPER See *Euonymus*
BARRENWORT See *Epimedium*
BEARBERRY See *Arctostaphylos*
BEARBERRY COTONEASTER See Cotoneaster
BIG BLUE LILY-TURF See *Liriope*
BISHOP'S HAT See *Epimedium*
BLUE LILY-TURF, BIG See *Liriope*
BUGLEWEED See *Ajuga*

CANBY PACHISTIMA See *Paxistima*
CAPE MARIGOLD See *Osteospermum*
CARPET BUGLE See *Ajuga*
CARPET JUNIPER, WILTON See *Juniperus*
CINERARIA See *Senecio*

CONVALLARIA
C. majalis (lily of the valley)

The white bell-shaped flowers of lily of the valley brighten areas of dense shade beneath trees and along north walls where few other plants will grow, much less bloom. In rich soil or poor, it will spread slowly to form a thick carpet of green that remains attractive from early spring to late summer. Hardy in Zones 2-7 and rarely troubled by pests and diseases, this easy ground cover requires virtually no care, although it benefits from a mulch to conserve moisture. The 8-inch-high foliage cannot be walked on and dies down in fall, leaving the ground bare until spring.

Lily of the valley multiplies from spreading underground stems, each plant sending up a pair of green leaves that envelop the upright flower stalk. New plants can be propagated by dividing clumps at any season. The delicately fragrant flowers are often used in wedding bouquets.

CORONILLA
C. varia (crown vetch)

A fast-spreading creeper 1 to 2 feet high, crown vetch is a vigorous ground cover that chokes out weeds and halts soil erosion on slopes with its tough nets of roots and underground stems. This drought-resistant plant requires no watering once it is established, and it does not need to be fertilized. It can be sheared to the ground in spring to encourage bushy new growth. It dies back to the ground in winter, but a single plant may become as large as 4 feet in diameter in a single season.

Crown vetch thrives in full sun and tolerates partial shade. It can be planted even in poor soil and will grow almost anywhere in Zones 3-10. It is, however, best planted away from lawns where its fast growth could make it a chore to keep under control. The glossy frondlike leaves of crown vetch are about 6 inches long. From late spring through fall the plant bears dense clusters of attractive pink-and-white flowers that resemble tiny sweet peas.

CORSICAN PEARLWORT See *Sagina*

COTONEASTER
C. dammeri (bearberry cotoneaster); *C. horizontalis* (rock spray, rock cotoneaster)

These graceful, deep-rooted ground-cover shrubs will cling tenaciously to steep banks and rocky hillsides and thrive in almost any rather dry soil. They seldom require watering, tolerate wind well and almost never need pruning. Cotoneasters can be planted in sunny areas or in partial shade and are hardy in Zones 5-10.

Bearberry cotoneaster, a prostrate evergreen, spreads in a dense mat 6 to 12 inches thick. Its trailing branches, bearing glossy 1-inch dark green leaves, will root at their leaf joints in moist soil. Small white flowers bloom in spring and are followed by brilliant red berries.

Rock spray grows faster than bearberry cotoneaster but is only semievergreen at the northern edge of its hardiness range. It produces mounds 2 to 3 feet high as it spreads up to 10 feet in diameter. It bears shiny green ½-inch leaves and, in spring, pinkish flowers. In colder zones the leaves turn reddish in autumn and may drop in winter, leaving the exposed branches covered with bright red berries.

CREEPING LILY-TURF See *Liriope*
CREEPING MYRTLE See *Vinca*
CROWN VETCH See *Coronilla*

DEAD NETTLE, SPOTTED See *Lamium*
DIMORPHOTHECA See *Osteospermum*
DWARF LILY-TURF See *Ophiopogon*

ENGLISH IVY See *Hedera*

EPIMEDIUM
E. grandiflorum, also called *E. macranthum* (bishop's hat, long-spurred epimedium, barrenwort)

CROWN VETCH
Coronilla varia

BEARBERRY COTONEASTER
Cotoneaster dammeri

For climate zones and frost dates, see maps, pages 148-149.

BISHOP'S HAT
Epimedium grandiflorum

BABY WINTER CREEPER
Euonymus fortunei 'Minima'

GALAX
Galax aphylla

Bishop's hat looks delicate but is not. It requires little maintenance and can survive temperatures as low as −40°. Tough rooted and slow spreading, this semievergreen can be grown successfully around tree trunks. Though a shady location is ideal, it will grow in full sun if kept moist. Plants are long lived and thinning is not necessary. They are not invasive and grow throughout Zones 3-8.

While a bed of bishop's hat can generally be ignored for years at a time, it will benefit from occasional mulching. Most leaves die between Thanksgiving and Christmas but do not drop, remaining as an attractive ground cover even in winter. Mowing or shearing once a year, in late winter, enhances the appearance of new foliage.

Bishop's hat is distinguished by 2- to 3-inch leathery, heart-shaped leaflets. Sprays of pink, pale yellow, white or violet flowers appear in late spring. The ½- to 1-inch blossoms are shaped like a bishop's miter. The dense foliage grows 9 to 12 inches high. Leaflets are pale green tinged with pink or red in spring, turning deep, glossy green in summer and reddish-bronze with the first frosts.

EUONYMUS
E. fortunei 'Colorata' (purple winter creeper); *E. fortunei* 'Minima' (baby winter creeper)

Winter creeper, a trailing evergreen vine, is a ground cover that is prized for its ease of care. Hardy in Zones 5-10, it thrives in either full sun or partial shade. It grows best in moist soil but is sufficiently drought resistant to survive in all but hot desert areas. It can be planted to hold slopes against erosion, or it can ramble over tree stumps or rocks. The stems root where they touch moist soil. Plants do not flower or produce fruit.

The leathery leaves of purple winter creeper are up to 2 inches long, oval shaped and deep green in summer. They turn vivid purple in fall and last through the winter. The plants grow 6 inches tall and spread up to 4 feet. Baby winter creeper grows only 2 inches tall; its leaves are green with white veins and are only ½ inch long.

Until the plants mature to form a dense, weed-choking carpet, the bed should be mulched to discourage weeds. Euonymus scale may infest winter creeper.

FLEECEFLOWER See *Polygonum*

GALAX
G. aphylla, also called *G. urceolata* (galax)

Attractive the year round, a dense carpet of galax makes an outstanding evergreen ground cover under rhododendrons and azaleas, where it is often found growing wild in southeastern woodlands. It is hardy in Zones 4-8, and requires little care if planted in a cool, moist, slightly acid soil in a shaded location. In a wild garden or a woodland rock garden, it spreads of its own accord by means of underground runners, but not intrusively so.

Although the heart-shaped glossy foliage is evergreen, it turns bronze in the fall except when it is planted in deep shade. The plants seldom grow more than 6 inches high, but in midsummer they produce 2-foot-tall stalks bearing tiny white flowers. Galax leaves, long-lasting when they are cut, are often used in floral decorations.

GALIUM See *Asperula*
GROUND PINK See *Phlox*
GROUNDSEL, SILVER See *Senecio*

HALL'S JAPANESE HONEYSUCKLE See *Lonicera*

HEDERA
H. helix (English ivy)

Of the species of ivy, the familiar English ivy probably makes the least demand on a gardener's time. This long-time favorite grows in Zones 5-10, adapts to any moist, well-drained soil and makes a handsome ground cover in sun or shade, although in deep shade its growth may be slow. It hosts no serious pests or diseases and is generally able to weather adverse growing conditions. In prolonged hot, dry spells, it may need to be watered, and in severe winters the normally evergreen foliage may be damaged.

English ivy takes several years to get established. Thereafter it spreads rapidly, forming a dense, dark green carpet 6 to 8 inches deep. English ivy is available in many varieties. Some have variegated leaves, others very small leaves (these grow slowly and are suited to small areas). Baltica is a particularly hardy variety.

HONEYSUCKLE See *Lonicera*

HYPERICUM
H. calycinum (Aaronsbeard St.-John's-wort)

With a strong root system that makes it an ideal ground cover for erosion-prone slopes, Aaronsbeard St.-John's-wort grows easily in well-drained soil and in full sun or partial shade. In Zones 9 and 10 its 2- to 4-inch oval leaves are evergreen; in Zones 6-8, they darken in winter. The plant does not need to be watered during a drought, although watering will make it look better.

The plants spread rapidly by underground runners, forming a dense weed-free mat 1 to 1½ feet high. In full sun the plants may become invasive, requiring the use of dividers to keep them from spreading. Large bright yellow flowers up to 3 inches across bloom profusely all summer.

IRISH MOSS See *Sagina*
IVY, ENGLISH See *Hedera*

JAPANESE FLEECEFLOWER, LOW See *Polygonum*
JAPANESE HONEYSUCKLE, HALL'S See *Lonicera*
JAPANESE SPURGE See *Pachysandra*
JUNIPER See *Juniperus*

JUNIPERUS
J. chinensis sargentii (Sargent juniper); J. conferta (shore juniper); J. horizontalis 'Wiltonii' (Wilton carpet juniper)

These low-growing spreading juniper shrubs make handsome ground covers for adverse conditions: they withstand harsh weather, city smog and poor soil. Their slow-growing branches with scalelike evergreen foliage seldom need pruning to keep them in bounds, and the foliage itself, once it has become established, is dense enough to discourage weeds. Female plants bear decorative berries in the fall if male plants grow nearby.

Sargent juniper and shore juniper are good choices for seashore property, for they thrive in sandy soil exposed to full sun and salt spray. Both form 1-foot-high mats 8 to 10 feet across. The Sargent juniper, hardy in Zones 4-9, has steel-blue foliage and blue berries. The shore juniper, hardy in Zones 5-9, has gray-green foliage and black berries. Wilton carpet juniper, also 8 to 10 feet across, grows in sunny, hot, dry locations and is hardy in Zones 2-9. Because of its blue needles and berries it is also called the blue rug juniper. It rarely grows more than 4 inches high.

KINNIKINNICK See *Arctostaphylos*

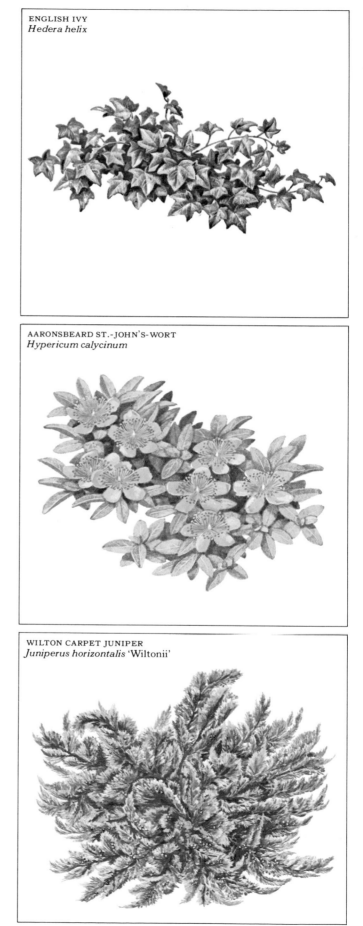

ENGLISH IVY
Hedera helix

AARONSBEARD ST.-JOHN'S-WORT
Hypericum calycinum

WILTON CARPET JUNIPER
Juniperus horizontalis 'Wiltonii'

For climate zones and frost dates, see maps, pages 148-149.

VARIEGATED YELLOW ARCHANGEL
Lamium galeobdolon 'Variegatum'

BIG BLUE LILY-TURF
Liriope muscari

HALL'S JAPANESE HONEYSUCKLE
Lonicera japonica 'Halliana'

LAMIUM

L. maculatum (spotted dead nettle); *L. galeobdolon* 'Variega-tum,' also called *Lamiastrum galeobdolon* 'Variegatum' (variegated yellow archangel)

A member of the mint family, this informal ground cover thrives on inattention. It grows in any average soil and although it does best in partial shade it will tolerate a sunny location if the soil retains moisture. It is hardy in Zones 4-10. Quick growing but not intrusive, the spotted dead nettle forms loose clumps 6 to 8 inches high, somewhat sprawling in appearance, although a midsummer shearing encourages more compact growth. Its foliage is dark green, usually with a white or yellow blotch along the midrib, although in some varieties the blotch is red or silver. In Zones 6-10, the foliage lasts into the winter. Its spikes of small pink or purple flowers begin to bloom in spring and continue through summer. Variegated yellow archangel, with silver-marked green leaves, forms clumps 12 to 18 inches tall. It is hardy in Zones 5-10 but loses its leaves in winter in northern regions. Its spikes of yellow flowers bloom in summer.

LILY OF THE VALLEY See *Convallaria*
LILY-TURF, BIG BLUE See *Liriope*
LILY-TURF, CREEPING See *Liriope*
LILY-TURF, DWARF See *Ophiopogon*

LIRIOPE

L. muscari (big blue lily-turf); *L. spicata* (creeping lily-turf)

These two evergreen lily-turf species have slightly different growth habits and degrees of hardiness, but both are favorite landscaping plants. Although they grow best in medium shade and in moist, well-drained soil, they will also grow in dry soils, in full sun, in deep shade and even in salt spray. Both of these lily-turfs flower most freely in a sunny location. Both plants form mounds of grasslike foliage. Usually the foliage is dark green, but in some varieties of the big blue lily-turf it is variegated.

Big blue lily-turf grows from 12 to 18 inches tall, forming clumps 2 feet across; it cannot be safely grown north of Zone 7. From midsummer to fall, it bears purple or lavender flower spikes followed by blue-black berries. Creeping lily-turf grows only 6 to 12 inches tall and bears pale lilac to white flowers from midsummer to fall. It resembles grass but cannot be walked on without damage; it is the hardier of the two species, growing in Zones 4-10.

LONG-SPURRED EPIMEDIUM See *Epimedium*

LONICERA

L. japonica 'Halliana' (Hall's Japanese honeysuckle)

Hall's Japanese honeysuckle is a vigorous twining vine that spreads rapidly—sometimes too rapidly—in either rich soil or poor. It is useful as a ground cover for large open areas in Zones 4-10. The plant is evergreen in mild climates, semievergreen in cold. It is adaptable to full sun or partial shade, and it is rarely bothered by pests or diseases. It should not be planted near shrubs or small trees, which it can climb and strangle.

The leaves of Hall's Japanese honeysuckle are deep green in summer; in the fall they may turn bronze. Fragrant flowers, white at first and then fading to yellow, blossom throughout the summer. Black berries appear in the fall. No maintenance is required except the pruning necessary to keep the plant in bounds. To produce dense, heavy growth, mow or shear Hall's Japanese honeysuckle to a height of 6 to 10 inches every two or three years.

LOW JAPANESE FLEECEFLOWER See *Polygonum*

MARIGOLD, CAPE See *Osteospermum*
MONDO GRASS See *Ophiopogon*
MOSS, IRISH See *Sagina*
MOSS PHLOX See *Phlox*
MOSS PINK See *Phlox*
MYRTLE, CREEPING See *Vinca*

OPHIOPOGON
O. japonicus (mondo grass, dwarf lily-turf)

Mondo grass, a turflike ground cover that grows about 6 inches high, is easy to grow in the mild climate of Zones 8-10. It thrives in either full sun or shade and will form a luxuriant carpet even when it is planted under trees. The plant does best in rich, moist soil, but it will grow in almost any soil. Mondo grass can endure drought, heat and salt spray. It becomes a tough-rooted mat that will hold banks against erosion, spreading somewhat slowly at first by means of underground stems. After it is established it grows faster and seldom needs weeding. Mondo grass can remain undisturbed indefinitely but may be divided in spring for propagation of additional plants.

Mondo grass has arching grasslike leaves that remain dark green all year in mild regions. Short stalks of inconspicuous lavender flowers in early summer are followed by tight clusters of ¼-inch blue berries.

OSTEOSPERMUM
O. fruticosum, also called *Dimorphotheca fruticosa* (trailing African daisy, Cape marigold)

Trailing African daisy, grown primarily on the West Coast in Zones 9 and 10, is suited for covering large open areas of level or sloping ground. It requires little attention and is rarely invaded by pests or diseases. It grows best in rich soil and full sun, and established plants tolerate drought. The plant spreads rapidly by means of long, trailing stems that root where they touch the ground. Occasional cutting back of old plants or pinching back of young stems encourages branching and keeps the plants from becoming straggly.

Trailing African daisy makes an attractive carpet about 18 inches high with leaves 1 to 2 inches long. The handsome lavender flowers with purple centers resemble daisies; they bloom in sunshine from November to March; a scattering of flowers may appear during the rest of the year. The daisy-like blooms are about 3 inches across.

PACHISTIMA See *Paxistima*

PACHYSANDRA
P. terminalis (pachysandra, Japanese spurge)

Pachysandra can be grown virtually anywhere in Zones 4-9, on slopes or level ground, and is especially valued as an evergreen ground cover for use in partial to deep shade where other plants will not grow. It thrives even in the dense shade of a Norway maple and competes successfully with the maple's shallow roots for nourishment. It prefers a rich, moist, slightly acid soil but requires no other care once it has become established. It is hardy to −30° and retains its green color through even the harshest of winters. The plant is rarely bothered by pests or diseases, although occasionally it is attacked by euonymus scale, which can be controlled easily with an insecticide.

Spreading readily by means of underground stems, pachysandra forms a lush, handsome carpet that is 6 to 8 inches tall. The saw-toothed leaves are a lustrous dark green; a

MONDO GRASS
Ophiopogon japonicus

TRAILING AFRICAN DAISY
Osteospermum fruticosum

PACHYSANDRA
Pachysandra terminalis

For climate zones and frost dates, see maps, pages 148-149.

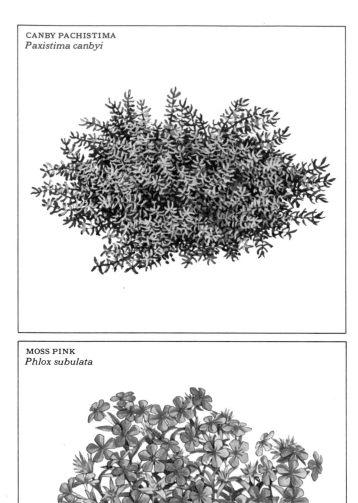

CANBY PACHISTIMA
Paxistima canbyi

MOSS PINK
Phlox subulata

REYNOUTRIA FLEECEFLOWER
Polygonum reynoutria

variegated form whose leaves are marked with white is also available. Pachysandra bears short, upright spikes of tiny white flowers in spring.

PAXISTIMA
P. canbyi, also called *Pachistima canbyi* (Canby pachistima)

Canby pachistima is an evergreen, shrubby ground cover that is particularly attractive when planted in front of rhododendrons, under trees or as an edging plant. It will grow in Zones 5-8 in full sun or partial shade; it needs partial shade in the warmer Zone 9. Once established in rich, moist, well-drained acid soil, the plants will grow for many years with almost no attention. They spread slowly by trailing branches that root where they touch the ground.

An established bed of Canby pachistima is about a foot high. Its ½- to 1-inch leaves are rich green in summer and take on a bronze hue in winter. Reddish flowers bloom in spring but are so small they are rarely noticed.

PEARLWORT, CORSICAN See *Sagina*
PERIWINKLE See *Vinca*

PHLOX
P. subulata (moss pink, ground pink, moss phlox)

The evergreen foliage of moss pink is attractive even in winter and the plant is spectacular when it flowers in spring, forming a dense carpet of color. This species will grow in almost any well-drained soil. Little maintenance is needed, although the stems may be sheared back to half their height after flowering to make the plants denser and more compact. The plant is hardy to −40° and does well in full sun in Zones 3-9. Pests and diseases are seldom a problem.

Moss pink grows 4 to 6 inches tall and spreads 2 feet or more with its creeping stems forming a thick mat that is weed free once the plant is established. It is most useful as an edging plant, for covering small areas in rock gardens or for cascading over retaining walls. The flower colors of different varieties range from white to pink, red and blue.

PINK, MOSS See *Phlox*

POLYGONUM
P. cuspidatum 'Compactum' (low Japanese fleeceflower); *P. reynoutria* (Reynoutria fleeceflower, dwarf polygonum)

Prolific plants that thrive in virtually any soil in full sun, the fleeceflowers spread quickly by underground stems. The plants are easy to grow but should not be used where they can encroach on other plants. Poor soil will slow their invasiveness. Fleeceflower plants can be left undisturbed indefinitely. They die to the ground in late fall. Pests and diseases are seldom a problem.

Low Japanese fleeceflower bears oval, 3- to 6-inch leaves on stems 2 feet tall. Clusters of small greenish-white flowers appear in late summer, followed by small red fruits in the fall. The plants are hardy in Zones 5-10. The 12- to 18-inch stems of Reynoutria fleeceflower flop over to form a carpet 4 to 6 inches tall. Plants bear great numbers of tiny pink flowers that open from red buds in late summer and fall; its 1-inch heart-shaped leaves turn brilliant red in fall. It is hardy in Zones 4-8 and in Zone 9 on the West Coast.

PURPLE WINTER CREEPER See *Euonymus*

REYNOUTRIA FLEECEFLOWER See *Polygonum*
ROCK COTONEASTER See *Cotoneaster*
ROCK SPRAY See *Cotoneaster*

SAGINA

S. subulata (Corsican pearlwort, Irish moss)

The dense, rounded tufts of Corsican pearlwort rapidly grow together to form a thick mosslike mat 3 to 4 inches high. The plant is useful in small areas, such as a retaining wall or rock garden, and can be planted in crevices between stepping stones. Corsican pearlwort thrives in moist, well-drained fertile soil. Little maintenance is required, and pests and diseases are seldom a problem. This hardy ground cover grows best in Zones 5-10, planted in partial shade. Tiny awl-shaped leaves cover slender, trailing stems that root where they touch the soil. In midsummer the tiny white flowers are often so profuse that they cover the thick evergreen foliage.

ST.-JOHN'S-WORT, AARONSBEARD See *Hypericum*
SARGENT JUNIPER See *Juniperus*

SENECIO

S. cineraria, also called *S. maritima, Cineraria maritima* (silver groundsel)

Easy to grow and propagate, silver groundsel is hardy in Zones 9 and 10. Though it grows best in full sun, it tolerates almost any light and any well-drained soil. In shaded areas where the soil is dry, silver groundsel grows where other ground covers fail. It is generally free of diseases. Propagation is by division or by stem or root cuttings.

Silver groundsel grows up to 2½ feet tall and is noted chiefly for its dense white woolly leaves, deeply lobed and blunt at the tips. Small yellow flowers bloom from late spring to fall. The variety named Silver Dust grows only 9 inches high. Its finely lobed fernlike leaves are silver-white.

SHORE JUNIPER See *Juniperus*
SILVER GROUNDSEL See *Senecio*
SPOTTED DEAD NETTLE See *Lamium*
SPURGE, JAPANESE See *Pachysandra*
SWEET WOODRUFF See *Asperula*

TRAILING AFRICAN DAISY See *Osteospermum*
TRAILING MYRTLE See *Vinca*

VETCH, CROWN See *Coronilla*

VINCA

V. minor (periwinkle, creeping myrtle, trailing myrtle)

This tough evergreen ground cover has been widely used in American gardens for over 200 years. It is especially useful for erosion control on banks. While it grows best in moist, acid soil enriched with peat moss or leaf mold, it will tolerate poor soil. Established plants will flourish with little care; they are rarely troubled by pests and diseases and they spread rapidly by means of prostrate stems that root where they touch soil. New plantings should be mulched to conserve moisture. Although periwinkle will grow virtually anywhere in Zones 4-10, it does best in light to deep shade, taking full sun only in Zones 4-7.

A mature bed of common periwinkle is about 6 inches tall. Its trailing stems are covered with small dark, shiny leaves. Five-petaled, lilac-blue flowers appear in early spring. Some varieties have white, red, pink or purple flowers.

WILTON CARPET JUNIPER See *Juniperus*
WINTER CREEPER See *Euonymus*
WOODRUFF, SWEET See *Asperula*

YELLOW ARCHANGEL, VARIEGATED See *Lamium*

For climate zones and frost dates, see maps, pages 148-149.

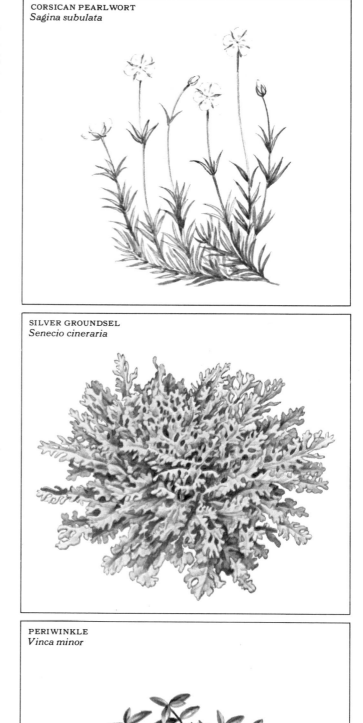

CORSICAN PEARLWORT
Sagina subulata

SILVER GROUNDSEL
Senecio cineraria

PERIWINKLE
Vinca minor

Appendix

Climate notes for the easy garden

The plants chosen for a low-maintenance garden should grow reliably year after year without any special coddling, indifferent to frigid winters or scorching summers, droughts or floods. The preceding encyclopedia chapter keys plants to the winter-hardiness map below that divides North America into 10 zones, based on how low the winter temperature, on average, is likely to drop.

There are a few plants—the perennial gaillardia, for example—that will grow in virtually any climate. But most can tolerate only a certain degree of winter cold (or, in a few instances, summer heat and humidity).

While some gardeners delight in testing their skill by pushing tender plants to the limits of their hardiness, the low-maintenance gardener is better advised to play it safe with plants that are known to be well adapted to a particular area. So after

you have used the encyclopedia to identify low-maintenance plants that should do well in your garden, winnow your list further by asking local commercial growers and neighboring gardeners about their experience with the plants.

Unfortunately, low maintenance does not mean no maintenance. The frost-date maps on the opposite page can be your guides in scheduling the few unavoidable garden chores. After the frost period has passed, you can set out new plants, attend to fertilizing, renew the weed-defeating mulches. Prepare the garden for winter after the first killing frost in fall, cleaning up perennial foliage as it dies back and raking up the fallen leaves. Or you may want to chop the nutrient-rich leaves with a power mower and let them stay on the ground where they lie. This is easy gardening at its best—but quite effective.

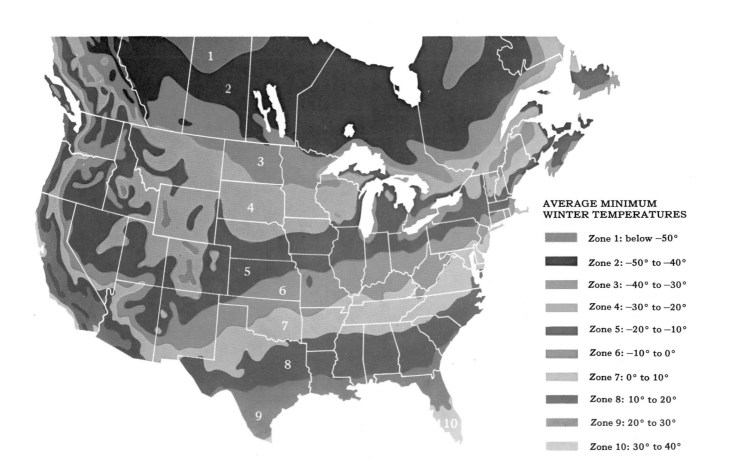

AVERAGE MINIMUM WINTER TEMPERATURES

Zone 1: below −50°

Zone 2: −50° to −40°

Zone 3: −40° to −30°

Zone 4: −30° to −20°

Zone 5: −20° to −10°

Zone 6: −10° to 0°

Zone 7: 0° to 10°

Zone 8: 10° to 20°

Zone 9: 20° to 30°

Zone 10: 30° to 40°

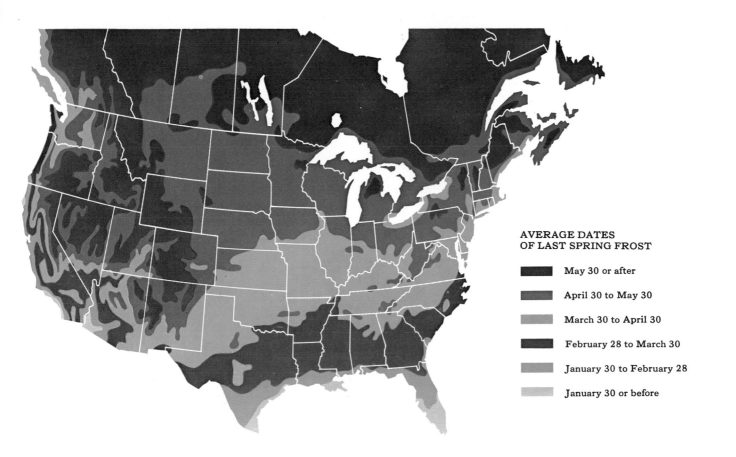

AVERAGE DATES
OF LAST SPRING FROST

May 30 or after

April 30 to May 30

March 30 to April 30

February 28 to March 30

January 30 to February 28

January 30 or before

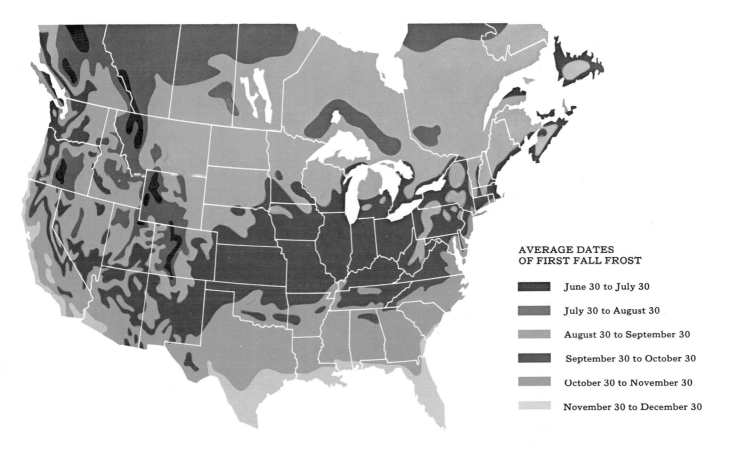

AVERAGE DATES
OF FIRST FALL FROST

June 30 to July 30

July 30 to August 30

August 30 to September 30

September 30 to October 30

October 30 to November 30

November 30 to December 30

Characteristics of 153 low-maintenance plants

Plant	Shrub	Tree	Perennial	Ground cover	Under 1 foot	1 to 3 feet	3 to 6 feet	6 to 10 feet	10 to 30 feet	30 to 50 feet	Over 50 feet	Grows in deep shade	Tolerates polluted air	Drought resistant	Tolerates wet soil	Resists pests and diseases	Slow	Fast	Deciduous	Evergreen	Sun	Partial shade	Dry	Moist
ABELIA GRANDIFLORA (glossy abelia)	●						●									●			●	●	●			●
ABIES CONCOLOR (white fir)		●								●			●	●		●		●		●	●			●
ACANTHOPANAX SIEBOLDIANUS (five-leaved aralia)	●						●						●	●		●		●	●			●	●	●
ACER PALMATUM 'ATROPURPUREUM' (bloodleaf Japanese maple)		●						●								●		●	●			●		●
ACER PLATANOIDES (Norway maple)		●							●				●			●		●	●		●	●		●
ACHILLEA TOMENTOSA (woolly yarrow)			●		●									●				●		●	●		●	●
AJUGA REPTANS (bugleweed)			●	●								●						●	●			●		●
AQUILEGIA CANADENSIS (American columbine)			●		●	●												●	●			●		●
ARCTOSTAPHYLOS UVA-URSI (bearberry)				●	●									●		●			●	●	●	●	●	
ASPERULA ODORATA (sweet woodruff)				●	●							●						●	●			●		●
ASTER NOVAE-ANGLIAE (New England aster)			●				●								●			●	●		●			●
ASTILBE ARENDSII 'ROSY VEIL' (astilbe)			●			●									●			●	●			●		●
AUCUBA JAPONICA 'PICTURATA' (variegated Japanese aucuba)	●						●					●	●					●		●		●		●
BERBERIS THUNBERGII 'AUREA' (yellow Japanese barberry)	●					●	●							●		●			●		●			●
BETULA PAPYRIFERA (canoe birch)		●							●				●			●		●	●		●	●		●
BUXUS SEMPERVIRENS 'SUFFRUTICOSA' (common dwarf box)	●					●								●	●		●			●	●	●		●
CAMELLIA JAPONICA (common camellia)	●						●								●					●	●	●		●
CAMPANULA CARPATICA (Carpathian harebell)			●		●													●	●		●	●		●
CEDRUS ATLANTICA 'GLAUCA' (blue Atlas cedar)		●							●					●				●		●	●			●
CEDRUS DEODARA (deodar cedar)		●							●									●		●	●			●
CENTAUREA MONTANA (mountain bluet)			●		●													●	●		●	●		●
CERCIDIPHYLLUM JAPONICUM (katsura tree)		●							●	●								●	●		●	●		●
CERCIS CANADENSIS (eastern redbud)		●						●										●	●		●	●		●
CHAENOMELES JAPONICA ALPINA (alpine Japanese quince)	●			●	●													●	●		●			●
CHAMAECYPARIS LAWSONIANA (Lawson's false cypress)		●							●				●		●			●		●	●	●		●
CHAMAECYPARIS OBTUSA 'GRACILIS' (slender hinoki false cypress)	●						●								●	●	●			●	●			●
CLADRASTIS LUTEA (yellowwood)		●							●						●			●	●		●			●
CLETHRA ALNIFOLIA 'ROSEA' (pink summer sweet)	●						●								●				●			●		●
CONVALLARIA MAJALIS (lily of the valley)			●	●											●	●		●			●		●
COREOPSIS GRANDIFLORA 'SUNBURST' (big-flowered coreopsis)			●		●													●	●		●		●	●
CORNUS ALBA 'SIBIRICA' (Siberian dogwood)	●							●						●				●	●		●			●
CORNUS FLORIDA 'RUBRA' (pink flowering dogwood)		●						●								●			●		●	●		●
CORNUS MAS (Cornelian cherry)	●							●								●			●		●	●		●
CORONILLA VARIA (crown vetch)			●		●									●				●	●		●	●	●	●
CORYLUS COLURNA (Turkish filbert)		●							●				●					●	●		●		●	
COTINUS COGGYGRIA 'NOTCUTT' (smoke tree)	●						●	●										●	●		●		●	
COTONEASTER APICULATUS (cranberry cotoneaster)	●				●										●				●		●			●
COTONEASTER DAMMERI (bearberry cotoneaster)			●	●											●				●	●	●	●		●
CYTISUS PRAECOX (Warminster broom)	●					●								●			●		●		●		●	
DAVIDIA INVOLUCRATA (dove tree)		●							●							●			●		●	●		●
DEUTZIA GRACILIS (slender deutzia)	●					●	●									●			●		●	●		●
DICENTRA SPECTABILIS (common bleeding heart)			●		●														●		●	●		●
DORONICUM CORDATUM 'MISS MASON' (Miss Mason Caucasian leopard's-bane)			●		●														●		●	●		●
ELAEAGNUS PUNGENS 'VARIEGATA' (variegated thorny elaeagnus)	●						●	●						●					●		●	●		●
EPIMEDIUM GRANDIFLORUM (bishop's hat)			●	●								●				●			●	●	●	●		●

150

Name	LANDSCAPE USE				MATURE HEIGHT							SPECIAL TRAITS					GROWTH RATE		FOLIAGE		LIGHT		SOIL	
	Shrub	Tree	Perennial	Ground cover	Under 1 foot	1 to 3 feet	3 to 6 feet	6 to 10 feet	10 to 30 feet	30 to 50 feet	Over 50 feet	Grows in deep shade	Tolerates polluted air	Drought resistant	Tolerates wet soil	Resists pests and diseases	Slow	Fast	Deciduous	Evergreen	Sun	Partial shade	Dry	Moist
EUONYMUS ALATA 'COMPACTA' (dwarf winged euonymus)	●						●							●	●				●		●	●	●	●
EUONYMUS FORTUNEI 'EMERALD 'N GOLD' (Emerald 'n Gold winter creeper)	●						●						●			●				●	●	●	●	●
EUONYMUS FORTUNEI 'MINIMA' (baby winter creeper)			●	●										●						●	●	●	●	●
FAGUS SYLVATICA (European beech)		●							●					●	●				●		●			●
FORSYTHIA INTERMEDIA 'LYNWOOD' (Lynwood forsythia)	●						●						●			●		●	●		●	●	●	●
FOTHERGILLA MAJOR (large fothergilla)	●						●									●			●		●	●		●
FRANKLINIA ALATAMAHA (franklinia)		●						●								●			●		●	●		●
FRAXINUS HOLOTRICHA 'MORAINE' (Moraine ash)		●							●	●				●				●	●		●			●
GAILLARDIA ARISTATA 'GOBLIN' (blanketflower)			●		●									●				●			●		●	●
GALAX APHYLLA (galax)			●	●		●														●		●		●
GERANIUM SANGUINEUM (blood-red crane's-bill)			●		●									●				●		●	●	●	●	●
GINKGO BILOBA (ginkgo)		●							●		●		●		●	●			●		●			●
GLEDITSIA TRIACANTHOS INERMIS 'MORAINE' (Moraine thornless honey locust)		●							●				●		●			●	●		●		●	●
HAMAMELIS MOLLIS (Chinese witch hazel)	●							●					●						●		●	●		●
HEDERA HELIX (English ivy)			●	●										●		●		●		●	●	●	●	●
HEMEROCALLIS 'PRIMROSE MASCOTTE' (dwarf Hyperion day lily)			●		●											●		●			●	●		●
HEUCHERA SANGUINEA (coral-bells)			●	●	●													●			●			●
HIBISCUS SYRIACUS 'WILLIAM R. SMITH' (rose of Sharon)	●						●	●					●			●		●	●		●			●
HOSTA 'ROYAL STANDARD' (plantain lily)			●		●													●				●		●
HYDRANGEA MACROPHYLLA (big-leaved hydrangea)	●					●										●		●	●			●		●
HYPERICUM CALYCINUM (Aaronsbeard St.-John's-wort)			●	●										●				●		●	●	●	●	●
IBERIS SEMPERVIRENS (evergreen candytuft)			●	●										●						●	●			●
ILEX CORNUTA 'BURFORDII' (Burford holly)	●						●							●						●	●			●
ILEX CRENATA 'HELLERI' (Heller Japanese holly)	●				●	●								●	●					●	●			●
ILEX OPACA (American holly)		●						●						●						●	●			●
ILEX VERTICILLATA (winterberry)	●						●								●				●		●			●
JUNIPERUS CHINENSIS 'COLUMNARIS' (blue column juniper)		●					●							●		●				●	●	●	●	●
JUNIPERUS CHINENSIS 'TORULOSA' (Hollywood juniper)	●						●													●		●	●	●
JUNIPERUS HORIZONTALIS 'WILTONII' (Wilton carpet juniper)			●	●										●				●		●	●		●	●
JUNIPERUS VIRGINIANA 'CANAERTII' (Canaert red cedar)		●						●						●				●		●	●			●
KALMIA LATIFOLIA (mountain laurel)	●					●						●				●				●	●	●		●
KALOPANAX PICTUS (castor aralia)		●							●						●			●	●		●			●
KOELREUTERIA PANICULATA (golden-rain tree)		●							●				●	●				●	●		●		●	●
KOLKWITZIA AMABILIS (beauty bush)	●						●											●	●		●	●		●
LAGERSTROEMIA INDICA (crape myrtle)	●						●									●		●	●		●			●
LAMIUM GALEOBDOLON 'VARIEGATUM' (variegated yellow archangel)			●	●												●		●		●		●	●	●
LEUCOTHOË FONTANESIANA (drooping leucothoë)	●					●						●	●				●			●		●		●
LIGUSTRUM JAPONICUM 'SUWANNEE RIVER' (Suwannee River privet)	●					●									●	●		●		●		●		●
LIGUSTRUM OBTUSIFOLIUM REGELIANUM (Regel privet)	●					●								●		●		●	●		●			●
LIGUSTRUM VICARYI (Vicary golden privet)	●						●									●			●		●			●
LIQUIDAMBAR STYRACIFLUA (sweet gum)		●							●						●			●	●		●			●
LIRIODENDRON TULIPIFERA (tulip tree)		●								●								●	●		●			●
LIRIOPE MUSCARI (big blue lily-turf)			●		●															●	●	●	●	●
LONICERA JAPONICA 'HALLIANA' (Hall's Japanese honeysuckle)			●	●										●				●		●	●	●	●	●
LONICERA TATARICA 'SIBIRICA' (Siberian honeysuckle)	●						●							●				●		●	●	●	●	●

Plant	LANDSCAPE USE				MATURE HEIGHT							SPECIAL TRAITS					GROWTH RATE		FOLIAGE		LIGHT		SOIL	
	Shrub	Tree	Perennial	Ground cover	Under 1 foot	1 to 3 feet	3 to 6 feet	6 to 10 feet	10 to 30 feet	30 to 50 feet	Over 50 feet	Grows in deep shade	Tolerates polluted air	Drought resistant	Tolerates wet soil	Resists pests and diseases	Slow	Fast	Deciduous	Evergreen	Sun	Partial shade	Dry	Moist
LUPINUS 'RUSSELL HYBRIDS' (Russell hybrid lupine)			●		●														●		●	●		●
MAGNOLIA ACUMINATA (cucumber tree)		●								●				●		●			●		●	●		●
MAGNOLIA GRANDIFLORA (southern magnolia)		●								●				●		●	●			●	●	●		●
MAGNOLIA LOEBNERI 'MERRILL' (Merrill magnolia)		●						●						●		●			●		●	●		●
MAHONIA AQUIFOLIUM (Oregon holly grape)	●						●					●				●				●	●	●	●	●
MALUS ARNOLDIANA (Arnold crab apple)		●						●								●		●	●		●			●
MYRICA PENSYLVANICA (bayberry)	●					●	●								●					●	●	●	●	●
NANDINA DOMESTICA (nandina)	●						●													●	●	●		●
NERIUM OLEANDER (oleander)	●							●	●				●	●						●	●		●	●
NYSSA SYLVATICA (pepperidge)		●							●					●	●	●			●		●	●		●
OPHIOPOGON JAPONICUS (mondo grass)				●	●									●			●			●	●	●		●
OSMANTHUS HETEROPHYLLUS (holly osmanthus)	●						●									●				●	●	●		●
OSTEOSPERMUM FRUTICOSUM (trailing African daisy)				●	●									●		●		●		●	●		●	●
OXYDENDRUM ARBOREUM (sorrel tree)		●						●								●	●		●		●	●		●
PACHYSANDRA TERMINALIS (pachysandra)				●	●							●								●		●	●	●
PAEONIA LACTIFLORA 'PHILIPPE RIVOIRE' (Chinese peony)			●		●	●													●		●	●	●	●
PAPAVER ORIENTALE (Oriental poppy)			●		●	●										●			●		●	●	●	●
PAXISTIMA CANBYI (Canby pachistima)				●	●												●			●	●	●	●	
PHELLODENDRON AMURENSE (Amur cork tree)		●							●					●		●			●		●	●	●	●
PHILADELPHUS VIRGINALIS 'GLACIER' (Glacier mock orange)	●						●	●								●			●		●	●	●	●
PHLOX SUBULATA (moss pink)				●	●											●				●	●		●	●
PICEA GLAUCA 'CONICA' (dwarf Alberta spruce)		●					●										●			●	●	●		●
PICEA OMORIKA (Serbian spruce)		●								●							●			●	●			●
PIERIS JAPONICA (Japanese andromeda)	●						●													●	●	●		●
PINUS CEMBRA (Swiss stone pine)		●						●						●			●			●	●			●
PINUS RESINOSA (red pine)		●							●					●				●		●	●		●	
PITTOSPORUM TOBIRA (Japanese pittosporum)	●						●							●				●		●	●	●	●	●
PLATYCODON GRANDIFLORUS 'MARIESII' (Maries' balloonflower)			●		●										●	●		●			●	●		●
POLYGONUM REYNOUTRIA (Reynoutria fleeceflower)				●	●											●			●	●	●	●	●	●
PRIMULA POLYANTHA (polyanthus primrose)			●		●											●			●	●		●		●
PRUNUS LAUROCERASUS 'SCHIPKAENSIS' (Schipka cherry laurel)	●						●									●				●	●	●		●
PSEUDOLARIX AMABILIS (golden larch)		●							●	●						●	●		●		●			●
PSEUDOTSUGA MENZIESII (Douglas fir)		●							●	●						●		●		●	●	●	●	●
PYRUS CALLERYANA 'BRADFORD' (Bradford pear)		●							●					●		●		●	●		●			●
QUERCUS ALBA (white oak)		●								●							●		●		●			●
QUERCUS PHELLOS (willow oak)		●							●	●		●			●			●	●		●			●
QUERCUS VIRGINIANA (live oak)		●								●								●		●	●	●		●
RHAMNUS FRANGULA 'COLUMNARIS' (Tallhedge alder buckthorn)	●								●					●	●			●	●		●	●	●	●
RHODODENDRON 'EXBURY HYBRIDS' (Exbury azalea)	●						●												●		●	●		●
ROSA HUGONIS (Father Hugo's rose)	●						●	●								●			●		●		●	●
ROSA RUGOSA (Rugosa rose)	●						●									●			●		●		●	●
RUDBECKIA FULGIDA 'GOLDSTURM' (rudbeckia)			●		●									●	●	●		●	●		●	●	●	●
SAGINA SUBULATA (Corsican pearlwort)				●	●											●				●	●		●	●
SCIADOPITYS VERTICILLATA (umbrella pine)		●							●							●	●			●	●	●		●
SEDUM SPECTABILE 'METEOR' (showy stonecrop)			●		●									●		●	●		●		●	●	●	●

	LANDSCAPE USE				MATURE HEIGHT							SPECIAL TRAITS					GROWTH RATE		FOLIAGE		LIGHT		SOIL	
	Shrub	Tree	Perennial	Ground cover	Under 1 foot	1 to 3 feet	3 to 6 feet	6 to 10 feet	10 to 30 feet	30 to 50 feet	Over 50 feet	Grows in deep shade	Tolerates polluted air	Drought resistant	Tolerates wet soil	Resists pests and diseases	Slow	Fast	Deciduous	Evergreen	Sun	Partial shade	Dry	Moist
SENECIO CINERARIA (silver groundsel)			●	●										●						●	●	●	●	●
SKIMMIA JAPONICA (Japanese skimmia)	●					●	●					●	●							●		●		●
SOPHORA JAPONICA (Japanese pagoda tree)		●								●			●	●		●		●	●		●		●	●
SORBUS ALNIFOLIA (Korean mountain ash)		●								●				●				●	●		●		●	●
SPIRAEA BUMALDA 'ANTHONY WATERER' (Bumalda spirea)	●					●								●				●	●		●	●		●
SPIRAEA PRUNIFOLIA (bridal wreath)	●							●						●				●	●		●			●
STACHYS BYZANTINA (lamb's ears)			●		●									●						●	●		●	●
STEPHANANDRA INCISA 'CRISPA' (dwarf cut-leaved stephanandra)	●													●				●	●		●	●		●
TAXUS MEDIA 'HICKSII' (Hicks yew)	●					●	●	●	●					●						●	●	●	●	●
THUJA PLICATA 'FASTIGIATA' (columnar giant arborvitae)		●								●					●					●	●			●
TILIA CORDATA (little-leaf linden)		●								●			●				●		●		●			●
TSUGA CANADENSIS 'PENDULA' (Sargent's weeping hemlock)	●						●	●	●			●	●							●	●	●		●
TSUGA CAROLINIANA (Carolina hemlock)		●								●	●	●								●	●	●		●
VERONICA SPICATA 'MINUET' (spike speedwell)			●		●									●							●		●	●
VIBURNUM CARLCEPHALUM (fragrant snowball)	●							●						●					●		●	●		●
VIBURNUM PLICATUM TOMENTOSUM 'MARIESII' (Maries' doublefile viburnum)	●							●						●					●		●	●		●
VINCA MINOR (periwinkle)			●	●	●							●								●	●	●	●	●
WEIGELA 'VANICEKII' (weigela)	●							●	●					●					●		●	●		●

Bibliography

Bailey, L. H., *The Cultivated Conifers in North America*. The Macmillan Co., 1933.

Berrisford, Judith, *The Weekend Garden*. Faber and Faber, 1978.

Biles, Roy E., *The Complete Book of Garden Magic*. J. G. Ferguson Publishing Co., 1961.

Bloom, Alan, *Perennials for Your Garden*. Charles Scribner's Sons, 1974.

Bonnie, Fred, ed., *Growing Lawns and Ground Covers*. Oxmoor House, 1975.

Brockman, C. Frank, *Trees of North America*. Western Publishing Co., Inc., 1968.

Brooklyn Botanic Garden, *Container Gardening*. BBG, 1978.

Brooklyn Botanic Garden, *Gardening Guide*. BBG, 1976.

Brooklyn Botanic Garden, *Handbook on Flowering Shrubs*. BBG, 1964.

Brooklyn Botanic Garden, *Handbook on Mulches*. BBG, 1957.

Brooklyn Botanic Garden, *The Hundred Finest Trees and Shrubs for Temperate Climates*. BBG, 1957.

Brooklyn Botanic Garden, *Nursery Source Guide: A Handbook*. BBG, 1977.

Brooklyn Botanic Garden, *The Year's Highlights in Gardening*. BBG, 1978.

Bruning, Walter F., *Minimum Maintenance Gardening Handbook*. Harper & Row, 1961.

Bush-Brown, James and Louise, *America's Garden Book*. Charles Scribner's Sons, 1965.

Chittenden, Fred J., ed., *The Royal Horticultural Society Dictionary of Gardening,* 2nd ed. Clarendon Press, 1974.

Clark, Robert B., *Flowering Trees*. D. Van Nostrand Co., Inc., 1963.

Cloud, Katherine M-P, *Evergreens for Every State*. Chilton Co., 1960.

Collingwood, G. H., and Brush, Warren D., *Knowing Your Trees*. The American Forestry Association, 1947.

Cumming, Roderick W., and Lee, Robert E., *Contemporary Perennials*. The Macmillan Co., 1960.

Dietz, Marjorie J., *The Concise Encyclopedia of Favorite Flowering Shrubs*. Doubleday & Co., Inc., 1963.

Dirr, Michael, *The Manual of Woody Landscape Plants,* 2nd ed. Stipes Publishing Co., 1977.

Dudley, Stuart, *Taking the Ache Out of Gardening*. Phoenix House, 1962.

Eckbo, Garrett, *The Art of Home Landscaping*. F. W. Dodge Corp., 1956.

Everett, Thomas H., *Living Trees of the World*. Doubleday & Co., Inc., 1969.

Faust, Joan Lee, ed., *The New York Times Book of Trees and Shrubs*. Alfred A. Knopf, 1964.

Fenten, D. X., *Clear and Simple Gardening*. Grosset & Dunlap, 1975.

Fish, Margery, *Ground Cover Plants*. Collingridge, 1964.

Flemer, William, III, *Nature's Guide to Successful Gardening and Landscaping*. Thomas Y. Crowell Co., 1972.

Flemer, William, III, *Shade and Ornamental Trees in Color*. Grosset & Dunlap, 1965.

Fletcher, H. L. V., *Popular Flowering Shrubs*. Drake Publishing Co., 1972.

Foley, Daniel J., *Gardening for Beginners*. Funk & Wagnalls, 1967.

Foley, Daniel J., *Ground Covers for Easier Gardening*. Dover Publications, Inc., 1961.

Hay, Roy, and Synge, Patrick M., *The Color Dictionary of Flowers and Plants for Home and Garden*. Crown Publishers, Inc., 1969.

Hebb, Robert S., *Low Maintenance Perennials*. The New York Times Book Co., 1975.

Hellyer, A. G. L., *Shrubs in Colour*. Doubleday & Co., Inc., 1965.

Hill, Amelia Leavitt, *Gardens and Grounds That Take Care of Themselves*. Prentice-Hall, Inc., 1958.

Holmes, Sandra, *Trees of the World*. Grosset & Dunlap, 1975.

Hull, George F., *The Know-Nothing Gardener's Guide to Success*. Hawthorn Books, Inc., 1969.

Huxley, Anthony, ed., *Garden Perennials and Water Plants*. The Macmillan Co., 1970.

Jenkins, Dorothy H., *The Weekend Gardener*. Rinehart & Co., Inc., 1950.

Kains, M. G., *Gardening Shortcuts*. Greenberg, Publisher, Inc., 1935.

Leathart, Scott, *Trees of the World*. A & W Publishers, Inc., 1977.

Lees, Carlton B., *Budget Landscaping*. Holt, Rinehart and Winston, 1961.

Levinson, J. J., *The Home Book of Trees and Shrubs*. Alfred A. Knopf, 1949.

McCurdy, Dwight R., Spangenberg, William Gray, and Doty, Charles Paul, *How to Choose Your Tree*. Southern Illinois University Press, 1972.

McDonald, Elvin, and Power, Lawrence, *The Low-Upkeep Book of Lawns and Landscape*. Hawthorn Books, Inc., 1971.

Maino, Evelyn, and Howard, Frances, *Ornamental Trees*. University of California Press, 1966.

Malkin, Robert, *How to Landscape Your Own Home*. Harper, 1955.

Midgley, Kenneth, *Garden Design*. Pelham Books, 1966.

Mossman, Tam, *Gardens That Care For Themselves*. Doubleday & Co., Inc., 1978.

Nehrling, Arno and Irene, *The Picture Book of Perennials*. Hearthside Press, Inc., 1964.

Northen, Rebecca T. and Henry T., *The Secret of the Green Thumb*. The Ronald Press, 1954.

Novak, F. A., *The Pictorial Encyclopedia of Plants and Flowers*. Crown Publishers, Inc., 1966.

Ortloff, H. Stuart, and Raymore, Henry B., *A Book About Soils for the Home Gardener*. M. Barrows & Co., Inc., 1962.

Perry, Frances, *Flowers of the World*. Crown Publishers, Inc., 1972.

Perry, Frances, ed., *Complete Guide to Plants and Flowers*. Simon and Schuster, 1974.

Pettingill, Amos, *The White-Flower-Farm Garden Book*. Alfred A. Knopf, 1971.

Pirone, Pascal P., *What's New in Gardening*. Hanover House, 1956.

Powell, Thomas and Betty, *Your Garden Homestead*. Houghton Mifflin Co., 1977.

The Reader's Digest Association, ed., *Reader's Digest Encyclopedia of Garden Plants and Flowers*. The Reader's Digest Association, Ltd., London, 1975.

Reader's Digest Association, *Reader's Digest Practical Guide to Home Landscaping*. The Reader's Digest Association, Inc., 1972.

Rockwell, Frederick, and Grayson, Esther C., *The Rockwells' Complete Guide to Successful Gardening*. Doubleday & Co., Inc., 1965.

Schery, Robert W., *The Householder's Guide to Outdoor Beauty*. Pocket Books, Inc., 1963.

Schuler, Stanley, *Gardening From the Ground Up*. The Macmillan Co., 1968.

Schuler, Stanley, *Gardening with Ease*. The Macmillan Co., 1970.

Schuler, Stanley, *Planning and Planting the Small Garden Plot*. The Dial Press, 1972.

Shewell-Cooper, W. E., *Mini-Work Gardening*. English Universities Press, 1973.

Staff of the L. H. Bailey Hortorium, Cornell University, *Hortus Third: A Dictionary of Plants Cultivated in the United States and Canada*. Macmillan Publishing Co., Inc., 1976.

Stark, Francis, and Link, Conrad B., eds., *Flowering Trees and Shrubs in Color*. Doubleday & Co., Inc., 1969.

Stout, Ruth, *Gardening Without Work*. Simon & Schuster, Inc., 1974.

Stout, Ruth, *How to Have a Green Thumb Without an Aching Back*. Exposition Press, Inc., 1955.

Sunset Editors, *Basic Gardening Illustrated,* revised ed. Lane Publishing Co., 1975.

Sunset Editors, *Garden Trees*. Lane Publishing Co., 1975.

Sunset Editors, *Lawns and Ground Covers*. Lane Publishing Co., 1964.

Sunset Editors, *Low Maintenance Gardening*. Lane Publishing Co., 1974.

Symonds, George W. D., *The Shrub Identification Book*. M. Barrows and Co., 1963.

Taylor, Norman, ed., *Taylor's Encyclopedia of Gardening*. Houghton Mifflin Co., 1961.

Thomas, Graham Stuart, *Perennial Garden Plants*. David McKay Co., Inc., 1976.

Viertel, Arthur T., *Trees, Shrubs and Vines*. Syracuse University Press, 1970.

Wallach, Carla, *The Reluctant Weekend Gardener*. The Macmillan Co., 1973.

Weiner, Michael A., *Plant a Tree*. Macmillan Publishing Co., Inc., 1975.

Wilson, Charles L., *Gardener's Hint Book*. Jonathan David Publishers, 1978.

Wilson, Helen Van Pelt, *Successful Gardening with Perennials*. Doubleday & Co., Inc., 1976.

Wyman, Donald, *Dwarf Shrubs*. The Macmillan Co., 1974.

Wyman, Donald, *Ground Cover Plants*. The Macmillan Co., 1970.

Wyman, Donald, *The Saturday Morning Gardener*. The Macmillan Co., 1962.

Wyman, Donald, ed., *Shrubs and Vines for American Gardens*. Macmillan Publishing Co., Inc., 1969.

Wyman, Donald, *Trees for American Gardens*. The Macmillan Co., 1965.

Wyman, Donald, *Wyman's Gardening Encyclopedia*. Macmillan Publishing Co., Inc., 1977.

Zion, Robert L., *Trees for Architecture and the Landscape*. Reinhold Book Corp., 1968.

Zucker, Isabel, *Flowering Shrubs*. D. Van Nostrand Co., Inc., 1966.

Picture credits

The sources for the illustrations in this book are listed below. Credits from left to right are separated by semicolons, from top to bottom by dashes. Cover: Henry Groskinsky, designed by Oehme, Van Sweden Associates. 4: Courtesy Dr. Donald Wyman; Jane Jordan. 6: John Neubauer, designed by Oehme, Van Sweden Associates. 8, 10: Drawings by Kathy Rebeiz. 12: Tom Tracy, designed by Chaffee-Zumwalt and Associates. 15: Drawing by Kathy Rebeiz. 17: Tom Tracy, designed by Chaffee-Zumwalt and Associates. 18, 19: John Neubauer. 20, 21: A. E. Bye & Associates. 22 through 27: Tom Tracy. 28: © Derek Fell. 31: Drawings by Kathy Rebeiz. 35, 36, 37: Henry Groskinsky, courtesy Garden of Aden. 38 through 45: Drawings by Kathy Rebeiz. 46: Tom Tracy, designed by Lang and Wood, Inc. 49 through 54: Drawings by Kathy Rebeiz. 59: John Neubauer, designed by Oehme, Van Sweden Associates. 60: Tom Tracy, designed by Martin Stoelzel. 61: Tom Tracy, designed by Chaffee-Zumwalt and Associates. 62, 63: Lee Lockwood from Black Star, designed by Elliot Rhodeside and Suzanne Dworsky. 64, 65: Jim Olive. 66, 67: Tom Tracy, designed by Martin Stoelzel. 68: John Neubauer, designed by Oehme, Van Sweden Associates. 71, 73: Drawings by Kathy Rebeiz. 75: Peter B. Kaplan. 76: © Peter B. Kaplan, 1978. 77, 78: Peter B. Kaplan. 81, 83, 85: Drawings by Kathy Rebeiz. 87: Drawings by Joan McGurren. 90 through 147: Artists for encyclopedia illustrations listed in alphabetical order: Norman Adams, Adolph E. Brotman, Richard Crist, David Hodges, Mary Kellner, Gwen Leighton, Harry McNaught, Rebecca Merrilees, Raoul Minamora, John Murphy, Trudy Nicholson, Carolyn Pickett, Allianora Rosse, Eduardo Salgado and Barbara Wolff. 148, 149: Maps by Adolph E. Brotman.

Acknowledgments

The index for this book was prepared by Anita R. Beckerman. For their help in the preparation of this book, the editors wish to thank the following: Paul Aden, The Garden of Aden, Baldwin, N.Y.; Robert Armstrong, geneticist, Longwood Gardens, Kennett Square, Pa.; Joe and Peggy Bailey, Houston, Tex.; J. Paul Barefoot, Superintendent of Grounds, Soldiers' and Airmen's Home, Washington, D.C.; George Bookman, Vice President, The New York Botanical Garden, Bronx, N.Y.; William Bowman, Hershey Nurseries, Hershey, Pa.; Stanley F. Bulpitt, Brookside Nurseries, Inc., Darien, Conn.; Fred K. Buscher, Cooperative Extension Service, The Ohio State University, Wooster, Ohio; A. E. Bye, Landscape Architect, Old Greenwich, Conn.; Henry M. Cathey, horticulturist and Chief, Ornamentals Laboratory, U.S. Dept. of Agriculture, Agricultural Research Center, Beltsville, Md.; Lester A. Collins, Washington, D.C.; Mr. and Mrs. William Collins, Moorestown, N.J.; John Creech, Director, National Arboretum, Washington, D.C.; Barbara Cunningham, B. G. Cunningham & Associates, Atlanta, Ga.; Edward L. Daugherty, Atlanta, Ga.; Francis DeVos, Director, University of Minnesota Arboretum, Chaska, Minn.; Suzanne Dworsky, Cambridge, Mass.; EDAW, Inc., Alexandria, Va.; Barbara H. Emerson, Technical Information Coordinator, Amchem Products, Inc., Ambler, Pa.; John and Marilyn Feild, Washington, D.C.; William Flemer III, Princeton Nurseries, Princeton, N. J.; Carol Levy Franklin, Andropogon Associates, Philadelphia, Pa.; Dan Franklin, Atlanta, Ga.; Betty Freudenheim, Chicago, Ill.; Fred Galle, Director of Horticulture, Callaway Gardens, Pine Mountain, Ga.; Arthur Goldberg, Goldberg & Rodler, Inc., Huntington, N.Y.; Mrs. Righton Gordy, Atlanta, Ga.; William Graham, Superintendent, Morris Arboretum, Philadelphia, Pa.; F. Otto Haas, Philadelphia, Pa.; Doris and Richard Held, Cambridge, Mass.; Mrs. Edith Henderson, Atlanta, Ga.; Jerry Hill, Hill's Nursery, Arlington, Va.; Allen Hirsh, Potomac Garden Center, Potomac, Md.; Dr. Sam Jones, Botany Department, University of Georgia, Athens, Ga.; William Klein, Director, Morris Arboretum, Philadelphia, Pa.; Frederick M. Lang, Lang and Wood, Inc., Landscape Architects and Planners, South Laguna, Calif.; Carlton B. Lees, Senior Vice President, The New York Botanical Garden, Bronx, N.Y.; Martha Lewellen, Martha's Landscapes, Fairfax Station, Va.; Richard W. Lighty, Associate Professor of Plant Science, University of Delaware, Newark, Del.; Edward L. Lindemann, Pennsylvania Horticultural Society, Philadelphia, Pa.; Jeannette Lowe, W. Atlee Burpee Co., Doylestown, Pa.; Bruce McAlpin, The New York Botanical Garden, Bronx, N.Y.; Frederick McGourty Jr., Editor of Handbooks, Brooklyn Botanic Garden, Brooklyn, N.Y.; Mrs. James E. McLeod, Burke, Va.; Robert S. Malkin, New York, N.Y.; Thomas Mannion, Campbell & Ferrara Nurseries, Inc., Alexandria, Va.; John W. Monday, Assistant Director, Office of Horticulture, Smithsonian Institution, Washington, D.C.; Monrovia Nursery Co., Azusa, Calif.; Klaus Neubner, Senior Vice President, George W. Park Seed Co., Greenwood, S.C.; William Niering, Director, Connecticut Arboretum, Connecticut College, New London, Conn.; Wolfgang Oehme, Baltimore, Md.; C. W. Eliot Paine, Director, Garden Center of Greater Cleveland, Cleveland, Ohio; David Patterson, horticulturist, Longwood Gardens, Kennett Square, Pa.; Brian K. Payne, Urban Forestry Research Unit, U.S. Dept. of Agriculture, Amherst, Mass.; James Pendleton, Chief Landscape Designer, Good Earth Nursery, Burke, Va.; The Pennsylvania Horticultural Society, Philadelphia, Pa.; David R. Phillips, George W. Park Seed Co., Greenwood, S.C.; David G. Pitt, Extension Landscape Architect, Maryland Cooperative Extension Service, University of Maryland, College Park, Md.; Mrs. Robert Potamkin, Philadelphia, Pa.; Thomas and Betty Powell, The Avant Gardener, New York, N.Y.; Elliot Rhodeside, EDAW, Inc., Alexandria, Va.; Helen Roback, Newtown Gardens, Newtown Square, Pa.; Robert H. Rucker, College Station, Tex.; Leslie Jones Sauer, Andropogon Associates, Philadelphia, Pa.; Robert W. Schery, Director, The Lawn Institute, Marysville, Ohio; Jacqueline Schmeal, Houston, Tex.; Elizabeth Scholz, Director, Brooklyn Botanic Garden, Brooklyn, N.Y.; Allen Seidel, Editor, American Nurseryman, Chicago, Ill.; Sidney Shore, The Toro Co., Minneapolis, Minn.; Alan Shulder, Executive Director, Professional Grounds Management Society, Pikesville, Md.; Henry T. Skinner, Bowie, Md.; Rachel Snyder, Editor-in-Chief, Flower & Garden Magazine, Kansas City, Mo.; Dorothy Sowerby, American Horticultural Society, Mount Vernon, Va.; Jane Steffey, American Horticultural Society, Mount Vernon, Va.; Martin Stoelzel, San Rafael, Calif.; Ruth Stout, Redding Ridge, Conn.; Mrs. Sally Taylor, Department of Botany, Connecticut College, New London, Conn.; Terry Thompson, Lima, Pa.; Mr. and Mrs. Charles Truitt, Haverford, Pa.; James A. Van Sweden, Washington, D.C.; Glenn Vincent, Executive Director, Men's Garden Clubs of America, Des Moines, Iowa; Mr. and Mrs. Leo Vollmer, Baltimore, Md.; Wayside Gardens, Hodges, S.C.; Robert A. Wearne, Extension Service, U.S. Dept. of Agriculture, Washington, D.C.; Bruce Whiton, extension agent, Alexandria, Va.; Mr. and Mrs. Matthews Williams, Haverford, Pa.; Joseph A. Witt, Curator of Plant Collections, University of Washington Arboretum, Seattle, Wash.; A. Rex Zumwalt, Chafee-Zumwalt and Associates, Tacoma, Wash.

Index

PRINTED IN U.S.A.